Environmental Psychology
in Building Design

ARCHITECTURAL SCIENCE SERIES

Editor

HENRY J. COWAN

Professor of Architectural Science
University of Sydney

Previously published

Thermal Performance of Buildings
by J. F. VAN STRAATEN

Models in Architecture
by H. J. COWAN, J. S. GERO, G. D. DING and R. W. MUNCEY

Architectural Acoustics
by ANITA LAWRENCE

Spatial Synthesis in Computer-Aided Building Design
edited by C. M. EASTMAN

Wind Loading on Buildings
by A. J. J. MACDONALD

Design of Building Frames
by J. S. GERO and H. J. COWAN

Building Services
by P. R. SMITH and W. G. JULIAN

Sound, Man and Building
by L. H. SCHAUDINISCHKY

Man, Climate and Architecture—2nd ed.
by B. GIVONI

Architectural Aerodynamics
by R. M. AYNSLEY, B. J. VICKERY and W. MELBOURNE

An Historical Outline of Architectural Science—2nd ed.
by H. J. COWAN

Scientific Basis of Air Conditioning
by KEN-ICHI KIMURA

Computer Applications in Architecture
edited by J. S. GERO

Solar Radiation Control in Buildings
by EDWARD L. HARKNESS and MADAN L. MEHTA

Environmental Factors in the Design of Building Fenestration
by B. P. LIM, K. R. RAO, K. THARMARATNAM and A. M. MATTAR

Indoor Climate
by D. A. MCINTYRE

Environmental Psychology in Building Design

by

JOHN BREBNER

*Department of Psychology, University of Adelaide,
South Australia*

APPLIED SCIENCE PUBLISHERS LTD
LONDON

APPLIED SCIENCE PUBLISHERS LTD
RIPPLE ROAD, BARKING, ESSEX, ENGLAND

British Library Cataloguing in Publication Data

Brebner, John
  Environmental psychology in building design.—
  (Architectural science series)
  1. Environmental psychology
  2. Architecture
  I. Title II. Series
  155.9092′472 BF353

  ISBN 0-85334-969-X

WITH 6 TABLES AND 25 ILLUSTRATIONS

© APPLIED SCIENCE PUBLISHERS LTD 1982

94163

Printed in Great Britain by Galliard (Printers) Ltd, Great Yarmouth

Acknowledgements

Many people have assisted in the preparation of this book, and many have contributed to it in different ways. Amongst those whose material is reproduced in the text, David Sless and Peter Cairney, Kerry Jaeger and Robert Sommer deserve thanks. The kindness of the Standards Association of Australia and the British Standards Institution, some of whose recommendations concerning the disabled are reproduced in Chapter 5, is acknowledged. At the same time, the danger of taking portions of Standards out of context is noted, and anyone directly concerned with these recommendations should consult the complete Standards.

My colleagues Jenny Burt and Chris Cooper, whose pictures appear in the text, gave their permission for this with the good grace which is characteristic of them. Michael White, Michael Clark, Mara Olekalns and Phil Smith commented sensibly on particular portions of the book, and I am grateful to them for their views. A number of our University librarians have been of inestimable help to me and, in singling out our subject librarian Marg Hosking for special thanks, I would like to recognise the fact that without the library staff this book could not have been written.

Finally, in actually producing this manuscript, three people have worked with me, making light work of a demanding task. Len van Ruth did all the photographic work, Judy Fallon did the illustrations and much of the compilation, and Margaret Blaber not only typed the manuscript but brought order and sequence to the handwritten scraps and jottings which she received. Their contribution, and my sincere gratitude to all three is recognised here.

This book is dedicated to my wife Jill and my children Candida, David and Christine, and to the memory of Anna Clare

Foreword

Most of the books in the Architectural Science Series have dealt with the application of the physical sciences to architectural design. There have been some exceptions to this rule. Professor Givoni's *Man, Climate and Architecture* and Professor Schaudinischky's *Sound, Man and Building* introduced the physiological basis of thermal and acoustic design, respectively, and Dr Canter's *Psychology for Architects* dealt with perception and the use of space from a psychologist's point of view.

Few architects today doubt the relevance of physiology and psychology to their work. Ultimately the object of design is to satisfy instrumentation. Dr Brebner's book is therefore particularly welcome because it combines, as far as I know for the first time, the application of physiological and psychological principles to architectural design.

The coverage is comprehensive, ranging from heat, light, sound and odour, through traffic in buildings, to colour theory and aesthetics. While Dr Brebner does not produce solutions for all the problems he discusses, because science has not advanced that far, he has provided a great deal of stimulating material for architectural designers on most aspects of ergonomics and environmental psychology.

HENRY J. COWAN
*Professor of Architectural Science,
University of Sydney, Australia*

vii

Note: Because SI units are used in this book some rounding off of values and amounts quoted by other people has been done where that seemed appropriate.

Contents

Chapter 1

Introduction

This book is about environmental psychology and the workability of the built environment. In large measure it is concerned with aspects of the environment which impinge on us directly, the spaces we live in, the objects we look at, handle, sit upon, and generally use. But it is also about how people appreciate their environments, and how they can and do behave within them. Concern about how functional built environments and the things in them are, goes by various names in different countries: human engineering or human factors in America; ergology in Japan; and ergonomics in Europe, Australia and New Zealand. This latter term, from the Greek '*ergos*' (work) and '*nomos*' (science), is sometimes used in the narrow sense of the study of workplaces, but throughout this text ergonomics is used in its broadest sense of what empirical studies can tell us about the workability of environments. Some of the areas treated in later chapters are: the forces people are capable of exerting, the ergonomic requirements which well-designed seating must meet, principles in designing for disabled people, some of the effects the built environment has on social interaction, and a consideration of the role of aesthetics in the environment. Within the text, ergonomics and environmental psychology shade into one another, as they do in the world around us. The difference between them, such as it is, is that ergonomics is directed more at performance, while environmental psychology focuses on behaviour. This distinction is a meaningful one, the fuzziness of which is justified by the reality that, though they originated at different times, and in different ways, the two areas link up when almost any particular environment is studied. The principles of seating dealt with later provide a good example of this. Under the banner of Environmental Psychology, the interest of researchers has mainly been in the effects various spatial arrangements have on social interaction. Ergonomists, on the other hand, have studied how a chair should work in terms of the seated person's blood circulation, muscle fatigue, and spinal support. Both sets of information are important when designing settings in which seats are a major feature, and ignoring either can render the setting unworkable.

More generally, the application of ergonomic principles may not overcome all possible problems, but it usually minimises mistakes, risks and fatigue, and maximises speed, reliability and ease of operation. This is achieved by using an empirical rather than a rational, or 'common-sense' approach, so that we know rather than believe, because our beliefs have been put to the test. Common-sense views of the world tend to be incapable of disproof, partly because they are widely shared, but also because any problems or difficulties which arise are not traced back to the incorrect rationalisation of the world which is their source. Many common-sense views about human behaviour are ill-founded, and from time to time some of these are enshrined in the stonework of our buildings. The gambler's fallacy that the likelihood of a particular 'heads' or 'tails' outcome increases with each successive occurrence of the other outcome, is one example of a mistaken belief which is widely held. In fact, looking forward to the next throw, the chance of 'heads' or 'tails' remains 50–50 on each occurrence.

In our buildings it may seem reasonable, even desirable, to design open plan and/or windowless accommodation. Yet there is evidence both that clerical performance is worse in open plan settings than in smaller offices, and that costly refenestration programmes may be avoided by heeding the eight out of ten people who, it was found, considered windows to be necessary (Wells, 1965). This point leads us to another problem, namely, the reliability and validity of information which is obtained when people's views are sought whether by interview or questionnaire. Those concerned with designing buildings are only too aware how difficult it is to discover what the eventual users will want, and that simply asking them does not necessarily give a true picture. The main difficulty is that buildings are far more complex than most people can conceptualise before actually experiencing being in and around them. The ergonomic answer to this and to related problems, is to improve techniques by which the information is acquired so that it is more reliable. The value of ergonomists and behavioural scientists to design teams is as much their knowledge of techniques they can apply to specific circumstances, such as collecting valid data about behaviour, as it is in the store of facts provided by their training. Arriving at good design decisions probably more often requires the former techniques, although the tendency remains to try to rely upon the latter body of information. Because of this, it is paradoxical that the greater part of ergonomic research is performed in universities, colleges and government departments, rather than by ergonomists working on 'real-life' design problems.

It is common to find that, in an attempt to bridge the information gap, those faced with design decisions rely on the recommendations of their national Standards Association or of some 'cookbook' of ergonomic information. This is to be commended. But, unfortunately, some problems remain. In the first place, such information is often static, and has not necessarily been obtained under the same conditions which apply in the designer's situation, and is, therefore, commensurately inapplicable. An example may make this point. It has been suggested (Gregory, 1973), that, since the colour to which the normal, dark-adapted eye is most sensitive, is green, we should paint photographic dark rooms in that colour. This idea is entirely reasonable, but we should note the implicit assumption that the photographer will remain dark-adapted for prolonged periods. If a photographer tends to use the dark room for short periods only, he will not achieve dark-adaptation which requires 30–40 min. Moving out of the dark room into normal lighting will destroy the dark-adaptation and with it the photographer's sensitivity to green, leaving him worse off than with white walls. Similarly, if there is a thin line of light under the dark room door when it is closed, as sometimes happens, this trivial feature will be enough to prevent dark-adaptation.

This simple example illustrates a fundamental feature of human functioning, variables which affect performance do not act independently but interact together. The effect of this is that, sometimes, a new, perhaps seemingly unimportant variable, may have a disproportionate effect upon performance.

The slightest distraction can totally disrupt highly organised skills like putting at golf or serving in a tennis match. The slightest evident addition to a painting or song can render it unpleasing. And, by the same token, the slightest additional demand made on the individual's information processing or response organising capacities, may make performance impossible.

Lapses in our control of our own performance occur daily and, although we tend to see them as the result of external factors, so that tripping on a staircase may be ascribed to worn or uneven steps, or steps of different height, it is very often more accurate to say that we were unprepared for that situation, but that, if we had recognised or expected it, we would have acted differently and without loss of control. The minor difficulties everyone experiences from time to time in avoiding obstacles; accurately judging rates, quantities, distance or time; remembering; and in all the other human modes of functioning, are unimportant failures of our information processing. Given a different outcome, however, a mistake in distance judgement can become a car accident. Many such accidents are best understood in terms of the limitations and vulnerabilities of human information processing, and it is one of the tasks of ergonomics to avoid them. Here, all that need be said is that the central process receives information from all sensory sources and, even though it has no relevance for other stimuli which are present, any additional stimulus will affect the ongoing central process, and may alter performance. To give one example, a number of research workers have obtained evidence that sensitivity to green–blue colour increases, but sensitivity to red–orange decreases, when some additional non-visual stimulus is present while colour thresholds are being measured (Kravkov, 1936, 1939*a*, 1939*b*; Jakovlev, 1940; Allen and Schwartz, 1940). This particular effect though stable is a weak one, and makes no great impact on our everyday life. Nevertheless, where fine colour judgement is required, as in reproducing material used in testing for colour vision defects, in high quality colour photography, or in chemical chromatography, it might be possible to improve performance by including or excluding additional stimuli.

There are much more dramatic effects in everyday behaviour. The attention holding properties of regularly repeating, intense stimuli are used to good effect in ambulance sirens, firebells or flashing light warning devices. But the same interruption of activity, and the additional effort required to continue with what one is doing, is less acceptable when someone else's telephone is ringing or the fluorescent light flickers noticeably. It is possible to design protectively, in a fashion which safeguards the functions being performed from effects which interrupt, inhibit or make performance more effortful. The first step toward this is the realisation that the central mechanisms actively integrate all stimuli acting upon the person, and that there are performance penalties for unnecessary amounts or complexity of information affecting the person, or of the performance required of him or her. The second step is taken when it is understood that the applicability of static information such as is provided in building codes, standards of information or 'cookbooks' of ergonomic data, is circumscribed by the whole, dynamic environment within which that information is applied. The final step needed is to test the effectiveness of the design in use against norms for that function where these exist, or against performance under other designs, as well as measuring the satisfaction of the users. The advantage of replacing common-sense and intuition with an empirical and deductive approach, lies in harnessing our ability and creativity more effectively. Where common-sense does come in, and is very necessary, is in checking that the scientific data and principles which exist are really applicable to the problem in hand. There is no substitute for reason in evaluating and selecting what is most directly relevant from our store of empirical observations.

Chapter 2

Human Physical Characteristics

2.1. TYPICAL BODY MEASUREMENTS AND THEIR IMPLICATIONS FOR ENVIRONMENTAL DESIGN

It is one of those curious facts that while an enormous amount of anthropometric data exists (see Table 2.1.1) there never seem to be accurate and up to date figures for any population for which a designer is working. At best he or she can rely on information ten years old, and often obtained in a different country. Clearly, it is a prime requirement of workable environments that they should physically fit the people using them. Figure 2.1.1 shows, however, that the difference between countries is more important than the antiquity of the data. Calculating the gradient of the average heights given in different studies over fairly recent years, gives the same results in all cases, a slope of zero. So, average height does not appear to be

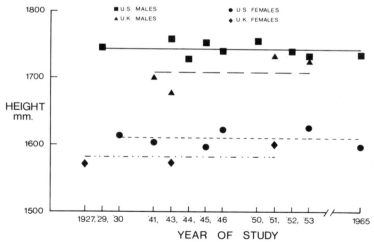

Fig. 2.1.1. The average height of American and British men and women in recent times.

6

Table 2.1.1
Some examples of anthropometric studies

BULLOCK, M. I. and STEINBERG, M. A. (1975) An anthropometric survey of Australian civilian male and female pilots. *Control*, **2**, 29–43.

CHURCHILL, E., CHURCHILL, T., McCONVILLE, J. T. and WHITE, R. M. (1977) *Anthropometry of Women in the US Army*, Report No. 2. The Basic Univariate Statistics, Webb Associates Inc.: Yellow Springs, Ohio.

CONNAN, A. and CNOCKAERT, J. C. (1975) Ecole Normale Superieure d'Education Physique et Sportive, Chatenay-Malabry, France, *Travail Humain*, **38**(2), 259–64.

DAMON, A., STOUDT, H. W. and McFARLAND, R. A. (1966) *The Human Body in Equipment Design*. Howard University Press: Cambridge, Mass.

DANIELS, G. S. (1952) *The 'Average Man'*. Aerospace Medical Research Labs., Wright-Patterson, AFB: Ohio.

HANSEN, R. and CORNOG, D. Y. (1958) *Annotated bibliography of applied physical anthropology in human engineering*. USAF, WADD, TR 56-30.

HENDY, K. (1978) Australian Tri-Service Anthropometric Survey, 1977. In: *Human Factors and Contemporary Society. Proc. 15th Ann. Conf. of the Ergonomics Soc. of A.N.Z.* Ed. T. J. Triggs, Printed at Monash University: Melbourne.

HERTZBERG, H. T. E., DANIELS, G. S. and CHURCHILL, E. (1954) *Anthropometry of flying personnel—1950*, USAF, WADC, TR 52-321.

HERTZBERG, H. T. E. (1972) Engineering anthropology. In: *Human Engineering Guide to Equipment Design*. Eds. H. P. Van Cott and R. G. Kincade. US Govt. Printing Office: Washington, D.C.

LAUBACH, L. L., McCONVILLE, J. T., CHURCHILL, E. and WHITE, R. M. (1977) *Anthropometry of Women of the US Army*. Report No. 1. Methodology and Survey Plan, Webb Associates Inc.: Yellow Springs, Ohio.

NATIONAL BUREAU OF STANDARDS (1977) *Power lawn mowers: Evaluation of anthropometric foot probes*. Human Factors Section, Consumer Product Safety Commission Report No. NBSIR-77-1294, Washington D.C.

OSHIMA, M., FUJIMOTO, T., OGURO, T., TOBIMATSU, N. and MORI, T. (1962) *Anthropometry of Japanese Pilot*. Japanese Air Self-Defense Force, Tokyo Aero-Medical Lab. Final report, March 1961–March 1962.

RAHE, R. H. and CARTER, J. E. L. (1976) Middle-aged male competitive swimmers. Background and body structure characteristics. *J. Sports Medicine and Physical Fitness*, Vol. 16 n.4. pp. 309–18. Naval Health Research Center: San Diego, Calif.

REYNOLDS, H. M. (1976) *A Foundation for Systems Anthropometry, Phase 1*. Interim Scientific Report, June 30–Nov 1976. Michigan Univ. Ann Arbor Highway Safety Research Inst.: Michigan.

ROBERTS, J. (1966) *Weight by Height and Age of Adults*. National Center for Health Statistics, Rockville, Md. Div. of Health Examination Statistics. Bureau of the Census: Washington D.C.

SHONYO, C. (1977) *Anthropometry: Basic Studies and Applications*. Vol. 1. National Technical Information Service: Springfield, Va.

SHONYO, C. (1977) *Anthropometry: Basic Studies and Applications*. Vol. 2. National Technical Information Service: Springfield, Va.

SNYDER, R. G., SCHNEIDER, L. W., OWINGS, C. L., REYNOLDS, H. M. and GOLOMB, D. H. (1977) *Anthropometry of Infants, Children and Youths to Age 18 for Product Safety Design*. Michigan Univ. Ann Arbor Highway Safety Research Inst.: Michigan.

STOUDT, H., DAMON, A., McFARLAND, R. and ROBERTS, J. (1965) *Weight, Height and Selected Body Dimensions of Adults*. National Center for Health Statistics, Rockville, Md. Div. of Health Examination Statistics. Bureau of the Census: Washington D.C.

WHITE, R. M. (1964) *Anthropometric Survey of the Royal Thai Armed Forces*. Army Natick Labs.: Mass.

changing over the time-span covered by these studies, although there is evidence that it is being reached earlier in life (Oxford, 1969; Tanner, 1968). There are rather fewer studies than one would wish for this procedure to be reliable, but is is probably safe to conclude that average height is not changing in any dramatic fashion in the more affluent nations. Where improvements in diet have occurred, as in some Asian countries, average height has increased, but this does not seem to have happened in the populations considered here. It may be assumed that measurements of length of other parts of the body tend to be equally stable, since it seems unlikely that our arms are tending to lengthen if our height is not altering. However, changes in girth, particularly of portions of the anatomy affected by food intake and exercise, are less stable and may change more quickly.

Those anthropometric measures which are most frequently taken are those related to seating; namely, stature, weight, height when seated, elbow height when seated, thigh length, lower leg length and the breadth of the bottom when seated. However, it is the dynamic anthropometric measures which are of real interest when designing for any human function.

The anthropometric differences which exist between different racial and national groups seem to be far more relevant than changes of anthropometric dimensions within any of these groups over time. For example, if we combine a number of studies of the height of the civilian population in Britain or in America, to provide a large sample of people who were measured, the mean differences between the two countries are as shown in Table 2.1.2.

Table 2.1.2
Average height of British and American civilians

	British		American	
	Number measured	Average height (mm)	Number measured	Average height (mm)
Men	28 426	1 680	35 344	1 740
Women	40 662	1 580	11 950	1 610

Because of the age of some of the data, only measurements of the white population were deemed comparable for the two countries.

Table 2.1.2 shows white American women to be 30 mm taller than British women on average, while the average white American man is some 60 mm taller than his British counterpart.

The studies which were combined to give the data in Table 2.1.2 were: for British men, Clements and Pickett (1952), Kemsley (1950); for British women, Cathcart *et al.* (1927), Kemsley (1957), Kemsley (1950); for American men, Diehl (1933), Hooton (1945), McFarland *et al.* (1954), Hooton and Dupertuis (1951); and for American women, O'Brien and Shelton (1941), Hooton (1945).

Even after maturity, the height of an individual does not remain constant, but decreases with ageing. Data from the American National Health Survey (1965), for example, show that, from about 25 years onward, height decreases by around 1·7 mm per annum, on average, for men and women. It follows from this that one should be cautious about using global averages as estimates of the height of groups of people who are preponderantly middle-aged or elderly. For example, the estimated population average will overestimate height by as much as 90 mm for groups of people who are all 75 years old or more.

It is common when presenting anthropometric data to provide the mean and some data about the distribution of measures. This provides information which will allow the designer to know the proportion of the population which can be accommodated by his design dimensions. Usually, the assumption is made that the physical dimension in question is normally distributed so that 68% of the population falls within the range $\pm 1\sigma$ from the mean (see Fig. 2.1.2). The information which is most often given with the mean is the upper and lower percentiles for the 10th and 90th percentiles, or the 5th and 95th percentiles. However, if the shape of the distribution of measures obtained from any user-population is not normally distributed, and the risk of this increases as the size of the user-population diminishes, then the means and percentiles from the general population are inappropriate. For example, May and Wright (1961) found that the average height for a sample of more than 2750 British company directors was 1780 mm, 100 mm taller than the average civilian man. Company boardrooms in the UK should perhaps consider raising the height of their tables and chairs in the light of this data, although their problem is eased somewhat by the fact (British Standard 3044:1958;

Human Physical Characteristics

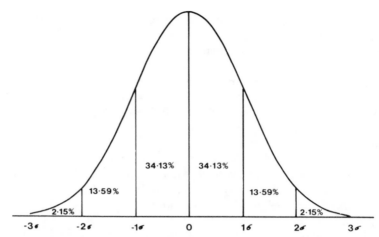

Fig. 2.1.2. Percentages of cases (areas) under the normal distribution shown in terms of σ (standard deviation).

Bennett, 1977) that the common 750 mm tables and 450 mm chairs used with them are too high for comfortable seating for most people. Murrell (1971) and Bennett (1977) both suggest that 450 mm is close to the 95th percentile for popliteal height, i.e. the height of the lower leg under the knee, for men as well as women. This means that only 5 % of people should find a 450 mm chair to be the correct height for them. However, these considerations do not take into account any effect of footwear which effectively lengthens popliteal height, and is widely used by people at the low end of the height range as a prosthetic device to bring them closer to the population mean.

Reviewing the published evidence on anthropometric data suggests that the means and ranges in Table 2.1.3 are reasonable estimates of the measures taken.

A slightly different approach to static anthropometric measures can be taken, e.g. Barkla (1961), which uses one actual measurement as the basis from which to estimate others. Height is the most commonly used base measure. This approach is better than having no information, and though less reliable than actually taking the relevant measures, can reduce time spent on finding relevant static measures. The prediction of body measures by this method is improved if we expand the base measures to include other information. Obviously, if

Table 2.1.3
The 5th, 50th and 95th percentiles for selected anthropometric measures

	Men (mm)			Women (mm)		
	5th	50th	95th	5th	50th	95th
Height						
1	1 626	1 727	1 854	1 499	1 600	1 702
2	1 615	1 735	1 849	—	1 598	1 704
3	1 626	1 727	1 829	1 456	1 600	1 702
Seated height						
1	838	914	965	787	838	914
2	843	907	965	785	848	907
3	851	914	965	749	851	876
Popliteal height						
1	406	432	457	381	406	457
2	394	439	490	356	399	445
3	394	419	445	368	394	419
Knee height, standing						
2	490	544	594	455	498	546
3	508	546	597	432	495	546
Elbow rest height above chair seat						
2	188	241	295	180	234	279
3	191	241	267	216	229	254
4	—	216	—	—	216	—
Buttocks to knee cap						
1	533	584	635	533	559	609
2	541	592	640	518	569	625
3	546	597	635	546	559	609
Height of thigh above hard seat						
1	127	152	178	—	—	—
2	109	145	175	104	137	175
3	127	165	191	127	165	203
Breadth across the buttocks						
2	400	356	404	312	363	434
3	333	356	394	318	368	406

1. From Bennett (1977).
2. From McCormick (1976).
3. From Murrell (1971).
4. *British Standard 3044:1958.*

as well as height we take the weight of the individual, our prediction of some measures, e.g. waist circumference, is markedly improved, but the prediction of others, e.g. leg length, is not. Using the proportionate estimate approach successfully, requires that relevant base measures be employed rather than simply using information which happens to be readily available as height is.

2.2. DYNAMIC ANTHROPOMETRICS

It is usual for ergonomics texts to describe the range of movements in anatomical and physiological terms. Here, the approach is varied purely to try to give the information in the easiest terms possible. To begin with, the body may be regarded as a system of bones (levers), which are moved by shortening or lengthening of the muscles attached to them (force), with the joints serving as the fulcrums of the lever system. Any of the bony movable parts of the body can be viewed in this way.

The extent of movements depends on limb length to some degree, but one must exercise some caution in interpreting the data on the length of possible movements. To give one example, Woodson (1957) quotes a forward arm reach of 750 mm for a person 1·56 m in height, and the comparable figure of 990 mm for a taller individual 1·98 m in height. These figures are fine for the standing position, but when seated, the difference in effective reach, even without adopting curious postures, for people at those two ends of the height range is closer to 100 mm, than the 240 mm cited in Woodson. The reason is straightforward. The taller person typically has a longer back so that, when seated, the shoulders are higher above the table with consequent loss of reach. Stretching out the arm, then drawing oneself up straight in one's chair may demonstrate this point. If one allows the individual to move and change position, then the differences in effective reach become even smaller. This point is clearly made by some authors, and in their comprehensive section on human body dimensions, Morgan *et al.* (1963) caution that their data are specific to the context in which they obtained them.

The force of movements also depends upon position and posture which are used to bring different muscle groups into play, so that different people achieve the same effects in different ways. It is a sign of good design when movements involving the same sets of muscles can be made by anyone and the same results ensue. For any specific movement the force which can be applied is a function of the muscle length and thickness and condition. Additionally, the condition of the joints may affect the strength and extent of movements if conditions like arthritis are present. Some atrophy of the muscles with ageing is normal and there is a decline in strength with an increase in the average age of the population. One of the features of ageing research is the increase in variability of functional capacity which accompanies ageing, as some people alter very much while others do not. To account for an ageing population as birth rates decline and life expectancy goes up, the only safe rule is to assume that everyone is a weakling suffering from a slipped disc and arthritis.

Choice of materials and equipment is sometimes made on grounds which ignore the demands these will place on strength. Heavy doors require strong mechanisms to close them and are hard to open. In the writer's place of work some of the doors require a force of 70 N to open them which means that some people find opening them effortful, and minor instances like this surround us. There are also more dramatic cases where the strength required exceeds the capabilities of the people involved. Female parachutists in Australia formed one-third of the fatalities during the period 1960–74, although only one-tenth of the total of parachutists. A possible reason for this has been suggested in a study by Bullock (1978) who tested the pull capabilities of females who were representative of registered women parachutists in Australia in terms of height, weight, build, and age. The specification governing many if not most sporting parachutes is the American Federal Aviation Agency's (FAA) order that the device used to open the parachute be, 'positive and quick functioning with no more than 98 N pull'. The location of the opening handle varies for different styles and manufacturers and Bullock took this into account and tested six different locations in her study. Table 2.2.1 shows the percentage of her subjects capable of exerting a 98 N pull for 0·25 s. These results show clearly that even without the added stress of jumping from an aircraft travelling relatively fast, which is like stepping into a high wind, many of the subjects were not able to match the upper limit of pull force allowed by the FAA.

Table 2.2.1
Percentage of female subjects able to exert a 98 N pull for
0·25 s

Handle location	(%)
Left shoulder	5
Right shoulder	72
Left pocket	86
Right pocket	55
Top for reserve parachute on chest	40
Right for reserve parachute on chest	5

Dramatic examples like this are, fortunately enough, the exception rather than the rule. But the point made above stands, namely that many tasks performed in buildings have to be carried out with assistance from bigger muscle groups, or using the weight of the body, when the original intention was not for this to happen. Wherever awkward postures or strained efforts in unbalanced positions are called for, or the jerking or lifting of heavy objects is necessary, the possibility of permanent damage exists. It is probably true, though not necessarily fashionable, to say that the lack of a full understanding of all the possible ways in which the spine can be damaged, leads to exaggerated accusations of malingering and suspicions that compensation is sought which is not deserved. In fact, as research proceeds, it is becoming clear that a host of conditions other than the slipped disc give rise to symptoms, such as pain in the legs, which are part of recognisable syndromes which indicate treatment of a different sort than for a slipped disc (Crock, 1978). Awkward posture often means that the spine is used as a lever instead of being supported by the thigh muscles as in the 'knees together and bent, and back straight' advice on lifting. Whatever the weight of the trunk and head is, perhaps almost half the weight of the body, that weight is added to whatever is being picked up in a poorly balanced lifting position, and the effect is multiplied at the base of the spine. Back injuries can just as easily occur by lifting an almost weightless object in a particularly stressing way, as they can by lifting especially heavy objects.

Apart from damage, effortfulness can have all sorts of other effects from slowing of performance to overheating and fatigue, all of which tend to reduce rather than enhance the endeavours of people.

While stressing the fact that the following values should only be regarded as very rough guidelines, a review of some of the relevant literature suggests that for the types of movement discussed the figures given are reasonably representative.

The approaches to human movement within ergonomics tend either to detail the distances and forces required to use equipment or other objects, or take the operator's standpoint and outline the characteristics of the movements he can make. In practice, it may be helpful to have both, and a mixed approach is taken in this short section; where actual values are mentioned as guidelines these emerge from reviewing the literature and, wherever conflicting results occurred, favour the more conservative values.

2.2.1. Some Types of Movement
Head movement
The actual head, not the eyes which are capable of extending the distance travelled, moves about 40–50° left–right, down–up or side-to-side (Glanville and Kreezer, 1937; Murrell, 1971). But, for material to be viewed, the preferred location is in front of the person and within an arc of 30° downward from horizontal eye level. If the material is offset to one side, it needs to be higher within this region as the degree of offset increases.

Hand movement
The hand can be rotated to about 90° either palm up or palm down without moving the forearm. 'Chopping' movements with forearm steady give around 30° downward movement and 15–20° upward. Many grasping tasks force the hand into this upward movement and play some role in wrist injuries. Handle sizes and some forces that can be applied with the hand are mentioned in a later section. But the middle range for strength of grip for men using their dominant hand is between 335 and 470 N. For women, much lower values obtain, and average differences as great as 195 N have been found going on figures from Fisher and Birren (1946). Nor is it safe to assume that the range is as great as for men.

Arm movement
The extended arm can move forward and back through 220° from

a vertical starting point, and sideways upwards through about 130° starting from touching the side. Stretched out sideways, as in full-span, and moving at right angles to the head, an arc of about 180° can be inscribed. This implies the various arcs of reach within which controls and other devices to be touched can be located. But as soon as combinations of these movements, like reaching forward and down, are allowed, there is a roughly spherical area surrounding the individual which he can reach. Estimates vary on how far the boundary of the reachable area is, but as guidelines, 550 mm will be within reach of most short people, and 700 mm will be comfortable for tall people. There is some indication, e.g. Grandjean (1973), that shorter distances are required if a purely female population is considered. Again, in very general terms, around 50 mm seems to be the average difference for a wide range of reaching distances. Some more specific information is included in Chapter 5.

A number of references give detailed information about reach from the seated position (King *et al.*, 1947; Thorsden *et al.*, 1972) and much of it is summarised in Morgan *et al.* (1963). Many studies of reach in industrial and specific settings have been performed (e.g. King, 1948; Schnewlin, 1959; Easterby, 1964); and Grandjean's (1973) masterly work on ergonomics applied to the home environment is a rich source of useful data for anyone involved in designing these and similar environments.

Lifting

The bending and straightening of the back which takes place in stooping to pick things up, or to reach cupboards and shelves, requires space for good lifting, as well as keeping the weight of objects lifted to a minimum. Figures of about 1200 mm have been suggested, but this may be judged a minimum for tall people. The manner of lifting determines the strength, and three times as much force can be exerted with the legs bent and back straight, as can be with legs straight and bending from the waist to pick up an object.

Foot and leg movements

The movement of the feet and legs when seated or standing is needed in order to avoid circulation difficulties, regardless of whether foot-operated controls are being operated. This raises the question of whether footrests should be provided where sitting is prolonged, and is the main reason why adequate legroom is needed. The forward leg space under desks and tables is given as 600 mm by some writers (e.g. Woodson, 1957), but as noted under *Seating* (Section 5.5), 650 mm seems a more satisfactory guideline for many seated positions.

The extent of leg movements which individuals can make varies more than their arm movements and, apart from pedals and foot switches which are dealt with later, it is rare to find foot-operated mechanisms. The force of leg movements depends upon the particular muscles being used, and whether the person is braced against a seat or not. For this reason ranges of forces from a minimum of 110 N to a maximum close to 4450 N can be found in the literature if both sexes are taken into account.

As a final word, it is worth pointing out that we are all taught to be extremely conservative in our selection of movements. The use of elbow-operated handles on doors to operating theatres testifies to their effectiveness, but their usage remains restricted, and there are many other unusual but very workable ways of making things happen other than by use of the hand. A moment's reflection of how some disabled people succeed in their environments with loss or impairment of hand movements, will produce a whole range of alternatives. Typically, however, conservatism will render these alternatives unacceptable unless they are perceived as being necessary.

More detailed treatments of anthropometrics may be found in Grandjean's (1971) '*Fitting the Task to the Man: An Ergonomic Approach*', or Plagenhoef's (1971) '*Patterns of Human Motion—A Cinematographic Analysis*' which gives a great deal of information about forces of movement in sporting activities, and includes a computer program of kinetic analysis of human motion.

2.3.   FREQUENCIES OF OTHER BODY FUNCTIONS

2.3.1. The Circadian Rhythm

It is an important feature of most animal behaviour that it tends to follow a pattern in time. Time is not a causal factor, but it does have direction for us, and we are affected by events which repeat regularly over time.

The cycle which affects us most obviously is the circadian, night and day or diurnal rhythm. Most organisms show patterns of behaviour which are adaptations to the 24-h solar day and which are characteristic of their species. Not only is it adaptive that some animals become nocturnal, but it is also adaptive that, within a species, tolerance for toxic substances, for example, or resistance to electromagnetic radiation fluctuates, and that there is some inter-individual variability in state at any moment in the night–day cycle which, as the Latin-based term suggests, is only approximately (*circa*) a 24-h day (*dies*). Variability increases the likelihood of there being some survivors if changes in the environment become dangerous.

Circadian rhythms are important ergonomically in so far as human performance is better at some times of the day than others, and also because if resetting of the internal 'biological clock' becomes necessary, it takes time before performance regains its characteristic level.

Unfortunately, however, these simple statements disguise a multitude of conflicting results and divergent interpretation. While we can show convincingly that performance is at its worst in the small hours of the night (Bjerner *et al.*, 1955), it does not seem possible simply to infer from this result that productivity will necessarily follow the pattern of the curve throughout the daylight hours. Murrell (1971) reviews work curves, obtained between 1920–1953 effectively concluding that little of value for real-life settings had been learned. To some extent the studies reviewed by Murrell may reflect the sort of confusion that can arise where, instead of one universal pattern, more than one trend is occurring over the same period for different people. Several writers have suggested this, but the problem remains that given enough trends one can explain anything. The long-term studies by Bjerner *et al.* may, like carefully controlled studies such as Blake's which is described below, wash out short-term interference effects and provide a picture which is accurate, but which is easily invalidated for use in any short-term situation.

A very general picture of performance at different times of day is shown in Fig. 2.3.1.

The decrement in performance in the middle of the day has

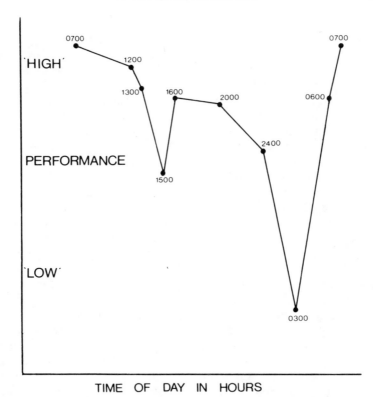

Fig. 2.3.1. A general representation of performance at different times of day.

sometimes been assumed to be related to the digestion of a 'mid-day' meal (Kleitman, 1963; Murrell, 1971). Certainly, drowsiness after meals might occur through changes in insulin levels or other effects. But the explanation for a period of relative inactivity in the middle of the day varies from avoiding the heat of the mid-day sun in countries where the siesta is socially acceptable, to the need to rest after having worked for several hours in countries with colder climates. Also controlled experiments by Blake (1967*a,b*) (reported in Colquhoun, 1971), call into question the dependence of the dip in performance upon the time of the 'mid-day' meal.

Other factors like body temperature have been shown both to be related to human performance and to vary with time of day (Kleitman, 1963). But again this is a general finding, and it is not the case that you can control the level of human performance in the same way you can vary the output of an electric oven by twiddling the temperature control knob.

The main mediating factor between performance and time of day, however, appears to be the presence or absence of light, and experimentation varying the timing of light and darkness periods while holding temperature constant (Kleitman, 1963), has shown that the body cycle tends to follow the light–dark cycle.

Where the established biological cycle is interfered with abruptly, as in changing from day to night shiftwork, or in the 'jet-lag' which follows rapid transportation to an incompatible time of day zone, the times shown in Fig. 2.3.1 are effectively misplaced right or left along the curve. From this we can see that it is conceivable that the lowering of performance and behaviour after mid-day has some biologically adaptive value. For example, if through the necessity to remain awake and alert throughout the night (perhaps to avoid some primaeval predator) the curve is misplaced by 12 h, the 'mid-day' and 'mid-night' dips partially coincide and may allow resynchronisation to occur more quickly. Richter (1965) has shown that the biological clock in the normally nocturnal rat shows a 12-h cycle as well as the longer 24-h cycle, and this gives some credibility to the hypothesis that the 12-h dip has adaptive value. This speculation depends on the degree of displacement and offers little comfort to the modern air traveller lying wide awake for most of the night in a foreign city.

Shiftwork has been studied since 1917 when the British Ministry of Munitions published an interim report on the health of munitions workers, though much of the work has consisted of statistical reviews of absenteeism and sick leave (see Conroy and Mills, 1970; Murrell, 1971). Experimental manipulation of different shiftwork systems has more recently been undertaken by Colquhoun in Cambridge (Colquhoun, 1971) and has shown the need for longer-term experimental investigations into the adaptation to shiftwork patterns.

Jet-lag has also been the subject of research and it has been found that it takes a week or more to adapt to the new time zone (Strughold, 1952), although adaptation occurs more rapidly if the travel is in an eastward rather than a westward direction (Hauty and Adams, 1966).

From an ergonomic point of view circadian rhythms are important for several reasons, one is the increasing move toward shiftwork, another the rise in artificial environments from space capsules to windowless buildings, and a third is the number of people involved in jet travel to incompatible time zones. As things are at present, shiftworkers still tend to be out of phase with other members of their family, and many show signs of fatigue and irritability while on nightwork. Jet aircraft crews tend to be constrained by regulations aimed at preventing them from being required to perform the most complex skills while at the lowest ebb of alertness and responsiveness. Typically, the degree of concern to control or avoid disrupting the circadian rhythm is a function of the risks and costs involved. We can send skilled men to the moon, but as the NASA clinical reports show (Berry, 1969), the impairment of efficiency due to disruption of the circadian rhythm, can be a real hazard to such space missions. There is no reason to suppose that performance is less affected when the task is less dramatic, or the risks less important.

2.3.2 *The Menstrual Cycle*

There is a voluminous literature on the cyclic changes in the reproductive state of the female human. Rather little, however, is relevant to ergonomics. Many assertions are made all of which would be true for some women. The studies of most interest in the present context have been reviewed by Redgrave (in Colquhoun, 1971). There, she points out, that two phases of increased activity have been observed during the menstrual cycle. The first is the premenstruation phase which is characterised by increased tension and irritability (Israel, 1938; Dalton, 1964). Associated with these changes there is often a marked alteration in personality shown as heightened emotionality and a tendency toward irrational behaviour. The expression of emotionality appears to reflect the basic personality of the individual so that normally withdrawn women can become depressed, while outgoing, extraverted women are more likely to behave in a generally aggressive manner. Some loss in planning and organising ability has been reported during the menstrual period (Schwarz, 1959), as has a loss in co-ordination (Johnson, 1932). Output in assembly operations has been found to be lowered during the premenstrual phase (Sfogliano, 1964), and the beginning of menstruation. However, there is some evidence that women paid according to output and accuracy may be able to overcome the effects (Eayrs and Glass, 1962), perhaps by increased effort to compensate for any loss in skill (Lewin and Freund, 1930), though such findings are likely to be task-specific.

The second phase, around the time of ovulation, is often marked by feelings of well-being and elation (Benedek and Rubinstein, 1939; McCance *et al.*, 1937), but the contradictory finding of increased tension has also been reported (Greene and Dalton, 1953).

While too important to ignore, the effects of menstrual cycle on performance are so individual that the only safe general approach seems to be actively informing people that the symptoms which occur just before, and in the early part of menstruation, can be treated.

2.3.3. *Other Cycles and Rhythms*

The cycles dealt with above are obvious and their effects are widely recognised. Other cyclic activities, however, tend to be taken as inherent in the individual, or the social organisation, to a degree that they are unchangeable. Yet this is not usually true. Two obvious distinctions can be made in considering the control of cycles in activities. The first is between rapid and slow cycles, and it is conventional to break these into infradian cycles which have a frequency below 1 cycle per 28 h, and ultradian cycles with a frequency higher than 1 cycle in 20 h. These cycles outside the circadian frequencies are currently the subject of much medical and scientific research (Halberg and Ahlgren, 1979) since, to take one example, when treating cancerous growths, the amount of healthy tissue also destroyed by chemotherapy or radiation can be reduced by plotting the time course of cell division in fast growing cells such as hair follicle cells and cells in bone marrow, or in the lining of the intestinal tract. Obviously, if the sensitivity of the body to any substance waxes and wanes, it makes sense to time the treatment to obtain the most beneficial result. It may also be possible to compare the effects of different treatments in this respect.

The second distinction is between cyclic activities which are determined by decisions made by people and others which are not. Much of human endeavour has been concerned with simulating conditions experienced in one part of a natural cycle during other parts of it. Without the experience of summer, or of high tides, the conception of greenhouses or canal and river locks would probably be much more difficult. Schurer (1978) discusses natural and man-made time patterns, pointing out that as transport and communication have taken on global dimensions, discrepancies in the timing of events, e.g. Friday being the weekly holy day in Muslim countries and Sunday in Christian countries, can result in less time being available for international commerce. Moreover, because of the religious basis of the timing of, many recurring events, standardisation at international level seems impossible to achieve. Having regard to buildings, controlling the timing of events to obtain the benefits this can give rise to, is neglected in the face of social and organisational pressures to conform, and also because temporal conformity itself offers benefits provided overload does not occur.

Returning to the first distinction, fast ultradian cycles permeate human functioning in ways which vary from trivial to critical. The fact that the extended finger shows a tremor around 8–12 s may be detectable just by extending the fingers, but the facts that downward pressing sorts of finger movements tend to be phased in with the downward part of the tremor (Travis, 1929), and that reaction times are faster and less variable if a signal to respond arrives when the tremor is at the top or bottom of the cycle (Tiffin and Westhafer, 1940), probably have little relevance except, perhaps, in microsurgery or other micromanipulative tasks. However, the fact that we can drive the brain by producing a synchronised response to regularly repeated stimulation, means that if we stimulate the visual or auditory system within the range 8–13 Hz, we may produce the alpha rhythm which is associated with altered states of consciousness. Loss of awareness can occur in this manner, and may well not be trivial. Of definite importance is the breathing rhythm which tends to be around 1 every 3 s. Any forced departure from this rate tends to be distracting, then distressful, before becoming incapacitating. Similarly, if heart rate departs markedly from, say, 70 beats per minute, the individual will usually show other signs of distress as well.

Somewhat slower ultradian cycles have also been found and Halberg and Ahlgren (1979) quote a 90-min cycle for light and deep sleep and the same periodicity for drifting in and out of dreaming. Still other cycles depend upon being triggered by events or activities under the control of the individual. The ingestion of food and liquids exemplifies this, and it may require about 24 h to complete the eating–excreting cycle though this is affected by many factors including the amount of food, its calorific value and, in the case of drinks, their status as diuretics, so that, depending on the nature of the food and drink, very much faster cycles also exist.

The time of day when food is taken has also been found to affect whether volunteer subjects gained or lost weight though taking in the same number of calories (2000 per day). This research, performed by the two authors cited above showed that when the only meal was taken as breakfast, rather than dinner, over a period of seven days, the subjects lost weight when breakfasting only compared to when they only ate an evening meal.

Infradian cycles of varying periodicities have also been observed. Many of these have been found as the result of research into medical aspects of chronobiology, e.g. a 7-day cycle in the rejection of kidney transplants has been found by Italian and American researchers. Some of the longer cycles are less easily studied simply because more variables can exert an influence during longer time spans, and more data tends to be lost as cycles move into months and years. But some annual patterns emerge, so that it is the case that the incidence of suicide among sufferers from depressive illnesses shows an increase in late spring although the cause of this is still unknown. Perhaps temperature is the relevant variable since Myers and Davies (1978), in a study of mania, which was found to peak in the summer and quieten in winter, could only relate this cycle to temperature. None of the other variables, like hours of sunshine, which they investigated, appeared relevant. However, the calculation of biorhythms predicted from the date of birth has no scientific standing. If such simplistic methods work at all, then they almost certainly do so through the suggestibility of the people who believe in them, and they probably have less effect than telling those people that they are looking particularly well, or complimenting them on the acuteness of their insight.

While making the distinction between cycles which result from decisions made by people and others which do not, it is worth bearing in mind that individuals may become geared, both physiologically and psychologically, to time courses, and the 'I keep thinking today is

Monday' effect is common after a long week-end. Ergonomically, the manipulation of cycles usually only occurs where some form of possible overload exists. Despite the existence of evidence that people differ in how early in the day they are capable of producing their best performance, from which it appears that extraverted people are at their best later in the day than introverts are at theirs (Colquhoun and Corcoran, 1964), allowing the person some choice of working hours is still the exception rather than the rule even where this is possible. Partly this is because flexible hours may increase operating costs, and any bills which reflect the duration of the working day rather than the number of people present, will militate against flexitime unless offset by greater productivity.

The simplest way of illustrating the time-course of a city is to plot some of the available information across time of day, day of week, and month of year. From this, some of the man-made cycles as well as some natural ones can be seen, and some of the most vulnerable times, such as the peak requirement hours for which electricity must be generated, are evident. A comprehensive treatment of time and behaviour is given by Parkes and Thrift (1980).

Chapter 3

Psychological Factors

In considering workable environments it is necessary to understand the process by which people arrive at their interpretation of the world. For the present purpose some of the finer points of psychological knowledge can be avoided and, by outlining a simple model of human information processing of a very general nature, we can ignore contending views on specific issues which are currently being researched. Figure 3.0.1 illustrates human information processing. Briefly, detectable changes in the sensory receptors are organised into

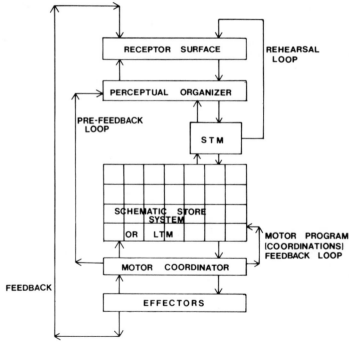

Fig. 3.0.1. A simple description of human information processing.

26

an integrated percept of the world which remains accessible to use for a very brief period in our short-term memory (STM). Some information is transferred from the short-term memory to our relatively permanent, long-term memory (LTM). If action is indicated, the information of the long-term memory maps on to response elements of programmes for motor activity, organising a response by the effectors. This response creates new stimulation at the receptor surface.

3.1. What is Stored?

The most important question is what is stored in the long-term memory which is the core of our experience? We know that acts of imagery are possible, allowing us to produce internalised representations of sensory experiences, so that we can conjure up images of familiar places or things, or of things very recently experienced. Some experiences are identified symbolically and in place of images, the symbols are manipulated as in 'yellow and blue make green'. Some symbols define the nature of the manipulation itself as in the instruction to 'imagine the Eiffel Tower ... *upside down*'. Most important, however, we do not simply have stores of disconnected images and symbols, but items are stored *in their relationships* to other items. These relationships are abstracted from our experiences and allow us to anticipate the next events. For several reasons this is of crucial importance for skilled performance of any sort. First, anticipation consists of feeding forward to the perceptual organiser a set of probable characteristics of the expected input. For example, our distance from and orientation to an object determines its appearance, and it is this information, known in advance, which permits the organisation of sensory input into a perception. Consider the structure of the eye, which not only has a 'blind spot' where the optic nerve leaves the retina, but also practically all the cells capable of detecting fine patterns are restricted to a tiny area near the centre of the retina. From this we might expect to look out at a world which is out of focus at the edges and has a hole in the middle. But not only is the missing information supplied from the LTM to organise our perception, it is very accurately given.

Secondly, anticipation can allow sampling for particular features at specific times. The absence of these features or the presence of unexpected information tends to interrupt the smooth flow of behaviour. Delaying the auditory feedback of speech by around $\frac{1}{3}$s, for example, can have a dramatically disruptive effect on the ability to read aloud. The words fed back are temporally at variance with all the other information available to the speaker about what he should be hearing. Sampling is an economical procedure which reduces the amount of information processed, leaving capacity available to deal with other information.

Thirdly, anticipation is complex and covers all sensory channels, that is to say that what is anticipated is a complete and integrated percept. Missing or unexpected features of any kind can force reorganisation of a person's perceptual and cognitive interpretation of the world at the expense of time. This is an important point since even one new element can lead to a total reorganisation of the perceived world. A dramatic example of this is cited by Gregory (1973) describing the research of Ivo Kohler into the effects of wearing inverting lenses which turn the visual world upside down, but leave the auditory and tactual world as it was. A candle seen through the lenses was perceived as being upside down until the moment it was lit. Then, the heat from the flame, and the stored information that candle flames burn upwards, was sufficient to change the perceived orientation of the candle so that it then was *seen* the right way up.

Moreover, the intersensory transmission of relationships learned in one modality but transferred to other modalities seems to occur almost instantaneously. Gregory (1973) again gives critical examples of this. A patient, S.B., blind very soon after birth, had his sight restored to him by surgery when he was middle-aged. Simple forms, e.g. upper case lettering which were tactually familiar to him could be recognised immediately using vision. More complex visual material, e.g. a lathe, could not be organised visually by S.B. when he first looked at it. Initially, all he could see was a handle, but, when he was allowed to run his hands over the lathe, keeping his eyes shut while he did so, then he was able to step back saying, when he opened his eyes, that he could now *see* it as a lathe. Once established, the tactual relationships had been translated, perhaps even simultaneously, for use visually. This multimodal transfer produces a vast range of relationships on the basis of which we structure the patterns of our expectations. It is the concordance throughout a set of relationships underlying our interpretations of sensory information which, when all the relevant relationships for a particular percept obtain, produces a stable and predictable environment. Ambiguities, conflicting or missing evidence can create illusions, reversible figures, or other effects which demonstrate the plasticity of our interpretation of sensory evidence, but, for the most part, sensory evidence can be integrated into stable and meaningful interpretations.

Fourthly, the perceptual and cognitive integration which is performed seems, in the absence of other strategies, to work probabilistically. This can be seen in laboratory studies of reaction times, word association, gambling, risk-taking and many other forms of behaviour in which items with the highest conditional probability seem to be the most easily accessible. Gambling is included in the list above since, when we do not know which possibility has the highest objective likelihood, we resort to other strategies, perhaps, as in the gambler's fallacy relying on recency rather than probability. Nevertheless, much of our anticipation is based on an assessment of the conditional probability of alternative Y occurring given that alternative X has already occurred.

Fifthly, although some re-interpretations take place immediately as we have shown above, this is not the same process as re-programming the LTM. The reversal of the candle's orientation happened because, given the new evidence provided by the heat of the candle flame, the LTM already possessed the other relevant relationships concerning the candle's true orientation. Acquiring new relationships can be done quickly and simply if they are in accordance with the existing relationships which, by generalisation, act as organising principles or rules for incoming information. Learning to ride a bicycle, getting one's 'sea legs', adapting to weightlessness in a space capsule, or even simply carrying an unaccustomed very heavy weight on one side of the body, all require extensions to previously learned sensory and motor relationships, and possibly the establishment of some new ones. If there is little in the way of relevant relationships stored in the LTM, it requires time and repeated experience to abstract and store the relevant relations. This is commonly accepted in learning situations but not always borne in

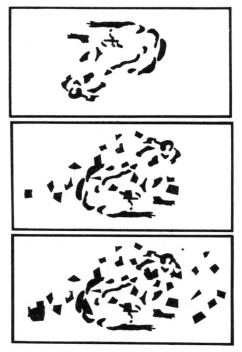

Fig. 3.1.1. Turn the page upside down, then try not to see the frog when you turn
the page the right way up again.

mind when considering perceptual experiences. An experienced
tracker following a trail, an Eskimo looking at ice floes in the early
spring, a radiologist looking at an X-ray film, or a modern abstract
painter looking at his or her own work, are all likely to perceive these
in ways we would not. Figure 3.1.1 demonstrates this. Once the frog
has been detected, the perceptual experience is quite different from
that before detection. Moreover, once organised in a meaningful way,
it is virtually impossible to disorganise the pattern once more.

Situations also arise where previously stored relationships have
become irrelevant, or worse, incorrect. Where this happens the
reprogramming of existing relationships can require very many
repeated experiences since, not only do new relationships have to be
abstracted and stored, but existing associations need to be broken

down and not applied—a task akin to learning not to see the frog in Fig. 3.1.1.

Such situations arise throughout the range of human activities, occurring when the demand for a particular skill, say driving tramcars, drops and the drivers have to retrain (Shooter *et al.*, 1972). Or again, the death of a close relative involves large scale alterations to the LTM which require time to occur. Time, not being a causal factor, does not heal, but adjustment of the LTM requires time.

Similarly, migrants in their new countries also go through a period of learning and adjustment to their new environment, as do residents in areas which undergo redevelopment. In some cases, particularly among old people, there is neither the time nor the opportunity to rebuild more appropriate cognitive structures, so that they tend to withdraw into whatever more limited existence they can manage.

A particular case of this, which is not restricted to old people, was studied by Fried (1963). The residents of a slum area in Boston were rehoused; but, instead of considering themselves better off, the reaction fairly generally, was best described as one of grief for their lost homes. This took the form of feelings of having experienced a painful loss, a generally depressive tone, some expressions of anger, and psychosomatic symptoms among other things. Almost half of the women interviewed reported sadness and depressive feelings lasting more than six months, and two years later one quarter of them still evidenced these emotions. Disruption of their social networks, resulting from the move, was implicated and three quarters of those who had had a very warm and positive relationship with their neighbours in their former locality experienced severe grief symptoms, whereas just over a third of those with a negative or neutral relationship with their previous neighbours were affected in this way. The fact that this third were still grief struck shows that it is not only the social network that matters but the whole range of familiar experience which has to be restructured. This process was typically painful for the residents studied by Fried.

Within this simple model, then, the LTM abstracts and stores relationships built up by experience, which may by generalisation become principles by which we predict, structure and sample sensory information, thereby integrating incoming data with the relationships abstracted from previous transactions with the world, and permitting

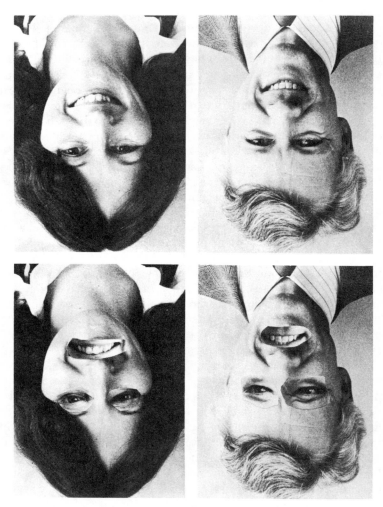

Fig. 3.1.2. Turn the page upside down. The importance of familiar salient features in determining the overall percept is shown by the effect of inverting the eyes and mouth.

the organisation of appropriate activities. The term 'schema', 'schemata' in the plural, has been applied to sets of abstracted relationships which are associated together. Each relationship implies some of the others, and all together operate as a rule by which incoming information is analysed on the basis of what has gone before, and motor activities which are necessary for effective interaction with the world are thus co-ordinated.

We may now consider the value of this simple and general model of human information processing in the area of ergonomics. Its function is to indicate what the capacities and limitations of human information processing performance are, so that systems, spaces and objects which are constructed are workable.

The main function served by this model is that it focuses attention on all of the most important processes so that, where difficulties arise, it is possible to identify the nature of the problem more accurately. For example, the LTM, over repeated experiences, builds up the expectation that visibly empty spaces are filled with nothing more harmful than air. This has led, on numerous recorded occasions, to people throwing cigarette ends or lighted matches into containers filled with petrol vapour, often with explosive results. Similarly, when pilots are drilled in their earliest training that the undercarriage control is on the right side of the cockpit, and the air-brakes or flaps control on the left; then it is scarcely surprising that, if these arrangements are reversed in more advanced aircraft, the pilots occasionally revert to their earliest training, and land without the undercarriage being down. Accidents like this usually happen when the pilot is fatigued or stressed and regresses to earlier habits which have been stored in the LTM.

One aspect of perceptual organisation is illustrated in Fig. 3.1.2. Viewed upside down, my colleagues, Ms J. Burt and Dr C. Cooper, look much as usual, even though there is something odd about one of the photographs. Turn the photographs the right way up, however, and a quite different impression is gained. We accept the eyes and mouth not being inverted when the face itself is, because we are accustomed to perceive them the right way up. But we do not accept the inversion of these salient features when the face is the right way up.

The short-term memory's limited capacity and vulnerability to distraction can be demonstrated using a string of random numbers. If one person reads them out at a reasonably rapid pace, while another starting when, say, the third number is spoken responds with the number which was first, then given the fourth responds with the second, the difficulty of continuing such a task becomes apparent. But, using higher loadings, e.g. starting on the fifth or seventh number, the task can be rendered virtually impossible. Psychologists often employ secondary tasks to gauge spare capacity, and this approach can be taken here if, in addition to the task described, the person responding is to do something else simultaneously. Pointing left or right according to the odd or evenness of the first, second or third number, disrupts proceedings admirably, when added to the ongoing memory task, and indeed any interference, such as someone entering the room and asking a question, renders the task impossible.

Many examples could be added, but perhaps these few will suffice to show that even a simple description of human information processing can prevent us assuming that people have greater capacities than they do, or that they are more easily reprogrammed than is the case.

Chapter 4

Ambient Conditions

4.1. LIGHTING AND VISUAL PERFORMANCE

It is usual to regard our sensitivity to light radiated electro-magnetic energy as the main sensory input for information, so that vision is the preferred channel for maintaining contact with the environment. Reducing visual contact, or substituting information in other modalities often impairs performance making it slower and more effortful, particularly if more mental manipulations become necessary, e.g. the reader may care to try assembling even a single jig-saw by touch alone. Exceptions exist, as in the use of auditory signals for warnings or alarms, but vision remains the principal source of information about the world with other modalities complementing it.

What the ergonomist mainly needs to know about the human visual system is the range of its functions and the limitations to its capacities. For this purpose it is helpful to have some understanding of how the visual system works.

4.1.1. The Structure of the Eye

Figure 4.1.1 shows the eye itself. Light falling on the protective corneal layer passes through the aqueous humour and then through the pupil of the eye which is a contractible, round opening in the iris. Behind the pupil stands the lens of the eye suspended on either side by the ciliary muscles. Light projected through the lens crosses the interior of the eye through the vitreous humour until it reaches the retina where the photoreceptor cells are. There are two types of photoreceptors: rods which are extremely sensitive to light, and cones which form the basis of our pattern and colour vision. There are many more rods in the retina than there are cones, some 120 000 000 rods to 6 000 000 cones. Practically all the cones are concentrated in the fovea where there are as many as 150 000 mm^2. The fovea is a small depression on the retina which is located more or less in direct line with the centre of the lens. There are no rods in the fovea, their

35

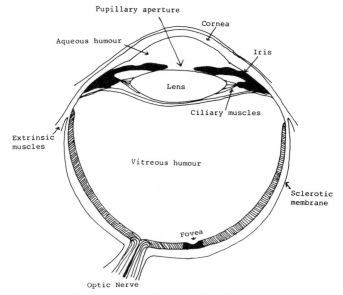

Fig. 4.1.1.   The human eye. See Appendix 1 for glossary of terms.

concentration being greatest, again about $150\,000\,\text{mm}^2$, between 10–20° either side of the fovea. Foveal vision is required for the detection of fine-grain patterns where a high degree of visual acuity is required. Rod vision on the other hand, given the rods' greater sensitivity to low intensities of light, forms the basis of vision in dark conditions. There are some cones in the periphery of the retina, numbering less than $10\,000\,\text{mm}^2$, but, although these peripheral cones are shorter and thicker than the cones in the fovea, this difference seems to be due to the relative concentrations of photoreceptors in different areas of the retina rather than to any difference in their function. There seems to be no evidence for the obvious possibility that peripheral cones are more sensitive to low intensities of light than foveal cones are.

Moving parts of the eye

There are three moving parts of the eye. First, the eyeball can move within its socket, tracking stepwise across a line of print or inspecting different areas of the visual field. These saccadic movements occur at a rate around 4·5 s, and it is difficult to inhibit them for more than a few seconds even when attempting to maintain a continuous visual fixation. In the writer's experience this can be important if inspection tasks are required to be performed at high speeds as can happen on some production lines. Saccadic eye movements continue in darkness or with the eyes closed if any form of visual inspection, as in imagery or dreaming, takes place.

Secondly, the pupil of the eye opens at low intensities of illumination and closes as the illumination increases. This pupillary reflex is a compromise between the sharpest possible focus, which is achieved with the smallest aperture, and the maximum amount of light for cone vision, which would require the pupil to be fully open. Looking through small artificial pupils can improve focusing, but for most practical purposes the opposite approach of magnifying what is being looked at is adopted.

Thirdly, the lens changes its thickness, and thereby its focal length, so that the object being viewed is focused on the retina not in front of it or behind it. Visual defects like short- or long-sightedness can result from the shape of the eyeball being such that the retina is too close or too far from the lens, so that the object is out of focus where the light reaches the retina (see Fig. 4.1.2).

A number of ergonomic considerations arise from the eye's moving parts. For example, since the area of the fovea is small, this forces us to redirect and refocus our gaze very frequently. This means

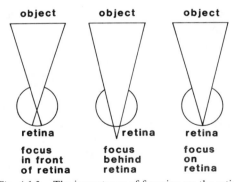

Fig. 4.1.2. The importance of focusing on the retina.

that the rate at which human information processing proceeds is constrained by the time taken up by the muscles extrinsic to the eye which move it within the eye socket, and the ciliary muscles inside the eye which change the shape of the lens. Moreover, changes in the lens occur within the normal ageing process which indicate that older people require higher illumination levels for tasks involving visual acuity. From such information we can, for example, predict and design road signs that are legible even to drivers passing them at high speed.

The retina and optic nerve

The rods and cones on the surface layer of the retina are linked to ganglion cells through a complex network of horizontal, bipolar and amacrine cells. From each ganglion cell one nerve fibre runs off to the optic nerve which conveys information about the firing of rods and cones to higher centres. Where these fibres leave the retina there is a 'blind spot' in the visual field. If the rods and cones were arranged so that their light-sensitive elements pointed forward, the connections to other cells, culminating in the neurons of the optic nerve, could all be behind the rods and cones, and there would be no 'blind spot'. However, the retina is not organised in this way, rather it is back to front with the light-sensitive elements pointing inwards to the brain, so that light has to pass through the connections to other cells and blood vessels before reaching the rods and cones. Considerable loss of intensity results from this set-up which appears to be due to the fact that rods and cones evolved from cells in the brain rather than directly from cells on the skin. However, the fovea is structured slightly differently so that fewer cells lie in front of the cones which are concentrated in that area, and the loss of signal is lessened.

The route taken by the optic nerve is shown in Fig. 4.1.3. From this it can be seen that if we are looking at a square, the right side of it projects onto the left hemi-retina, and the left side of the square onto the right hemi-retina. Similarly, the lower side projects onto the upper half of the retina, and the top side onto the lower half of the retina. When, in 1625, Scheiner removed the protective layer of the sclerotic membrane from the back of an ox's eye, he was able, looking from behind the retina, to see the image falling on it. What he saw then was that the image on the retina was upside down and reversed.

Overlapping visual fields

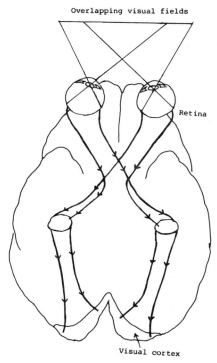

Retina

Visual cortex

Fig. 4.1.3. The pathway of the optic nerve.

The basic task for the ergonomist contributing to the design of the visual world is to ensure that there is sufficient illumination and sufficient time for viewing to occur. Other subsidiary requirements include avoiding glare, making sure that the visual world is not ambiguous or gives rise to visual illusions, ensuring that the visual world is stable which means avoiding flickering light, for example, and using colour in a manner which is consonant with all of these.

4.1.2. What is Sufficient Illumination?

Many people labour under the belief that, for any given task, there is a minimum level of illumination at which some particular task becomes possible and above which performance does not improve very much. This view may owe something to the fact that visual acuity is a logarithmic function of the illumination level (Weston, 1949; Lythgoe, 1932), and authoritatively expressed views that no more than $43 \, \text{lm m}^2$–$54 \, \text{lm m}^2$ (Tinker, 1949), or sometimes very much higher levels (Blackwell, 1959; Crouch, 1958), are required for adequate illumination. However, if you are measuring visual acuity, then level of illumination is not the only variable to be measured—the region of the retina stimulated, shape and colour of the target and its contrast with its background, the time available for viewing, and whether the target is stationary in a known position or moving somewhere in the visual field, all are relevant. No one would deny the importance of these factors, so the reason why leading research workers at different times, and in different countries (see Weston, 1961), arrive at grossly divergent values for adequate illumination levels, must lie elsewhere.

The people involved question each other's methods, and it seems likely that different approaches can yield widely differing results. One possibility which does not seem to have been explored concerns Blackwell's (1959) method. From the description given of the method used it seems that Blackwell's subjects viewed extremely fuzzy-edged discs projected against an illuminated translucent screen. Very careful testing took place varying the luminances of test disc and background along with other relevant variables, and appropriate illumination levels were arrived at which are much higher than those of most other workers in this area. However, in using this approach Blackwell may have eliminated one very important variable which operates in real-life settings, and in other laboratory procedures. By eliminating any well defined edges of his circles, Blackwell may have reduced the apparent brightness of his target discs. Figure 4.1.4 shows two circles which are in fact of equal brightness, but which, because of the presence or absence of a hard edge look very different in their brightnesses. This difference is ascribed to nystagmus (Lindsey and Norman, 1972), i.e. small wobbling movements of the eye make the hard edge produce a marked change in intensity between the inside and outside of the circle, and this is perceived as a large difference in brightness, whereas the more gradual change in intensity with the fuzzy edge is seen as a smaller difference in relative brightness. If the high levels required by Blackwell do derive from the particular approach adopted, this does not mean they are necessarily wrong. An

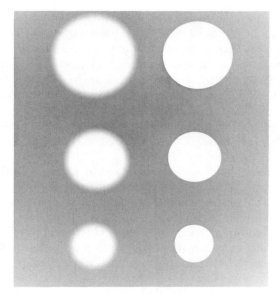

Fig. 4.1.4. The role of nystagmus in brightness perception.

eye surgeon involved in microsurgery on tissue about as strong as wet blotting paper, needs all the illumination that can be provided, and may even be performing something fairly close to Blackwell's task. However, where there are clear edges, outlines and contours present, then, as Fig. 4.1.4 shows, the perceived brightness can be markedly altered. This factor is not usually taken into account when recommended lighting levels are put forward, but is one good reason why *in situ* evaluation of the level and quality of illumination is desirable.

Two other points are worth making about illumination levels. The first is that most tasks are carried out under varying illumination. This is obvious when daylight contributes to lighting, but it still occurs in artificially lighted contexts because of different reflectances, contrasts and shadows. Some variation in level is desirable, but it is important to consider particular functions to be performed rather than making general statements such as 1·6 klx is the level recommended for kitchens. The second point is that the variability among people in their vision is such that it renders very general recommendations insecure. Such recommendations are very useful as rough indications of levels at which various tasks have been successfully carried out. However, where these recommendations have been based on minimal or threshold values, they are more vulnerable to specific and individual factors than levels based on values well above threshold. It is for these reasons that the highest of the various recommended levels is more likely to be trouble-free.

A comprehensive treatment of illumination, including glare, may be found in Murrell (1971), and particular levels for various rooms in the home are provided by Grandjean (1973). The topic is one of the greatest interest, and one which in recent years has led lighting engineers and architects to pay increasing attention to the quality of lighting as well as the amount of illumination. Using colour and brightness contrast, and surfaces with varying degrees of reflectance, as well as positioning the lights themselves in the best positions to give light where it is needed, all contribute to a good visual environment. As usual, however, some caution needs to be exercised. In the natural environment objects are lit from above and if, in our artificial environments, we decide to illuminate them from below, we can create illusions, e.g. that domes are craters and so on. Such effects may or may not be desirable, but they need to be heeded if there is any risk or impairment of performance due to them.

4.2.   Temperature and Humidity

In considering working environments, temperature and humidity should be looked at together. While temperatures around as low as $-70\,°C$ and as high as $50\,°C$ may exist in different parts of the world, people in common with other mammals maintain a more or less constant temperature, and performance is rapidly impaired if the individual has either to try to increase or conserve heat or to lose it. In many cases the effects on performance are simply interference ones, in the sense that the additional behaviour involved in conserving heat or losing it impedes or prevents the carrying out of some task. Some effects, however, result from the direct action of the mechanisms of heat exchange—slipperiness of hand grip due to sweating is a common one. Again in common with other mammalians, man controls his body temperature by changing his behaviours and by modifying his environment. Behaviourally, to gain heat, man may eat more, alter his diet to include more fat, exercise to generate heat, reduce activity to avoid heat loss, reduce exposed surface area by curling up, and so on. But more efficiently, through clothing, structures and heating devices, body temperature may be closely controlled. To lose heat, people sweat, pant, become inactive to avoid generating heat, seek to reduce skin temperature to create heat exchange, and all the things that are everyday observations in warm climates.

Adaptation does occur within individuals, and different groups respond in different ways physiologically to environmental conditions. Carlson and Hsieh (1974) for example, have shown that unlike European subjects the heat production of Australian aborigines did not increase as skin temperature decreased between 33 °C and 27 °C in overnight experiments. It may be some sort of index of comfort that the aborigines were able to sleep under these conditions while the white subjects could not.

The regulatory mechanisms maintaining a constant temperature can be described as

$$M \pm R \pm C_v \pm C_d - E = 0$$

where M is the metabolic rate producing heat,
R is the gain or loss by radiation,
C_v is the gain or loss by convection,
C_d is the gain or loss by conduction, and
E is the loss by evaporation.

Any one of these can become the main source of heat loss, but one is forced to agree with Murrell (1971, p. 261) that for the sorts of environments we are thinking about, the heat loss through the evaporation of water from skin and respiratory system is most important. It is for this reason that humidity enters the equation as an important factor. Evaporation through sweating is affected by the difference between the vapour pressure of water on the body surface and that in the air around it, which depends on the air temperature and the relative humidity.

Where humidity is high, it is likely that sweating will occur over more of the body surface as a means of maintaining the loss of heat by evaporation. And, in some cases, panting occurs or its rate is increased to compensate for increased vapour pressure. Adequate oxygen intake is so basic that obvious impairments of performance occur. If work is undertaken under very hot, humid conditions, sweating increases to maintain heat loss, but the temperature regulation mechanisms can break down in extreme conditions with serious consequences. Both young children and old people are very vulnerable in this regard, and cannot adjust their heat exchange, whether in cold or heat, as well as adolescents and younger adults. Deaths of babies do occur when loss of heat becomes irreversible in cold climates, or when heat exchange is inadequate in hot ones, without air temperatures being particularly unusual, mainly because some parents are unaware of the need to help in regulating infants' temperatures. A comprehensive and lucid account of the physiological effects of temperature is given by Carlson and Hsieh on cold, and Robinson and Weigman on heat and humidity in Slonin (1974).

In work contexts, and with buildings in mind, the question which usually has to be answered is what will be a comfortable temperature. Unfortunately, comfort reflects the influence of a host of variables. Looking at some of the research on working temperatures shows that tolerance for heat begins to decrease somewhere around 25 °C (Buettner, 1962). This is rather lower than the range of 27–30 °C within which Murrell (1971) suggests skilled performance will remain at a satisfactory level. However, Murrell was basing his conclusion on research in Cambridge by Mackworth (1950) and in Singapore by Pepler (1958), and he may be right since we also know from the studies of Buskirk and Bass (1957) that adaptation to higher temperatures not only occurs, but can be relatively good within the period of one week, and that it generalises to different humidity levels.

It has also been shown, as we might expect to happen, that relatively heavy work is affected earlier as temperature rises. Vernon and Bedford (1927) found the loading of coal tubs became progressively slower as the temperature increased above 19 °C, and that more frequent rest pauses were taken above 24 °C, and Eckenrode and Abbot (1959) cite data from the New York Ventilation Commission showing that weight lifting was impaired at 21 °C in comparison with lower temperatures.

The effect of clothing providing suitable insulation has been shown by Burton and Edholm (1955) to vary what is a tolerable temperature for 8 h exposure from 22 °C with light clothing down as far as −10 °C when equipped for Arctic conditions.

Murrell's range fits Mackworth's results which were obtained from subjects variously engaged in receiving Morse code, problem solving, attentional tasks, pursuit tracking, and light exercise (finger ergograph), and agrees with earlier findings by Viteles (1932) who showed that, at more than 30 °C, typing random letters, spatial ability, mental arithmetic, checking for errors in numbers, and co-ordination, were all carried out less well than at lower temperatures.

Given all the defensive strategies which people possess for dealing with temperature and humidity, it would seem that, as a general recommendation, that of the American Society of Heating, Refrigerating and Air Conditioning Engineers (ASHRAE, 1960)— which assumes a relative humidity not less than 25 % or more than 60 %, and air movement around 7·5 m min—a comfortable temperature should be achieved between 23–25 °C, seems as justifiable as we are ever likely to achieve. Specific tasks will continue to be studied under different conditions, local variations from this range will continue in the light of prevailing climatic conditions, and the effect of different *patterns* of temperature within buildings needs to be researched, but part of the answer has already been achieved.

Other performance measures affected by temperature and humidity include hand co-ordination and reaction time, though, as noted, the use of appropriate clothing can solve the problems of temperature. In extreme conditions, such as Arctic temperatures, merely providing a thick covering of insulating material is not the best approach. Goldman (1973) points this out, making the point that during physical work too much heat may be generated with this sort of clothing. The more modern approach to extremes of cold prefers lightweight insulating materials which are windproof, and possibly the provision of auxiliary heat to the hands and feet. In some specialised environments like military aircraft cockpits the pilot's flying suit is heat controlled. An additional advantage of lightweight alternatives is the increase in mobility which is achieved with them.

The opposite problem of clothing in extremely hot conditions depends for its solution on the duration of exposure to the heat source and intensity. If the source is exposure to sunlight, the traditional loose, well-ventilated light-coloured garments, worn with protective headgear and footwear, meets a variety of needs including protection from sunburn, insect bites, and contact with hot surfaces, provided the ambient temperature is not too much above skin temperature. The solar heat loading on the human form is predictable using the surface area of the individual, the areas intercepting the sun's rays, the intensity of the direct light and of radiation reflected back from the ground, together with other factors like the clothing worn (Breckenridge and Goldman, 1971). Though many factors need to be accounted for in particular settings, e.g. the shape and postural position of a person may suggest either the geometry of a vertical cylinder, or of a sphere, is more appropriate, the solar load has been shown to be closely approximated using the approach of these authors.

Where exposure to intense heat is prolonged, complete coverage is necessary and this may lead to the need for provision for ventilation or air conditioning, and even for an air supply. Such heat protective clothing is only used in very specialised areas, and the solution using lighter and less clothing is the everyday answer to exposure to heat.

4.3.   Noise Effects Upon Performance

It has become common to distinguish noise from sound on the grounds that noise is unwanted sound. Physiologically, it makes no difference, the mechanisms of hearing are the same. Psychologically, the degree to which one can select what is listened or attended to, depends on variables such as the intensity, predictability, and significance of the noise, along with other attention-getting factors. Ergonomically, the problems are to reduce the effects of noise and to maintain effective sound communication. As with vision, some inkling of how we hear is useful as a basis from which to try to serve these two aims.

Sound is mechanical energy impinging on the eardrum. Usually this takes the form of alternations in pressure on the eardrum, the changes in pressure being airborne (sometimes waterborne) and caused by some vibrating entity. The vibration at the eardrum is transmitted via the bones of the middle ear to the cochlea. In the cochlea, hair cells attached to the basilar membrane are set in motion by the vibrations, carrying the effect of the sound in a rippling, wave-like motion, along the basilar membrane. Different sound frequencies produce the greatest wave effect at different positions along the basilar membrane. The hair cells are part of the *organ of Corti*, and the movement in the *organ of Corti* caused by the original vibration, activates other neural fibres linked to the hair cells, and this neural activity is transmitted along the auditory nerve to the temporal lobe of the brain.

The frequency of vibration determines the perceived pitch of the sound heard, the operating range of hearing being from around 20 Hz (cycles per second) to about 18 000 Hz. Perceived loudness derives from the pressures on the eardrum which result from the amplitude of the vibration. Here, the range of pressures giving rise to hearing is roughly between 20×10^{-6} Pa and 100 Pa. The decibel (dB) measure of loudness is a logarithmic function of dynes per square centimetre which uses $0 \cdot 0002$ dynes cm^2 as a reference because that is conventionally taken to be the lower limit of hearing. Although decibels were widely used, intensity and frequency interact, so that, for example, for any given intensity, different frequencies (of pure tones, i.e. pure sine wave vibrations) will be perceived as differing in loudness. Fortunately for musicians, the same is not true for complex sounds. To account for frequency, a loudness scale using phons has been matched to our perception using a standard 1000 Hz tone. The 1000 Hz tone's intensity is increased or lowered until it matches the intensity of the stimulus tone. The intensity of the 1000 Hz tone in dB when the intensities appear equal is the phon level of the stimulus tone. Which scale one utilises depends on whether it is the pressure at the eardrum, or the perceived loudness, that is relevant. As very rough guidelines, the assumed dB level of some everyday noises are often presented for illustration. Tables such as Table 4.3.1 give some indication of noise levels which commonly occur.

What is not evident from tables like these, however, is that loudness tends to be additive. That is, if there are two sources of complex sounds, the loudness will be the sum of their loudnesses. Simple additivity only occurs with sounds of very different frequency, but there is still an increase in loudness for combinations of more similar sounds. Background noise is insufficiently considered in many

Ambient Conditions

Table 4.3.1
Some examples of noise levels

	Noise level (dB)[a]	
	140[b]	Pain, damage
Jet engine throttle	130[b]	Pressure felt at eardrum
fully open at 75 m	120[b]	Amplified music as in discos
Heavy metal press		
at 15 m	110[b]	Some weaving machinery
Heavy truck revving	100[b]	
up at 15 m		
	90[b]	Unacceptably noisy under normal conditions
	80	
	70	Noisy offices
	60	Actual levels recorded in several areas of a
	50	hospital (Falk and Woods, 1973)
	40	Recommended level for hospitals
	30	Whispering
	20	
	10	
	0	May be able to hear your own heart beat

[a] Re 0·0002 dynes cm^2.
[b] Hearing loss occurs with prolonged exposure.

work settings, although legislation to compensate people for industrial deafness has led to a vast improvement in what were previously very noisy situations, and to an increased acceptability of ear defenders among those still exposed to high noise levels for prolonged periods of work.

4.3.1. Effects of Noise
Hearing loss

Permanent loss of hearing is the major worry facing those who work in very noisy conditions. Partly, the problem of hearing loss derives from the capacity of people to tolerate noise levels which produce permanent damage, and to perform satisfactorily under those conditions. Also, until recently, there was widespread resistance to the use of protective ear plugs or defenders. 'Shop floor bravado' and ridicule commonly acted against the protection of hearing. But another reason people found ear plugs and like devices unacceptable is because they prevented auditory information from reaching them. The fact that we do not have to be oriented toward a sound source to hear it is an extremely valuable supplement to information from the visual field. Moreover, the states of many pieces of equipment are detected by the sound they emit while working. To shut out all auditory information, and make the person effectively deaf, is only acceptable when he or she has been educated to understand the serious risk of hearing loss and, even then, may only be acceptable for periods of intense noise if the noise is predictable.

To some extent the problem of hearing loss is complicated by the normal processes of ageing, which include some functional deterioration in hearing. The greatest loss occurs around 4000 Hz which is toward the top of the speech frequency range, and there is some indication that the effect is worse for men than for women. This could reflect a general difference in noise levels to which the two sexes have been commonly exposed in work and home situations. As women are accepted into a wider range of work situations the hearing loss difference would be expected to disappear.

Various experiments have sought to establish how great is the effect of exposure to high noise levels for different durations. Ogden (1944) tested the auditory thresholds of 66 American Air Force men before and after a gunnery training course which lasted six weeks. Up to 500 Hz no effect was evident, although the men had worn no hearing protectors. Slight increases in threshold of ~ 3 dB were noted between 500–2000 Hz. Beyond 2000 Hz, thresholds rose markedly, with a shift of 9 dB being found around 4000 Hz. These results do not tell us how permanent such losses are, and nowadays it is usual to distinguish between temporary threshold shifts (TTS), where there is recovery from hearing loss in less than 24 h, and permanent effects which, after a period of several weeks or months, have shown no return of hearing function. Some early researchers (Machle, 1945) suggested that gunnery instructors' hearing suffered permanent damage due to the continued exposure to high noise levels. In other noisy occupations, like boilermaking or weaving, hearing loss was regarded as an occupational hazard, and there was little doubt that the impairment was permanent and, in some cases, resulted in total deafness. Moreover, where the work environment is noisy, conditions are often poor in other ways. Horino (1977) looked at the general environment of foundry workers and found that while noise and dust were factors, the work load was adversely affected by poor arrangements of work-spaces, and bad working postures, as well as by noise and dust. This may reflect a tendency to generalise from one set of bad conditions to others, so that if an environment is very noisy, it may be more acceptable for it to be dusty. This is not necessary, of course, but any bad condition tends to devalue the whole environment.

Taylor (1972) studying hearing loss in the jute weaving industry in Dundee, which used to be a particularly noisy industry, found a very clear relationship between long-term exposure to intense noise and hearing loss. The noise levels produced by the flat, overpick looms, many of which had been installed just before the turn of the century, ranged between 95–102 dB re 0·0002 dynes cm^2. The weavers studied were women who had been continuously employed in the industry for 20 years or more. People with hearing problems which could have derived from other causes than noise at work, such as frequent exposure to loud amplified music in their leisure time, or with otological abnormalities, were excluded from the study. In this way a very pure sample of 96 female weavers was obtained, and their hearing compared with that of a control group, matched for age and sex, which had not been exposed to the high noise levels of the jute mills. Around 80% of the weavers admitted to hearing problems when conversing with others, although 53% of them used lip reading to compensate for their lost hearing. Among the controls, only 16% said they found such difficulty, and this figure decreased to 6% when asked about understanding telephone conversations, or hearing in churches or theatres, whereas the comparable figure for the weavers was around 70%. When the hearing thresholds of both groups were measured, the weavers' average loss between 0·5 to 2 kHz was 36·6 dB compared to 12 dB for the control group. Using a criterion of 45 dB loss for deafness, at frequencies between 2 to 8 kHz, the weavers were classified as deaf, the controls were not.

More clearly than many, this study implicates work noise as a cause of hearing loss, eliminating normal ageing or self-inflicted intense noise during leisure activities, as the source of the loss.

While the father of occupational medicine Bernardino Ramazzini, who studied the health hazards of various occupations, noted as far back as 1713 that bakers exposed to the continuous noise of wheels, millstones and water falling from a height, were usually hard of hearing, and that coppersmiths subjected to the perpetual noise of hammering became completely deaf, it was only in the 1960s that industrial compensation for deafness was introduced in Great Britain. With this legislation there was a rise of interest in treating noise at its source, which is the most effective approach, in screening or absorbing noise which cannot be reduced at its source, and providing ear defenders if neither of these approaches is possible.

Annoyance

Apart from loss of hearing whether permanent or temporary, noise has various other undesirable effects. The main ones are irritation, masking and distraction. Most reviews mention annoyance or irritation as a possible reaction to noise, but the conditions which produce irritation are dependent on so many, and such varied factors that some psychologists have concluded that it is outside the realm of experimentation (Carpenter, 1958). Nevertheless, various procedures have been devised in an effort to estimate the acceptability of noise. One of these procedures, produced by the International Organization for Standardization (1961), increases the estimation of likely annoyance if the noise is a pure tone or impulsive, and if it occurs at night or in rural neighbourhoods. How often the noise occurs is taken into account, as is how much adjustment has occurred to the noise. People living near a railway line usually exhibit this sort of adjustment and report being scarcely aware of trains running in the night.

As a very rough guideline, and bearing the points above in mind, Fig. 4.3.1, which is a modified presentation of the International Organization for Standardization's procedure, can be used to estimate the likely acceptability of noise. If the intensity of any frequency exceeds the curve shown, the likelihood is that the noise will be unacceptable unless there are extenuating circumstances.

Noise pollution depends not only on the intensity and frequency of the sound, but, rather, responses of annoyance are mediated by the individual's perception of the noise, whether it accompanies an activity he values—such as lawnmowing or flying model aircraft—or impedes something he is doing, whether it conveys information which is aversive (Kryter, 1970), whether he can control the noise or escape from it, and to some extent on personality factors such as introversion and anxiety (Stephens, 1970). Other factors are known to affect annoyance, and square wave noises, e.g. model aircraft engines,

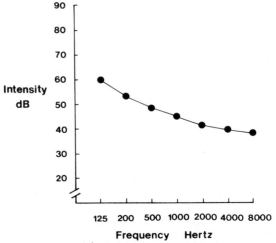

Fig. 4.3.1. Estimated upper levels for acceptability of noise (modified from International Organization for Standardization, 1961).

create stronger effects than wave patterns with slower rise times. The predictability of noise is also a relevant variable (Finkelman and Glass, 1974) and it is the unexpected noise which produces the startle response.

The strength of the startle response depends on how relaxed or aroused the person is, so that the person who is highly charged emotionally is more reactive to noise. This point may have a peculiar significance for noise in buildings. Whereas there is habituation of our responsiveness to most of the stimuli which affect us repeatedly, it has been suggested (Saegart, 1976) that the alerting, arousing effect of other people does not habituate. If this is the case, other people's presence may itself accentuate the effects of noise by increasing arousal. Whether this speculation is well-founded or not, people, along with devices, design, and noises which penetrate from outside, are the most commonly reported sources of annoying noises in buildings.

The most frequently reported symptoms other than irritability after exposure to noise are headaches, tenseness, sleeping problems and fatigue (McLean and Tarnopolsky, 1977).

Other people as sources of noise are not usually dealt with

separately. This is probably because people, without the aid of other devices, rarely produce noises of very high intensity. But annoyance or distraction does not require that. Some laboratory experiments have used loud speech, and Rotton *et al.* (1978) report that tolerance for frustration is lowered under these conditions. Also, the ability to discriminate people occupying different roles appeared to diminish.

There are three reasons for taking other people into account when considering noise. In the first place, people tend to make noises which are meaningful. Whether they are speaking or carrying out some activity, we can usually tell what is happening from the sound of it. This is important whenever any conscious act of attention which involves 'concentrating upon' a task is performed, because that implies attending selectively and filtering out or attenuating irrelevant stimuli. And it is more difficult to filter out meaningful information than random stimuli which have no significance for the person. People do vary in their ability to attend selectively, but almost anyone who is 'not listening' to what is going on around him will respond to the sound of their own name being spoken, or to some unusual noise. The occurrence of distraction by other people is so commonplace that it tends to be taken for granted or regarded as unavoidable. However, the judicious siting of activities, together with the use of absorbent materials, can produce settings which facilitate attending selectively when that is required. It should be pointed out that this is not the same as producing the 'silent' atmosphere of an old-fashioned library, where the slightest rustle of paper or footfall becomes a distraction precisely because of the extreme quiet. Rather, it argues that across a vast array of tasks, in fact wherever reduced speed of performance or making errors is either important or costly, protecting people from noises made by others will be productive. Estimates of how widespread annoyance by noise is vary from 65% of the people around London's Heathrow airport (McKennell, 1971), to 22% disturbed by noise at work (Burns, 1968), or 25% bothered by noise in their neighbourhood (Foveman *et al.*, 1974). Clearly, then, noise is an extensive issue.

Secondly, there is some evidence (e.g. Shaban and Welling, 1972) to suggest that people are more prone to annoyance if they locate another person(s) as the source of stress, than if they perceive an impersonal stressor. Presumably, this is linked to the perceived degree of voluntary control the other person has over their behaviour, though it may be more complex than just that, with the alerting, arousing by other people creating physiological effects, like raised heart rate or blood pressure, which usually accompany annoyance. Whatever the mechanism, it seems that other people should be regarded as a potent source of annoyance and distraction rather than left out of consideration.

The third reason is that where the activities of people, or groups of them, overlap in time, noises made are classified by most people in terms of the group making them. This allows identification with a particular group on the part of individuals, and the (usually unconscious) adoption of different standards of acceptability for noises made by one's own group and those produced by other groups. This mismatch of standards means that a group which is creating noise finds the sorts and levels of noise that they themselves are generating acceptable, whereas other groups do not. Given this scenario, the stage is set for intergroup conflict.

One study (Jaeger, 1980) into noise in hospitals showed that comparing people by occupation, only the domestic staff reported 'great annoyance' due to 'doctors and nurses conversations'. Both groups, domestics and doctors and nurses, were most affected by 'equipment being dropped' and 'maintenance repair work', but while the noise of 'mechanical polishers' was the most frequent source of annoyance for doctors and nurses, the same noise was only equal fourth along with six others in annoying domestic staff. This may illustrate different reactions to the noise created by one's own group's activities.

More important than who makes the noise is the effect upon patients, and Knowland (1976) quotes Florence Nightingale as stating 'unnecessary noise is the most cruel absence of care which can be inflicted on either the sick or the well'. Evidence for adverse effects of noise on hospital patients tends to be from correlational studies such as Fife and Rappaport's (1976) one which showed the length of patient stay in hospital was greater during a period when there was increased noise from construction work than either before or after it. More specific investigations of the exact functions affected by noise, e.g. sleep loss, raised blood pressure, and so on, are relatively rare though possible in principle.

Jaeger's (1980) study aimed at finding out, not only which noises were judged annoying, but whether these noises were related in any meaningful fashion. Using the simple technique which is outlined in Chapter 6 and described fully by Rump (1974), she was able to show which items correlated to form clusters of related noises in two different hospitals (Fig. 4.3.2). Three of the clusters which were obtained are reproduced here to show the coherent picture which emerged. Noise in hospitals from these results can be seen to be divided into patient-care noises (cluster 1), noises produced by patients (cluster 2) which could be most annoying during the night, and an excretory-function cluster (cluster 3).

It is worth noting that these hospital noises are not necessarily very loud, but they are still annoying. The degree of annoyance caused can be affected by the function the person is attempting to perform, which may explain the tendency for noise to be more annoying to people when they are in their own homes than when they are at work (Burns, 1968), or on the way to and from work (Levy-Leboyer *et al.*, 1977). But factors mentioned above, like lack of control over noise, and the inescapable nature of some noises, as well as the additional loading noise places upon our information processing capacities, can render even relatively quiet noises extremely irritating.

Where large groups of people are affected by noises, from airports, main roads or similar sources, there can be a form of 'social facilitation' of annoyance. Patterson and Connor (1973) may be demonstrating this with their finding that the number of times aircraft noise was discussed by people with their friends was a reliable predictor of their annoyance. There is a well-researched phenomenon of 'risky shift' in social psychology which indicates that, in larger groups there is a tendency to adopt the more extreme attitudes which are expressed, and the more risky courses of action which are advocated. This may dictate the direction of the effect facilitating annoyance rather than inhibiting it. Identification with those sources of noise such as pride in a national airport, or with a social group, like being proud of being a New Yorker, seems one effective social mechanism for reducing annoyance with noise. Alternative physical approaches of attenuating noise or insulating people from it may, then, be more or less necessary, given exactly the same noise,

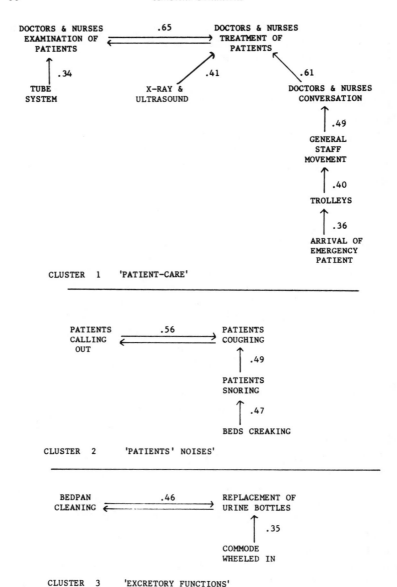

CLUSTER 1 'PATIENT-CARE'

CLUSTER 2 'PATIENTS' NOISES'

CLUSTER 3 'EXCRETORY FUNCTIONS'

Fig. 4.3.2. Clusters of hospital noises obtained using a simple correlation approach.

depending on the affiliations those exposed to the noise have with those producing it, and what it stands for.

Specific effects of noise upon performance have been found. Salame and Wittersheim (1978) required their subjects to memorise lists of numbers, and then to reproduce them by typing the lists out. Errors and omissions increased under noisy conditions, but not only that, the time for decisions was longer in noise, but the keying movements were faster. This combination seems likely to underlie the loss of accuracy. The effects were greater where stated annoyance was worse. This particular study points to the vulnerability of short-term memory to interference by noise affecting relevant information. It may also indicate that the additional emotional effects, which we can also regard as information of a different sort, affects short-term memory. It should not be concluded from this that reaction times are shortened in noise. The decision component of a reaction time appears to require more time, at least in loud noise (Kohfeld and Goedecke, 1978), even though the keying movements in the previous study were faster in noisy conditions.

Further evidence for noise impairing memorisation comes from Zimmer and Brachulis-Raymond (1978) who found that tape-recorded industrial noise reduced recall of standard prose passages. Moreover, short-term memory may be the function mediating the effects of noise, and Fowler and Wilding (1979) suggest that, under noise, the use of order cues increases. Learning in noise may, therefore, depend on the use of these order cues which are not needed for learning in quiet conditions.

In another experiment, Danhauer *et al.* (1978) showed that short-term memory for consonants decreased when their subjects were tested in noisy rather than quiet conditions. These specific effects may have applied significance wherever keyboards are in use, and verbal material is being processed. Laboratory experiments do not always translate directly to more everyday settings, but this was the subject of some work by Cohen *et al.* (1980) who examined the effects of aircraft noise on schoolchildren. Children in noisy schools were found to have higher blood pressure readings than their counterparts from quiet schools, and they were more likely to fail, or to give up, when given a cognitive task to perform. Mentally retarded children have been shown to score some 30 % lower on word intelligibility when tested with noise present, even though the level of noise was not unduly high. To what extent this should be attributed to distractability is not clear, but, in the light of the other studies, it should not be assumed that this is the answer. Interference with speech, and intermodal effects on subjects exposed to recorded aircraft noise while watching television, are invoked by Gunn *et al.* (1977) to explain the annoyance exhibited by their subjects. Further evidence that noise has more than merely peripheral effects is offered by Lord and Finlay (1978) who found that recalling previously learned lists of nonsense syllables (which are a standard tool in memory research) was impaired under noise. These researchers suggest that it is the process of retrieval from long-term memory which is affected, rendering their subjects unable to recall items which had been committed to memory using three consecutive errorless trials as the criterion for learning. Whether memory processes are involved in the worsening of performance at an anagram solution task is not certain, but Cole and Coyne (1977) showed that when inescapable noise was present, their subjects' ability to solve anagrams did decrease.

Some central effects are well-established, and it is known that, just as the brain can be driven by flashing lights causing synchronised activity of the cells, so auditory stimuli can control the rhythm of the brain. This phenomenon is called 'auditory following', and is the auditory analogue of 'photic driving'. These neurophysiological considerations may be implicated in disrupting the physiological processes which underlie recall, though it is not yet possible to demonstrate precisely how this occurs. Curious effects have been demonstrated which are not fully understood, but which may eventually be explained in terms of brain function. The fact that, in a word association test, noise acts to inhibit originality, by increasing the frequency of repeating an association, or alternating between associations, whereas some odours increase the originality of the associations (Pons and Baudet, 1978), is intriguing, but not easily explained.

4.3.2. *Sensitivity to Noise*

Sensitivity to noise has been regarded as a more or less stable feature of the individual although, comparing people's reactions in noisy and quiet residential areas, Delauzum and Griffiths (1978) failed to find evidence that noise annoyance is related to personality. Since the reliability of their methods was found not to be high when they retested their subjects two months later, it may be that their result reflects this, rather than there being no personality feature of noise sensitivity. Certainly, other authors claim that people high on noise annoyance show an increased risk of psychiatric illness (McLean and Tarnopolsky, 1977). They point to the converse relationship, that neurotic patients are more sensitive to noise than non-neurotic controls, and provide a list of organic functions which are altered by noise. Although, in a survey of 208 households, a link between noisy conditions and psychiatric disorders could only be shown for respondents with high educational levels (Tarnopolsky *et al.*, 1978), there was the expected association of annoyance and high noise levels.

Further evidence that noise sensitivity is a stable characteristic of the individual is provided by Weinstein (1978) who used a self-report measure of sensitivity to differentiate the most and least sensitive 30 % in a group of 155 college freshers. Self-reports were also obtained about their being disturbed by noise in the dormitory, first, early in the academic year, then again seven months later. The insensitive group, which was much less bothered by noise in the early survey, showed no change in the later reports, but the noise-sensitive group, initially more affected by noise, became increasingly bothered as the year passed. These students who were sensitive to noise appeared less secure in their social interactions, and it was suggested that their academic achievement may have been lower.

Individual differences in sensory thresholds are well-established, and it is known that introverted people tend to have lower thresholds. This does not necessarily mean they are noise-sensitive in the sense of being disturbed by it, but those introverts who are also high on emotionality measures tend to be anxious people in social interactions, and also to be emotionally very easily upset. It may be that another way of looking at sensitivity to noise would be through established personality differences likely to underlie that sensitivity. In any case, the noise-sensitive students tested by Weinstein failed to adapt to dormitory noise during their college year, suggesting that adaptation may depend upon the sensitivity of the person to noise. Another study which surveyed more than 2000 young people in Florida, suggests that cultural differences between Black and White

Americans may partly determine attitudes to environmental pollutants like noise. Even after statistical procedures to even out the effect of education, economic status, and other differences, it appeared that cultural differences existed. This sort of evidence needs to be treated very cautiously, but it may be that if the only environment that has ever been experienced is very noisy, then the adaptation level of the individual may be a resultant of this. In other words, sensitivity may be a function of attitudes and relativities rather than absolutes. Just as the Dundee weavers accepted deafness as an occupational hazard, to the extent that the Dundee accent is unique in Scotland, and may well have been affected by the effects of noise destroying the higher frequencies of hearing for speech. Whereas most Scotsmen say 'Aye', like (I), if they say it at all, in Dundee the pitch of the noise is always lowered, and 'Aye' becomes 'A'. Fascinatingly, this tendency to use lower frequencies is not only imitated by the children brought up in that specific location, but is also evident in surrounding geographical areas, and it is possible that frequency analysis of speech in those regions would provide a contour map with the lowest vowel frequencies in Dundee, and their gradual rising with distance from that city. Similar geographic studies could be conducted round cities with existing significantly high levels of occupational noise. But Dundee's dependence on the jute industry which was, in the past, a very noisy one, may make it one of those unique situations which it is impossible to find again.

The noise-sensitive individuals, judging by Weinstein's data, fail to show the adaptation to noise which seems to characterise some other groups. Failure to adapt to noise may have effects on the person but, equally, those effects can rebound on other people. In a complex experiment, Geen (1978) organised certain confederates who treated some of his subjects in a hostile fashion, by delivering 10 electric shocks to them, others were treated more neutrally by only receiving two shocks. The confederates were then given electric shocks by the subjects while the subjects were exposed to loud noise in one condition, or not, in another. Noise had no effect on subjects treated neutrally, but the presence or absence of noise did affect the aggressiveness of those previously dealt with in a hostile manner. This result does not stand alone, rather it reproduces earlier findings by Donnerstein and Wilson (1976) and Konečni (1975), and relates to other results showing both that animosity between individuals is greater in the presence of noise (Ward and Suedfeld, 1974), and that there is less helping behaviour under noise conditions (Matthews and Canon, 1975).

If noise-sensitivity is a feature of the person, whether it reflects a general sensitivity to sensory stimulation, and much neo-Pavlovian research done in Russia supports the idea that some people have 'strong' nervous systems, capable of withstanding high levels of stimulation, while others are 'sensitive' and relatively less intense levels of stimulation have more effect on them, then the need to escape from noise is greater for such people, and effective noise control at the level of the individual may need to take this into account. Noise-sensitivity, or insensitivity, may also be part of the reason why some people can work in the presence of music while others cannot. The particular music is important, but, more generally, it may be whether the person has the ability to turn the music into a background noise, or lacks this ability, which matters. This seems likely to be related to noise-sensitivity.

4.4. VIBRATION

The effects of noise and vibration merge into one another, but vibration is usually considered to involve contact with a moving object which creates mechanical displacement of all or part of the body. There are pressure-sensitive nerve endings in the skin, and the vestibular apparatus, for example, contains receptors which are differentially sensitive to linear and angular acceleration, but problems of vibration within buildings typically can be understood in terms of moving the body, or part of it, at frequencies which are uncomfortable or impair performance. What is uncomfortable, and the nature of impairments of skills, depends broadly on the rate and amount of displacement, which are both affected by body posture, e.g. whether the person is standing straight, bending forward, sitting or lying down. Discomfort effects begin with irritability, but can increase to produce sweating and nausea, or pain, and some researchers have pushed their subjects to the point where they refused to be vibrated any longer (Goldman, 1948). Tolerance for being vibrated at low frequencies is not high and any of the effects described may be found in buildings housing machinery.

Much of the research reports effects of vibration beginning at 1 Hz though lower frequencies are often also unacceptable. Whole body vibration does not have a uniform effect, but rather, because different organs and portions of the body have different resonant frequencies, and because the amount of displacement increases as the vibrating frequency approaches their resonant frequency, the effect of vibration varies throughout the body.

For example, resonance of the abdomen and chest occurs at frequencies between 4–8 Hz where the effects are worst for any given amplitude of vibration. The resulting stresses and strains (see von Gierke and Clarke, 1971) can produce pain in those areas at these frequencies as well as other effects such as increased blood pressure and heart rate (Hood *et al.*, 1966). Prolonged vibration can damage the internal structure of the body and protective devices such as shock absorbers, cushions, seatbelts, and so on, can be of great importance in damping vibration. However, it may be critically necessary to measure the actual effect of any device intended to reduce vibration, using accelerometers attached to different parts of the body, since it has been shown that cushions may lower the frequency at which resonance occurs, but in some types, like innersprung cushions, the effect at the lowered frequency may be worse than that at any frequency when no cushion at all is used.

The military implications of vibration have been extensively researched since vehicles like tanks, rocket launchers, and particularly aircraft engaged in low-level flight at high speeds, create serious difficulties for the human operator. However, most of this research has little bearing on vibration as it typically occurs in buildings where the source of vibration is a nearby machine. The three most likely problems within buildings are impairment of visual functions, interference with controlled movements which the person is required to make, and disorientation which may produce motion sickness. Speech can be impaired at reasonably high vibration frequencies, but long before this occurs, difficulties due to vibration will have become obvious. It follows that it is usually vibration of the head, or of the hands or feet, that gives rise to performance difficulties, even though the vibration may be transmitted through the seat of a chair or the floor.

Grether (1971) reviewed the effects of vibration within the range of frequencies 1–30 Hz excluding motion sickness on the grounds that the conditions creating motion sickness are generally below 1 Hz. Grether notes that visual acuity has been repeatedly shown to be adversely affected by vibration, particularly in the 10–20 Hz band (Lange and Coermann, 1962), and that problems in fixation create blurred images which make tasks like scanning or reading dials hard to perform. Scanning was most impaired around 3·5 Hz (Guignard and Irving, 1960), although other studies found the worst effect at higher frequencies, indicating that, depending on things like distance and whether it is the visual material to be read or the operator's head which is moving, it is the amount of relative motion between the eyes and the visual display which matters.

Reviewing 18 studies of the effects of vibration on manual tracking which covered a wide range of frequencies, amplitudes and different types of vibration, Grether concluded that decrements in performance were proportional to the amplitude of the vibration, and that vibration along the axis of movement increases the difficulty of tracking, i.e. a vertical tracking movement is more influenced by vibration along the vertical axis than along the horizontal axis. Tracking has also been shown to be worse when being vibrated in noisy conditions than when only being vibrated, indicating the interactive nature of these ambient conditions (Harris and Sommer, 1973).

The use of foot controlled mechanisms under vibration occurs commonly in vehicles. The ability to maintain foot pressure has been demonstrated to be impaired (Simons and Schmitz, 1958; Hornick, 1962), and although Schmitz (1959) later failed to show any effect on foot reaction time, this result cannot be generalised safely to everyday conditions. What it does imply, however, is that conditions can be engineered in which the reaction time of a foot movement is not slowed down under vibration. Similar caution needs to be exercised in interpreting laboratory studies of intellectual performance which, like that of Simons and Schmitz (1958) who studied mental arithmetic, show no deterioration under vibration.

Turning to motion sickness, while the vestibular system is the major mechanism causing nausea, it is interesting that disorientation in space and difficulty in focusing visually are also implicated. Both can occur under vibration, possibly creating the same sorts of effects that food or alcohol poisoning produce, and evoking the same reflex of sickness which is an adaptive response to many forms of poisoning. Maintaining visual contact with a fixed and stable horizon is often effective in preventing motion sickness by reducing disorientation. Notice this is more precise than the 'look out of the window' advice often given to queasy car travellers.

Like noise, vibration is best treated at its source but, where this is not practicable, damping the forces acting on the person, or restraining the body or part of it which is affected, are the usual approaches to vibration problems. Occasionally, other solutions offer themselves, like reducing the relative motion between the eyes and a viewed object by increasing the distance between them. But the more radical solutions are almost always more effective.

4.5. ODOUR

Less is written about the smell of buildings or worksettings than their visual or auditory quality. Legislation controlling air quality has improved health by reducing exposure to dangerous substances, but it has also greatly improved the olfactory environment. Although superseded in man by vision as the main directional sense, smell was the earliest of the senses, and in many mammals smell has retained pride of place. It is not surprising then that, precisely because smells have a very powerful influence on behaviour, acceptable conditions of smell are assumed more often than they are discussed. Within the specialised area of dealing with smells which derive from industrial processes, a variety of techniques are used to clean the air. Among the main ones are passing the dirty air through furnaces so that the smell-carrying particles are reduced to carbon dioxide and water. Water treatments may also be used, passing the dirty air through running water which contains material which will react with the smell-carrying particles, caustic soda or the more expensive water soluble chlorophyll are used in this way. Dirty air may also be passed through a bed of carbon to be cleaned by the process of adsorption. Electrostatic precipitation is used in smoke control to precipitate out soot particles in many industrial areas, and many other techniques exist.

Moncrieff (1970), in his highly readable and informative text on '*Odours*', cites a number of interesting examples of industrial odour pollution and the methods used to combat them. He illustrates the danger of not controlling for smell during the design of industrial premises, with a British court verdict against a firm engaged in stove enamelling, which not only cost them thousands of pounds in costs and damages, but closed down the spray shop where the smells originated, and in|the end the firm moved the whole operation to a different part of the country.

It is perhaps partly the association of bad smells with toxic effects which motivates people to take action about unpleasant odours, but the main reason is emotional not rational. The old 'smell brain' or rhinencephalon in man houses the emotional centres, and this may be related to the powerful effects smells exert on moods. The nostalgic memories evoked by specific odours reproduce the mood as well as the events of the past. On the other hand, it only needs one out of the 30 000 or so breaths we take each day to detect sulphur dioxide, or carbon disulphide, and to make us steer clear of that location in future if we can. If we can is important because, if motivated sufficiently, people not only accept unpleasant odours but do adapt to them (Berglund *et al.*, 1971). Workers in abattoirs, or tanneries, or other workplaces with bad smells, in many cases lose the acute awareness that most of us exhibit in such places. However, in the absence of any motivating factor, people tend to take action long before adaptation takes place.

Psychologists attempting to classify the different types of odours which people can discriminate tend to take the great botanist Linnaeus' 1752 classification into seven groups of smells, as their starting point. Linnaeus' categories were: (1) aromatic, e.g. carnation; (2) fragrant, e.g. jasmine; (3) ambrosaic, e.g. musk; (4) alliaceous, e.g. assafoetida; (5) foetid, e.g. goat; (6) virulent, e.g. night shade; (7) nauseous, e.g. gourds; though he did, in fact, offer several other ways of classifying odours. Bain (1868) the Aberdeen psychologist, tried to improve upon Linnaeus and offered a number of comments which are still quoted today, including the fact that his class of 'fresh' smells, like eau-de-cologne, tend to increase the activity of the lungs. His class of appetising smells has been overtaken by research, and modern classifications are given in terms of the chemical composition of the substances, though the best descriptions are still by common example. Bain's comments on 'flavour', however, have not really been taken much further, and his example of cinnamon having little taste but a flavour, i.e. an odour, brought out by chewing it, remains a compelling one.

Various other attempts have been made to classify the basic qualitites of smells. In 1924, Henning gave six which he termed fragrant, ethereal, resinous, spicy, putrid and burnt. Other workers have suggested more, or, in one case, fewer components—caprylic, burnt, acid, and fragrant. Many attempts have also been made over the years to provide ratings of the intensity of smells, and it is well established that extremely low concentrations of many substances are easily detected by smell. In fact, smell is the most sensitive of our chemical senses, another fact which renders it worthy of at least a brief mention in considering ambient conditions.

For buildings, the main odour concerns centre on air pollution effects from petrol burning traffic, air conditioning and ventilation and, to some extent, smells from other people. The last is dealt with by spacing and ventilation, and is treated in the literature, if at all, under personal space. Acceptable smells are determined by culture and convention and throughout the world the range of tolerability is enormous. About all that can be suggested ergonomically is that wherever people congregate for periods of time, ventilation needs to be take seriously, particularly if smoking is permitted in that area. Cigarette smoke has been shown to increase anxiety in some non-smokers, aggression in others (Jones, 1978). Ventilation by fan expellers may be more effective than air conditioning in removing odours, and the rate at which the air is changed can affect the comfort of rooms. Where conditions are reasonably stable a constant rate of air extraction may be satisfactory, as with the single extractor fan in many kitchens, but, in more variable and public situations, the ability to vary the rate of changing the air is the best way out of the dilemma posed by the fact that too fast rates of change, as well as too slow, can produce discomfort. The nature of the odour is at least as important, often more so, than its intensity in trying to select an appropriate rate. Diluting malodorous air by bringing fresh air in, rather than only expelling the tainted air, can be a highly effective approach and is underused in public buildings. Although temperature, humidity, and the quality of the air outside city buildings, both now and in the future, needs to be considered, the use of natural air may be as sensible as the use of natural lighting. Similarly, the deliberate cooling of buildings by ventilation at night to stop them heating up during the hot weather, which is widely used in private homes, can also be applied to other buildings, though often it is not.

Although excellent filters, like active charcoal, exist, air conditioning systems typically do not filter the air very effectively. If they did, the filters would need to be cleaned or replaced very frequently. But they do dilute offensive air with cleaner air. An implication of heating or refrigerating air conditions, which is noted by Moncrieff (1970) is the need, for economy's sake, to recirculate about 80 % of the air in the building, which may mean that the air becomes lower in oxygen and higher in carbon dioxide, with consequent effects on performance.

Pollutants and odour are linked together in the minds of most people. Yet many of the dangerous pollutants are odourless, for instance, carbon monoxide which is highly toxic is not detectable by smell. Most of the writers on smell make reference to the relatively recent improvement in the smell of our cities and quote descriptions of how bad things were in the 18th or 19th centuries. Much of the early problems stemmed from two sources, the disposal of sewage and other wastes, and the burning of coal. Indeed, burning coal was prohibited in the city of London in 1273 in an effort to clean the air. Later, problems derived from the industrialisation of countries which made them prosperous, and most recently from the exhaust systems of petrol driven vehicles. Ideally, the exhaust fume problem, which affects buildings from streets and parking areas, would be dealt with by improved engine design to ensure that all of the fuel burns, leaving only carbon dioxide, water and nitrogen. In practice, legislation may control exhaust systems to reduce the emission of petrol and dangerous gases, and to prevent the addition of tetra-ethyl lead which can be used to lower the octane number of the fuel required by the vehicle. Vehicle exhaust gases can affect whole cities as in the Los Angeles situation where the air is still, so that the gases do not disperse, the volume of traffic is great, and the action of ultra-violet light in the sunny climate combines the gases photochemically into new chemicals some of which irritate the eyes.

If odour or pollution from vehicles is severe, then windowless buildings may be acceptable, but fixed windows which do not open are likely to be a preferred solution along with other measures to exclude the contaminated air. Closed car parks may require close attention to adequate ventilation and even regular cleaning away of substances like the tars deposited on the floor. Since some of these are known to be carcinogenic, there is every reason for caution.

One final point that deserves to be made about smells is that they are not independent of the other senses. In fact, sources of unpleasant smells are more often identified visually than by smelling the object in question. The reverse is true for Bain's 'fresh' smells, which lead us to inhale deeply and sample the fresh sea or country air, and there is a large area of uncertainty. But people like their olfactory environment to be stable, not in the sense of always smelling exactly the same, but rather of being able to identify what the smell is and where it comes from, and smells do not have to indicate danger to be particularly nice or nasty to excite comment. Any novel smell will soon have people trying to identify and locate it.

Chapter 5

The Workable Environment

5.1. TRAFFIC WITHIN BUILDINGS

Mobility within buildings is equally as important as entry or exit. From an ergonomic point of view the spaces through which people move are simply extensions of the working areas themselves, and appropriate dimensions are arrived at by considering the major functions which will take place in corridors, stairways, lifts and other linking spaces. The first considerations are traffic volume and the type of goods or equipment that may have to be transported within the space. While there are a variety of recommendations for distances, workability can be achieved in many different ways. When projecting traffic volumes, a useful rule of thumb which fits both anthropometric and personal space data (Hall, 1966; Sommer, 1969), is to regard the minimum space occupied by the average person as a 600 mm square. This implies that the minimum width for two-way traffic is 1200 mm. In some cases even narrower corridors can be employed, but these are unlikely to be acceptable unless they are usually used only by one person at a time, or by people on intimate terms such as families, or else form part of what is perceived as an unusual structure. This last point highlights the differences which exist, and what would not be acceptable in most situations is found workable in some buses, trains, homes, boats, library stacks, and so on.

Other main aspects of corridor design concern

(1) visibility, which argues for straight lines or gentle curves, and adherence to lighting standards;
(2) avoiding intruding items which cause bottlenecks, e.g. fire extinguishers, doors which either open into the corridor or are placed across it, or using corridors as storage areas by locating, say, filing cabinets in them;
(3) activities taking place in adjoining spaces, which can determine the acceptable level of noise which will be transmitted from the corridor;

69

(4) junctions and terminuses of corridors which, in most cases, need to feed into wider areas to accommodate the increase in volume—again a 600 mm square per person is a reasonable approximation unless large items are normally transported by those using the corridors;

(5) signposting for everyday and emergency use, which may include fire exit directional arrows or markers, which are not only visible at floor level to avoid them being hidden by smoke, but can also be interpreted by touch in cases of complete blackout. A standard fire exit arrow does not yet exist, but a 25 mm deep hole in the shape of a 75 mm equilateral triangle, let into brick or other hard surface, just above floor level so it is easy to find in the dark, is one relatively indestructible means of pointing the way out which could be used under most conditions unless flooding occurred.

Aisles differ from corridors in that they are essentially for one-way traffic at peak loading which is often predictable. Here, proper signposting can avoid congestion and increase traffic flow. Aisles which are also used as waiting areas can be designed to encourage or discourage social interaction between those present. Sommer (1974a) makes the point that the side by side seating typical of airport lounges tends to discourage interaction. This, however, is not necessarily bad design since, although little evidence seems to exist on this point, people in airports, medical and dental waiting rooms, and even in public service or commercial waiting areas, are often in a state of heightened tension and prefer to be able to avoid casual, short-lived social interactions which in any case are relatively pointless.

Staircases normally connect different levels of a building if the change of height can be around 1 in 3. Where space is not available, and the staircase is used very little, steeper stairs of 1 in 2 are acceptable (Grandjean, 1973). Very much more or less than that, say 1 in 1·75 and 1 in 4·5, and ladders and ramps become appropriate. Ergonomic considerations in staircase design may be discussed under:

(1) traffic type and volume which determines the necessary width;
(2) safety, where the main considerations are the need for

handrails, non-skid stair surfaces, and clearly defined stair edges capable of supporting the full weight of any person, and fire doors;

(3) fatigue which is related to step height, length of stairway, distance between steps and the weight of any items normally carried.

Handrails need to be 850–900 mm high (Lehmann, 1962), not only to protect people from falling into stairwells, but also to be close to average elbow height. Spacing between vertical rails should not be more than 120 mm where there is any risk of serious falls. Handrails not only provide leverage but, like walls in staircases, allow the person to offset the side to side tendency to unbalance while descending. When used for leverage, it is important that the hand be able to grip the rail firmly, and diameters much greater than 40 mm are less effective, though some recommendations (e.g. Grandjean, 1973) are considerably thicker than this. Non-slip handrails may be useful if the thickened rail is used.

Many different non-skid surfaces are available and widely used, but stair edges are often less well defined than they should be. For example, edges which are the same colour as the step surface are difficult to detect and may be dangerous during descent. This is made worse if the stair treads are ribbed across their breadth since, during descent, the ribs can be confused with the edge, creating the worst of situations if the person is confident that his misperception is correct. Also, where thick carpeting is used, rounded stair edges can provide slippery and insecure footholds. Older people with their greater requirement for sensory information, and increased need to rely on vision (Szafran, 1948), are particularly at risk on badly designed stairways.

Fatigue results from prolonged climbing, and landings are desirable, but it is difficult to decide how frequently by estimating the amount of energy expended unless one knows the total number of stairs to be climbed. In practice, landings every 10 stairs avoid undue fatigue for most of the population. Fatigue can also be created by inappropriate step widths or heights. For example, widths greater than about 1 m force the individual to step up or down using the same foot each time. The person can, of course, deliberately change step, and it is arguable that only having to step up with every second step should be less fatiguing. Nevertheless, asymmetrical climbing is perceived as fatiguing, probably not because of the asymmetric fatigue of one leg rather than another, though this does not seem to have been tested, but more because very broad steps tend to lead the climber to step up flat footed rather than being on his toes. A relevant factor here is the inability to use reflected elastic energy or loss of upward impetus, if the person steps on each level step, but the relative importance of each of these factors is not known.

Too narrow step widths are obviously dangerous and widths of 300 mm are required to accommodate the largest foot. Very much more than this is unnecessary and shades gradually into the problems of too great width.

Step height is recommended to be between 150–200 mm with the middle of that range being close to an optimum measure. Too shallow steps are to be avoided just as much as too steep ones. The tread:rise ratio of 300:170 mm, which is based on that recommended by Grandjean (1973), has been shown to be less effortful than both steeper and shallower staircases.

Pedestrian traffic movement in and around buildings tends to follow certain predictable patterns. First, people usually try to use the most direct route which involves least effort (Preiser, 1972, 1973). This remains the case in some recreational settings, such as walking round a World Fair Exhibition (Weiss and Boutourline, 1962), though pace may be a function of time spent in inspection, arguing for wide pathways. Despite differences in age, in the reasons for walking and so on, Preiser (1973) suggests that people tend to match their walking speed to those around them. Perhaps the mechanism for this is that it is easier to maintain constant distances between yourself and others when moving at the same pace, and in so doing avoid invasions of your own personal space or that of others. If so, the effect of those setting the pace, whether through age, infirmity, load, or determination to get somewhere quickly, should not only be a function of the number of such people (which can be experienced in any rush hour), but also by the space available. This suggestion gains support from Konečni *et al.* (1975) who found pedestrians crossed the street faster the closer other people were to them. Their results (see Fig. 5.1.1) suggest that within part of the range of distances tested, the

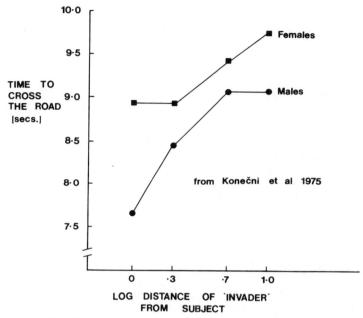

Fig. 5.1.1.   The effect of personal space invasion on the time taken to cross the road.

relationship between walking speed and distance can be shown to be a straight line on a logarithmic plot. But, also, that females begin to increase their speed when people are at a distance which has no effect on males. Finally, it may be that the women studied have already reached their maximum speed at a distance less than the minimum used in this experiment, whereas the men, who are consistently quicker anyway, do not show this levelling off of pace. Further research is needed along these lines to test this interpretation, but many experiments show male–female differences in response to personal space invasion.

The use of music to speed up or slow down pedestrians' walking speed is sometimes effective (Preiser, 1973), but other variables usually enter into everyday behaviour. Using slides of different areas of a suburban shopping area, le May and Aronow (1977) found that viewing time increased with the complexity of the area. This can be put to work if, by rating the complexities of the areas for movement, one can detect a need to reduce the complexity in order to reduce looking time and lingering behaviour.

The distances people keep from one another serve as cues to their relationship to one another, and this, together with their behaviour, signals whether individuals are part of a group or not. Where they are perceived as being a group, some other rules come into operation so that, for example, people tend to walk round the boundaries of groups rather than violating their 'groupspace', and this tendency is strengthened if the group is stationary rather than on the move (Cheyne and Efan, 1972; Knowles and Bassett, 1976). Moreover, people will more readily stop and join a group of people looking at something if they perceive the group as being made up of people not known to one another (Milgram *et al.*, 1969; Knowles and Bassett, 1976). These are easily observed patterns of behaviour, but the role of interpersonal distance is not always recognised as the powerful cue it is.

That people slow down as they approach barriers is another commonplace observation (e.g. Winkel and Hayward, 1971), but barriers such as changes of surface from pathway to lawn, or roadside kerbing can be more psychological than physical. Many factors affect pedestrians' speed round or through barriers but, where their motivation is very high, inappropriate speed can become dangerous, and some National Safety Councils now issue 'Watch that door!' stickers in an attempt to prevent accidents caused by hurrying people flinging doors open. The pedestrian version of a motorway pile-up accident does also occur, usually at very popular sporting events or rock concerts, where members of crowds entering or leaving a stadium are motivated to move so fast that each ignores the risk of tripping, or is frightened that if they slow down they will be the ones piled into. Ergonomically, the number of people involved is a key safety factor, and the number of entrances and exits available, and known to be open, must be geared to the number of people to avoid this serious situation.

Within buildings used as exhibition halls, some early studies suggest that more people tend to follow the right hand wall than perambulate in a clockwise direction (Robinson, 1928; Melton, 1936, 1972), and almost half the visitors walked along only one side of a rectangular room, preferring to use the doorway into the next gallery than complete their circuit. Suggestions of a 'gradient of attraction' to an exit have been made to explain this, and may well turn out to be correct. But, where more than one doorway exists, people may prefer to avoid the extra effort involved in backtracking or arriving where they started from, using a strategy of maximum inspected (including from a distance across the room) by the most direct and least effortful route. This rule appears to govern much pedestrian activity, and is often used to do away with the need for physical barriers to prevent people operating the rule illegally and taking shortcuts despite a designer's intentions.

5.2. LIFTS

Some features of both the design and usage of lifts are worthy of ergonomic scrutiny. For the most part lifts are well designed and pose relatively few problems, but some undesirable features do exist. Probably the most common are the effects of being decelerated too quickly, which can range from mild jolt to the giddiness and nausea which accompany disorientation in space. This disorientation can be produced by the activity of the semicircular canals which provide information which helps us to balance. Too sudden stopping makes the fluid in the semicircular canals flow in the direction opposite to that in which it has been flowing, and this produces the sensation of moving in the opposite direction. When this is in conflict with other sensory information which tells us we are not moving, then spatial disorientation may occur. The unpleasant effects of disorientation can be made much worse if the person moves and tilts his head while in motion. In fact, anything which tends to create spatial confusion or disorientation should not be used whenever people are in motion, so that, for example, op-art furnishings which often involve ambiguous cues for depth-perception are to be avoided. But as far as lifts are concerned, furnishings and decoration only very rarely have adverse effects although some curious practices exist, such as carpeting the walls and floors of lifts with the same thick shag carpet as on the floor of the rest of the building.

Carpeting can help with soundproofing, but noise in lifts is less of a problem than noise outside lifts, for example from lift machinery. Auditory indicators should be avoided except on ground floor levels where many lifts are dealing with a heavy volume of traffic, as happens in some retail stores and office blocks.

The current fashion for carpeted lifts may be due to the appearance of spaciousness which they give to a small lift, and the preference for light coloured, non-reflective wall surfaces which make the space seem larger. The small sizes of lifts will, nevertheless, still produce crowding by other people which, although not usually perceived as intensely unpleasant, produces effects like raised heart rate, raised blood pressure, increased sweating and other stress indicators. Behaviourally, people in lifts adopt the conventions surrounding invasions of personal space, that is, they avoid looking at each other, avoid touching each other, stand far apart if they can, prefer to stand side by side if they cannot, and exit from the situation as quickly as possible. The problems of crowding can be exacerbated if space is taken up with rails which function to protect the décor, or by giving floor space to ash trays or litter bins.

The most acute problem which can face the occupants of a lift, however, is power failure which, fortunately, only occurs infrequently. Back-up emergency lighting and power supplies and procedures usually mean that those people who are stuck between floors remain so for only a short time. Nevertheless, it is important that the lift occupants should not only be able to signal their predicament at once, but should be in contact with people outside the lift within a very short time. This implies that on the control panel the appropriate button should be clearly marked and within easy reach of everyone including children or disabled people in wheelchairs. Many lifts provide telephones which can be used to summon assistance, but these are commonly too high to be reached by everyone, and sometimes the handle on the door of the compartment housing the telephone is poorly designed, for example, by only being able to be grasped by finger and thumb when, perhaps through expansion or misalignment of the compartment's door, more force is required to open it than can be exerted.

As far as the control buttons and indicators inside and outside the lift are concerned, it is necessary to resolve the possible ambiguity about whether the information given represents what you want the lift to do in the future, or what it is doing at the moment.

This is usually resolved by having both directional 'call-accepted' buttons which light up when pressed, and 'hall-lantern' indicators showing the lift's direction of travel which are often located above the door of the lift. With these arrangements, it can be important that the hall-lantern indicators should not remain illuminated if the lift is ready to go either up or down. If the hall-lantern indicators remain on outside the lift, people interpret this to mean the lift is still going in that direction, as it usually is. This misinformation effectively reduces the volume of traffic by the proportion of missed opportunities which could have been taken. It may also reduce the credibility of the hall-lantern and, in at least one building known to the writer, may people check the directional indicators on the control panel inside the lift, or ask the passengers in which direction they are going, rather than trusting the hall-lantern, because it can be misleading in a very small proportion of cases.

Apart from the size of the lift, and the numbers of lifts warranted by the volume of expected traffic, features such as the width of door required, are determined by the function the lift plays in transporting material as well as people. Recently, the current interest in allowing access to buildings for people in wheelchairs has given rise to the recommendations by the Standards Association of Australia (Australian Standard, 1428-1977) which include a minimum clear doorway of 800 mm, and a square design with the sides not less than 1800 mm. The provision of a handrail adjacent to the control panel is also one of the recommendations.

Finally, because lifts are the main form of transport in many buildings, and are also relatively expensive, perhaps accounting for 10–15 % of some building costs, the logistics of how the lift system works is important. The main considerations are how many people travel per run and how long most people have to wait.

5.3. INFORMATION COMMUNICATION

5.3.1. *Alphanumeric Symbols*

Within buildings, the communication of information is primarily visual, and letters and numbers are more often used than other types of symbols. The main requirement is legibility, an area where there have been many studies, particularly into the legibility of dials and instruments. However, provided that the information display is correctly positioned, is large enough, and there is sufficient contrast between the background and the display, legibility is not difficult to achieve.

Positioning is a matter of meeting the user's expectations of where particular information is likely to be at the time when they require it, and avoiding obstructions covering up the information. The London Underground system of overhead, named and colour coded symbols for various lines, is a good example of traffic direction. One point worth noting is that the symbols are not really overhead when first noticed, but tend, when entering the system, to appear from below eye level descending by escalator or stairs. People look above their heads only infrequently unless they are alerted to the presence of information displays in that position.

Legibility of alphanumeric material has been researched in terms of making each letter or number unique by minimising the number of common features so that, e.g. instead of 3 and 5 with common lower halves, you can use 3 and 5. However, when Soar (1955) first studied the common confusions which occurred, and then went on to produce sets of characters with minimal common features, these were not widely accepted.

One can argue that the new characters 'looked funny', or were too unfamiliar, but there is another possibility. Common elements may direct our attention to critical differentiating elements, thus reducing the number of ways in which we can discriminate one character from another. That is, they reduce the amount of critical information we can process, so that until we are very heavily overeducated in the use of the unique characters, we may process more information than we need, and find them more effortful to use. The situation with new and unique characters may be rather like the first time one drove a motor car, when we all sought too much information visually, like looking for the position of the gear lever, and the skilled activities had not been integrated by familiarity and anticipation. In any case, British Standard 3693, which deals with alphanumeric symbols, accepts common elements between characters, as does the US Military Standard AND 10400 (1957) (described in McCormick, 1976, p. 90) which contains a more comprehensive review of alphanumeric research than is warranted here. However, it is worth noting that some 'unusual' sets of characters, such as the numerals devised by Landsell (1954), have been shown to be easily learned and highly legible (Foley, 1956). These are only indicated for use where legibility is a problem, and most important, when being read by operators using them over a long term. They are merely confusing to casual readers like the passer-by. But special alphabets do exist for special problems.

Ratio of strokewidth to height

Beyond the shape of alphanumeric characters, various combinations of strokewidth and the height of character have been examined. Based on Berger's (1944) data, the distance at which black numbers on a white ground could be discriminated ranged from 25 m for a 1:40 ratio to 33·5 m for a 1:8 ratio. Within the range of ratios 1:6–1:10 the distance at which they could be read did not fall below 32 m. Differences are observed where white characters against a black ground are used. Here, the longest distance achieved—36·5 m—was for the ratio 1:13·3 and, within the range of ratios 1:10 to 1:20 the shortest distance observed was 33·5 m. These, however, were threshold measures for numerals measuring 42 × 89 mm, and while the ratios are relevant, larger character sizes are indicated for above threshold performance. It is also true that the vision of the individual is relevant for legibility, and while that cannot be controlled, increased illumination can compensate for loss of acuity to some degree. As previously stated, this is particularly important for older people with failing eyesight.

Another ratio which has occupied the time of applied psychologists is the width–height ratio. On the basis of military research in America, recommended ratios for width to height have emerged which are 1:1 for most letters (obviously not I) (US Military Spec. No. MIL-M-18012 B, 1964), or 2:3 (US Military Standard AND 10400, 1957). These recommendations were formulated for capitals, and are familiar to most people through the ARMY, NAVY lettering on US military vehicles. Variations away from these strict recommendations do not produce immediate illegibility; in fact, numerals with a width–height ratio of 3:5 are frequently used.

The actual size of lettering needed depends upon the person's acuity of vision, their colour vision, the viewing distance, as well as on factors which the ergonomist can control. On distance, reasonably high detectability rates will be found where the angle subtended by the object in view is not less than 1 minute. With high degrees of contrast or very bright stimuli, much smaller targets are visible, but in the present context we are not concerned with the lower limits of vision.

One widely quoted study by Peters and Adams (1959) has attempted to allow for illumination conditions, and the importance of the information being viewed, by using the formula:

$$H = 0{\cdot}0022D + K_1 + K_2$$

where H is the height of the letter or numeral,
   D is the distance from the viewer,
   K_1 is a correction for illumination and conditions of viewing given as 0·06 (above 10 lux, good conditions), 0·16 (above 10 lux, poor conditions, or less than 10 lux, good conditions), and 0·26 (below 10 lux, poor conditions), and
   K_2 is a correction for importance which is 0 or 0·075 depending upon the classification of the information as everyday or important.

5.3.2. Symbolic Representations

Although less common, the use of non-verbal symbols is a matter of importance and may make the difference between successful communication or failure. Obvious indications for use are where not everyone can read the language, where there is insufficient time for more than a symbol, and even to save the person time in discovering that this is not the information he requires.

Ergonomically, symbolising the world in non-verbal ways is a challenging task, and one which requires validating either by research or by *in situ* observation. The types of symbols used, and the functions they are meant to perform, have been categorised in various ways, and not only is there agreement on the need for non-verbal symbols, but in the case of road signs (e.g. McCormick, 1976, p. 104), there is agreement on the need for standardisation. The advantages of standardisation are very real and may even outweigh small improvements in comprehensibility. The most interesting symbols are those which attempt to represent some feature of the world, whether the likely presence of wild animals on the road, the existence of toilet facilities, or the fact that you are entering a minefield. Other arbitrary symbols, such as the yellow diamond indicating 'Priority Road' in parts of Europe, require to be discriminable under a wide range of conditions, but otherwise depend upon widespread publicity for their significance to be learned.

However, there are studies showing that the meaning of visual symbols can, under some circumstances, be learned extremely quickly (Haber and Erdelyi, 1967), though equally, where there is any ambiguity or possibility of confusion, meanings of symbols can be forgotten or mistaken.

Representational symbols have been studied in military or air traffic contexts (Provins *et al.*, 1957; Smith and Thomas, 1964), to find the speed and accuracy which can be attained with such material, and Hitt (1961) has investigated performance of different sorts, e.g. locating, counting, for different types of non-representational symbol.

More recently, Easterby (1967*b*) has reminded us that the most effective displays are those which exemplify the principles which govern the processes by which we organise sensory input into a perception. Among such principles Easterby mentions contour, closure, symmetry, unity and form. But the visual properties of individual signs are also determined by the relationship of that sign to others, and by the meaning which that set of signs carries, e.g. informational, spatially directional, precautionary, mandatory. A great deal of information can be condensed into one sign provided it belongs to a standardised set. Such information can be processed very quickly, sometimes more quickly than the verbal symbols of our written language (Walker *et al.*, 1965). It is also necessary to consider the sign's function in relation to human performance, this can affect size, location, colour and contrast between the symbol and background; and the conditions under which the sign needs to be used, like whether it needs to be illuminated or not. All of these considerations are important for the effective use of symbols, but perhaps the very first consideration is when a sign is needed at all, and whether it should be a non-verbal symbol.

Easterby (1970) makes the point that it is paradoxical that, with increasingly complex technology, we must sometimes revert to symbolic representation like that used in the earliest pictographic languages.

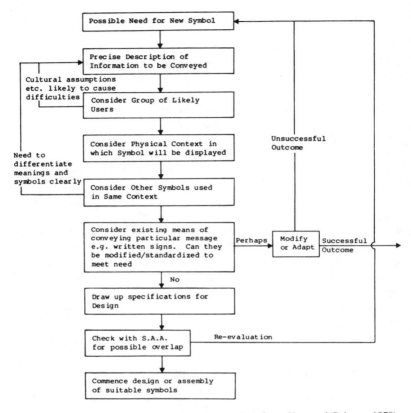

Fig. 5.3.1.   Determining the need for a new symbol (from Sless and Cairney, 1978).

Despite the obvious need to know when to use symbols, until recently no accepted method of deciding when symbols were necessary has existed. In 1978 an evaluative procedure (Sless and Cairney, 1978) to determine the need for new symbols, which has been endorsed by the Standards Association of Australia (SAA) and recommended by them to the International Standards Organization (ISO) was developed. Figure 5.3.1 shows the suggested procedure. These authors have also been concerned with the perceived meaning of symbols.

In one study, which was carried out to test the procedures which were under consideration for adoption by the Standards Association, they used a set of symbols for use in indicating occupational hazards. Their subjects were all people with problems of literacy, in some cases because they were recent migrants with little or no English; some Vietnamese and other migrants of European origin took part in the study, as did a group of Australians who had literacy difficulties. The straightforward recognition approach of showing the sign and asking what it meant was adopted. If incorrect answers were given, the experimenter corrected them by explaining what the sign was intended to signify. A second test took place about one week later to establish how good the recall of the meanings was. A coefficient of concordance was calculated for both tests, which proved that the people tested showed a high degree of consistency in both the initial and recall tests. The Vietnamese subjects proved to have most difficulty initially in recognising the symbols, but improved significantly more than all other groups in the test of recall.

Since these particular signs should have been likely to have clear meanings, and since some of the meaning is communicated, as in road signs, by the shape and colour of the sign, so that mandatory signs are circular, hazard signs triangular, some of the problems which emerged are of interest. The conventional Radiation Hazard symbol, a three-bladed propeller-like sign, was not well-recognised and it was most frequently identified as indicating danger from a fan or moving machinery. Nor was it easily learned.

While not knowing what a symbol stands for is one of the difficulties that can arise, so is misidentifying its meaning. Misinterpretations of the sign prohibiting naked flames—a lighted match with the prohibitory red diagonal band across it—were common, often being dangerously confused with an instruction not to drop spent matches. These two cases point very clearly to the main problems with signs. Cairney and Sless suggest that at least three sets of factors need to be considered to avoid such problems. The nature of the message needs clearly to refer to some object or action which is unambiguously meaningful to the viewer. Second, standardisation of types of sign, mandatory, cautionary and so on, by shape and colour, needs to be established. Finally, the ambiguity of signs must be taken into account. It is not enough for there to be clear meaning for a symbol, instead there needs to be only one clear meaning rather than several, so that the translation of the symbol to its referent is inescapable.

Essentially the same findings were reported (Cairney, 1979) in a study which, in addition, included roadside information symbols. In this latter report, Cairney identifies having some portion of the referent missing from the symbol as another source of difficulties. Thus, rather than using the sign for no naked flames mentioned above, also to mean no smoking, it is less ambiguous to use a separate no smoking sign like a lighted cigarette with the prohibitory diagonal red band running through it. Where such signs have to be seen and understood quickly, as in travelling at high speeds, it becomes vital that signs are used which are of known effectiveness. Unfortunately, this does not always happen, many signs are accepted on the rational basis that their meaning is obvious when, in fact, as the Sless and Cairney research proves, this turns out to be wrong when the signs are subjected to empirical test.

The move to international, standard signs requires research on an international scale. Easterby and Zwaga (1976) tested people in Australia, Canada, Spain, Argentina, India and The Netherlands, in an effort to evaluate their procedures as well as obtaining information about six referents. The referents were: drinking water, stairs, taxi, waiting room, information, and toilet; for each of which a number of different symbols were originally used, e.g. eight versions of waiting room and 35 versions of toilets. The symbols used were drawn from a wide variety of texts including Dreyfus (1972). The symbols were rated for preference, and their numbers reduced to six versions of each referent through tests in the UK and The Netherlands. The selected versions were then administered for matching and recognition in the various countries. Relatively small numbers of about 25 were used as subjects in each country for the initial testing. While, from a practical point of view this is sometimes all that is possible, ideally very large samples are desirable, like the 4000 people tested by Easterby and Hakiel (1977) in their study of safety labelling in consumer products. However, enough information was obtained in this study to show there were differences between countries, and to reduce the number of versions to a final three for each referent.

Not only are there cross-cultural differences in recognition, there are also differences of acceptability. The red crescent is far more appropriate and acceptable in Muslim countries than the red cross is, though they both have the same referent of first-aid or medical treatment.

Moreover, it is sometimes wise not to insist on absolute standardisation if the actual referent varies from country to country. Thus, for example, while a sign for 'danger, native animals on the road' could be produced, the extra information of what sort of animal is highly relevant. It is for this reason that while similar in shape and colour, deer are represented on the sign in Scotland, reindeer in Sweden, and kangaroos, wombats or koala bears in Australia.

Apart from meaning, Easterby (1970) offers one summary of principles of symbol design. He suggests that:

(1) the figure–ground relationship should be clear and stable,
(2) contrast boundaries to figures are preferable to line boundaries,
(3) solid rather than outline geometrical shapes are to be preferred,
(4) that contour figures should always be closed with a continuous outline, and be as simple and symmetrical as possible,
(5) using the same sizes and proportions of individual elements which are repeated will help to create a unified figure, and
(6) the outlines of the symbol should follow the horizontal and vertical axes as far as possible.

Many of these principles are to be seen at work in road signs which often have to be comprehended in a short space of time. Following these principles, and considering the other factors mentioned above, should produce effective symbols but, unfortunately, one does not have to look far to find examples of poor signs which do not follow them. As interest grows in testing the effectiveness of symbols, and in achieving standardisation where that is useful, the quality of poor symbols can be expected to improve, but there is already a great deal of useful information which can be utilised.

5.3.3. *Auditory Information in Warning Signals and Direct Communication*

Although public address systems are widely employed, their main function is to provide up to the minute information, and the use of the auditory channel is more usually restricted to warning or emergency signals. The reasons for this are self-evident, visual information can be made more or less permanent and can, if necessary, be changed and updated like auditory information as, for example, in airport arrival and departure details shown on closed circuit television. Auditory signals, on the other hand, are not dependent on any particular direction of attention and are, therefore suitable for warning signals like fire alarms or the sort of burglar alarm designed to alert the neighbourhood and scare off intruders. Since we are considering workability, it is necessary to note that any ergonomically organised warning system not only indicates the nature of the emergency, but should also tell those being warned what action they should take. This frequently requires drills and practices to familiarise people with the warning signal, and with what is appropriate behaviour for them. Otherwise, typical reactions to an unaccustomed firebell include assuming the system has triggered accidentally or is under test, or puzzled consultations between people which are not helpful if none of them knows what the alarm signifies or what to do about it.

The other main uses for auditory information are mostly determined by the difficulty of using visual presentations so that, e.g. where lighting is poor, or the person's head is being vibrated so strongly that it makes reading visual information impossible, it may be necessary to operate in an auditory mode. There are, however, some specialised situations in which the direction and rate of change of state may most quickly and accurately be signalled by using the hearing system's great sensitivity to changes in the pitch of an auditory stimulus, or the temporal acuity of the system, which may be capable of hearing clicks which are separated by as little as 0·001 s. Such specialised auditory displays tend to be used for unusual tasks like sonar detection in submarines, or as auditory airspeed indicators in carrier-based aircraft.

Morgan *et al.* (1963) suggest that the human auditory system also has other useful capacities. It can selectively attend to some portion of a complex, total pattern of auditory stimulation, and can localise the source of sounds. This is certainly true but, unfortunately, only within limits; and attention-holding auditory warning signals lose their value and become a distraction and an annoyance when trying to listen to some other source. Similarly with auditory localisation, which most people believe they are far more capable of than they really are. Practical difficulties arise because in everyday settings expectations and non-auditory sensory data also play a role in locating the sources of sounds. Geissler (1915) illustrated the importance of expectancy by showing a 30–40 % increase in incorrect localisations when subjects were told to expect a sound in one half or quarter of the auditory field, but the stimulus occurred elsewhere. In a more homely example, Jackson (1953) employed the sight of steam issuing from the whistle of a whistling kettle which, in fact, made no audible sound, to see whether people's judgements of where the whistling sound came from were affected by the visual information. As might be expected, people showed a tendency to be less accurate when sight and sound were in conflict. How much more inaccurate judgements would be where it is not suspected that the possibility exists that the viewed source is not the actual source of the sound, is a matter of conjecture, but localisation is clearly affected, and its accuracy cannot be relied upon where such factors enter into the situation.

Interestingly enough, using artificial model ears which were plugged into his subjects' own ears, Oldfield (1979) has demonstrated that by turning the artificial ears up or down in relation to the real ear, the apparent locus of an auditory stimulus follows the position of the artificial ears. Thus, the outside portion of the ear—the pinna—i.e. the part we hang our spectacles from, appears to play an important role in our localisation of sound. This can be generalised back to situations without artificial ears indicating that the orientation of the head and ears to a sound source may affect its accurate localisation. Lifting the head to listen may help, but factors like these, as well as problems of reflected sound, make potentially simple ergonomic principles like 'Always site your fire alarm where those hearing it should gather, using their prearranged routes' far less simple than they seem. That is not to say that, with training, very good fire alarm systems, perhaps using firebells to indicate the area in which the fire had occurred together with another signal or signals to indicate a safe area or route, could not be designed. But, apart from the problems raised, a moment's reflection will show that, just because of their virtue as warning signals, most of the auditory signals which we know, e.g. foghorns, klaxons, sirens, firebells, all carry the wrong meaning to be used to indicate that people should move toward them for safety, and this approach could have disastrous effects because of what we have come to expect those sounds to mean.

A number of writers on ergonomics have suggested other situations in which the use of auditory signals is indicated than those above. McCormick (1976), for example, includes cases where the original signal is itself a sound, where people move about from one place to another, and where speech channels are fully loaded. This is because the masking of auditory information is a function of the similarity of the two or more sets of stimuli, as well as of intensity. Many experiments have been done on human capacity for dichotic listening using different information delivered separately to the two ears. If the person's attention is fully taken up by one source of speech, and psychologists try to ensure this in some experiments by making their subjects 'shadow' a continuous spoken message to one ear by repeating it aloud, then the listener is usually able to tell whether a non-verbal stimulus like a bell tone or whistle was delivered to the other ear. Similarly, other non-verbal aspects of the additional stimulus can be recognised, whether there was some speech presented to the unshadowed ear, that the speaker was male or female and so on. What are normally not discriminated are the verbal aspects, and the listener cannot tell you what was said in the additional message, whether the message was sense or nonsense, or even what language was used. Ergonomically, findings like these underlie the use of tones, bells, sirens and a whole host of other non-verbal signals in buildings to avoid the masking of spoken messages. However, the shadowing studies also point out that speech masking is far more complex than just not being able to hear the voice. Anyone who has tried in vain to catch a train announcer's message in a cavernous, echoing railway station has experienced this, though the significance of it for designing more effective systems may not have been obvious.

The more traditional approaches include:

(1) warning the listeners that a message is about to be delivered,
(2) trying to stop all other speaking while the message is given,
(3) using higher rather than lower pitched voices for increased intelligibility, and
(4) repeating the message several times.

Apart from these, the use of auditory non-verbal signals in and around buildings has increased somewhat in recent years, as in the 'bleepers' carried by some hospital staff which are used to contact the person more directly and efficiently than by a public address announcement. But verbal contact has increased rather more whether the contact is indirect, as in recorders used to man telephones during periods of absence of people, or is direct through two-way radios, intercom or other systems. The main reason for this is that the greatest increase in need has been for the exchange of information between people in contexts where the behaviour of one depends on the information supplied by the other. Telephone recorders may defer this exchange, and protect an individual from too much access, but it is still the same need.

Where communication by speech is required, there are few general principles which apply. A comprehensive discussion of speech communication is given in Morgan *et al.* (1963) which includes the topic of intelligibility and intelligibility testing. Where an environment is being created around the spoken transfer of information, an ergonomic approach to the design considers the characteristics of the human participants, and the surrounding auditory environment, as well as the physical and psychological nature of the speech. On the participants, it may be important to bear in mind that some hearing loss with ageing is normal, and that the effect of this on speech perception shows more clearly when visual cues are removed, as in the commonly reported problems old people have with telephone conversations. The role of vision in the understanding of speech in older people has shown their unwitting dependence on lip-reading (Farrimond, 1959). But more recent research (MacDonald and McGurk, 1978) has revealed that associating the sound made by a person saying 'da', with a video picture of him when he is saying 'ba', makes us perceive the person saying something which is neither 'da' nor 'ba', but in this case perhaps 'pda'. Learning to understand speech is obviously not entirely an auditory process.

5.4. Control Mechanisms

In this section we shall attempt to review some of the controls and displays in most common usage and to consider how far these match users' expectations. At the outset it is worth stating six very general principles concerning controls.

(1) The first is that the function which the control performs should be obvious.
(2) With that, the mode of operation should be clear.
(3) The mode of operation should also be in accord with the users' expectations of how the control works.
(4) The state or setting of the control should be evident without the need for interpretation.
(5) The force required to operate the control should normally not be great.
(6) Lastly, where there is a display associated with the control, other than the position of the control itself, the workability of the control–display relationship must be considered as well as the design of the control and display being evaluated separately.

Some further discussion of control–display relationships follows in a later section to illustrate their importance, which goes beyond just having a good control and a good display.

Taking controls first, the range of different types of control is truly enormous, but fortunately, for the present purpose the most commonly used types of controls within buildings are relatively few and can be categorised as: handles, knobs, locks and catches, keyboards and pushbuttons as the most frequently found controls, with a second group of less frequent controls comprising: levers, pedals and handwheels.

5.4.1. Handles

Problems with controls which meet the six principles above generally arise because of design or location faults. Recurrent design faults for handles include being too small to be gripped by the hand, or too large for the thumb to overlap the fingers when holding the handle, protruding in such a manner as to catch people's clothing, and having right angles in cross section which create undue pressure on a small area of the hand. The first and last points may be illustrated by stating that many suitcase handles are too narrow, and leather handles, as on brief cases, should have the sewn seam on top or outside, rather than on the inside portion of the handle.

5.4.2. Knobs

Knobs pose some special difficulties because they can be considered to move in all directions round the central shaft at the same time. An example of this is taken up under control–display relationships. Considering just the knob design alone, difficulties can arise if there is insufficient space around the knob, if knurling is insufficient to grip the knob sufficiently strongly, or is great enough to allow such a strong grip that the knob may be broken off the shaft, or if the knob has to be identified by touch alone in the dark or operated with gloved hands. Special designs exist for identification of control knobs by touch alone (Jenkins, 1947) where this is important, and in some circumstances it is desirable to indicate a control knob's function, either by naming it on or underneath the knob, or by some symbolic indication of what it does. Problems of symbolic representation were noted above and the need for standardisation pointed out. Even some accepted standard representations may, however, prove to be unnecessarily confusing, e.g. the widely used indication of the type '10^{-3}' on a piece of equipment, means less to most users than it does to the engineer who designed the machine. Other common errors include writing on the rim of the knob, which means that the information vanishes with rotation, and labelling the knob with material which wears off leaving a mute and anonymous knob for users to puzzle over.

Other forms of coding by colour, by size, or by shape, are usefully employed to identify knobs which perform similar functions, but one of the best methods, which is to locate together control knobs in the sequence in which they will be operated, is not as frequently used as it could be. The size of control knobs varies but it is widely recommended (e.g. Morgan *et al.*, 1963), that knobs to be operated by the fingertips only be not less than 6 mm or more than 100 mm in diameter, while those to be operated by the whole hand should have a diameter of somewhere between 40 mm and 80 mm.

5.4.3. Switches

Switches pose few problems for the user provided the general principles above are borne in mind, but their location and accessibility can mean unnecessary walking or awkward bending, which is undesirable. Where an effect can be controlled by more than one switch, it is desirable that this be indicated on the switch since the normal 'down for on' (or the reverse in some countries) ruling is invalidated. It is rare to find that this information has been provided, and no standard way of indicating that more than one switch controls the function is in current use.

Switches for special purposes like shutting down the power for a whole plant or building, require protected access. Some electricity authorities offset ease of access for meter reading against protection of the light and power switches for private homes and many other buildings which are open to potential interference, but in most commercial, industrial or public buildings the mains switch is one example of special function devices whose operation not only needs to be clearly indicated, but also to be controlled only by particular people. It is desirable to locate such switches close to responsible individuals if such switches need to be used frequently, or if the speed with which they are operated may be in some way critical.

5.4.4. *Locks and Catches*

For some curious reason locks and catches are not treated in most of the literature on ergonomics even though they are among the most commonly found mechanisms in buildings. They are grouped together here because they share the same function although they achieve it in different ways. The effectiveness of particular locking devices is not considered except to note that tongues which are rectangular, rather than curving to a sharp front edge, are generally somewhat less easy to open without a key. Thin, curved and flexible material, such as a part of the side of a round plastic carton, can often be inserted into the space above a tapering type of tongue and the lock opened by drawing the plastic against the tongue. Where safe locking is a matter of concern the combination of ill fitting doors and curved tongues is to be avoided.

The three most general comments that can be made on the ergonomics of locks are: first, that it is unfortunate that one cannot tell the state of most locks without trying them. This is such an everyday occurrence that it may seem trivial, but ergonomics is concerned with simple convenience such as being able to tell a door is locked at a distance, as well as more dramatic, dangerous and exciting situations. Where the keyhole rotates when the key is turned, as in some padlocks, this objection does not apply. Secondly, people expect the tongue of the lock to move in the same direction as the movement of the key. Often the reverse is true, and where both types of lock exist together it is not true that people learn and remember what to do for particular doors, and even if it were, it should not be necessary to do so; standardisation is much preferable to the confusion that mixing types creates. The third ergonomic comment concerns keys used to operate locks. These vary more or less with the size of the lock but centuries of design mean that, provided the materials used and specific design provide enough strength to withstand the force applied, the main everyday problem is identifying one key in the presence of many others.

The variety of catches is great and, for the most part, being simple devices they accord with the general principles noted at the start of the section. Two features of catches are worth bearing in mind, first that their size should be related to the force which needs to be applied to them, and second that when used, and in their open position, they should not damage the surface of the door, window or whatever they are on.

5.4.5. *Keyboards*

Most keyboard designs are modelled either on the typewriter or the electronic calculating machine, and both types are increasingly common for entering data, producing an output and controlling machine operations. In some cases, the rate at which the person can operate the keyboard is an important criterion of workability, as in the speed of the typist, but often accuracy is the most important factor. In general, keyboards are not particularly well designed and require the hands to be held in a position which is more fatiguing than some others. Having said that, and although keyboards have been designed which are better from an ergonomic viewpoint, the standardisation afforded by the QWERTY keyboard, which has been standard for all makes of typewriters for many years, militates strongly against accepting any alternative except for very specialised tasks, and Klemmer (1971) has stated that the standard keyboard is suitable for most purposes. As in the case of some alphanumeric designs, ergonomically better keyboards may run into problems of acceptability.

While some arrangements are better than others, it is not safe to advocate the simple rule that the most frequently used keys should always be in the nearest and most accessible positions. This is a good principle for situations where there is no precedent for the operator to follow, but wherever a habitual way of responding has been built up, speed is decreased and errors increased if it is opposed. This may

Table 5.4.1
*Pushbutton layout for calculators
and telephones*

Calculator			Pushbutton telephone		
9	8	7	1	2	3
6	5	4	4	5	6
3	2	1	7	8	9
	0			0	

occur by the person being forced to inhibit heavily overlearned response tendencies. A good example of this happening is seen in the study by Conrad and Hull (1968) in which they compared the different layouts for numerals used by most calculators and pushbutton telephones. Table 5.4.1 shows the two layouts. The telephone layout was shown to be very slightly faster, about 0·5 digits per minute, but gave rise to almost 2 % fewer mistakes. Performing at slower rates allows accuracy to be traded for speed, and it should not be concluded that the telephone format is necessarily superior in all situations. But an arrangement which is in accord with normal patterns of eye movement during reading, seems to be preferable when operating quickly. Testing whether the opposite result would be found for those who habitually read from bottom right to left could serve to confirm or disprove the reading eye-movement hypothesis.

Alternative keyboards, rather like piano keyboards, on which more than one key may be struck simultaneously, exist, and have been shown to allow faster operation (Conrad and Longman, 1965) than the QWERTY type. Ergonomically, the existence of the piano and the typewriter prove that both keyboards can be used and high levels of skill may be achieved with either. The problems which exist are those of how to present information to the chord keyboard operator, and how to train operators for either type most efficiently. Glencross (1977) has outlined a rational teaching method based upon learning the most frequently required movements and combinations first; this is currently being developed.

Since keyboards are used in a seated position, the issues of seating and keyboard height are important. The former is considered separately, and the latter is treated when problems with visual display units (VDUs) are dealt with below.

5.4.6. *Pushbuttons*

Pushbuttons are used to operate so many devices that they are often regarded as characteristic of our mechanised civilisation. It is, therefore, not surprising that recommendations exist to cover all aspects of their functioning for both hand and foot operation. Morgan *et al.* (1963), for example, note that hand pushbuttons are reasonably easily coded, are easy to operate in the midst of an array of controls and require little space. Murrell's (1971) recommendation that pushbuttons should be larger than the fingertip used to operate them, sets the size at 10 mm or more, except for emergency buttons for which a minimum diameter of 25 mm is given. Many writers (e.g. McCormick, 1976) follow Chapanis (1972) in suggesting a concave surface and a minimum movement of 3 mm (Murrell prefers 6 mm), a minimum resistance of 3 N (corresponding to a mass of 300 g) and a maximum of 115 N (corresponding to a mass of 11·5 kg); however, Murrell suggests a minimum of 2 N and a maximum of 8·5 N. The displacement minimum is suggested at 30 mm (Chapanis) or 60 mm (Murrell), but the maximum displacement of 400 mm given in McCormick (1976, p. 478) is probably a misprint for 40 mm (Murrell, 25 mm). There is agreement generally that either a click, or sudden change in resistance, is important to indicate when the button has been operated. Murrell makes the additional point that to reduce the risk of being pressed accidentally, pushbuttons can be recessed or surrounded by a protective rim. The recess or rim should permit operation by the largest fingertips. If one takes this further to include gloved hands in cold climates or protective clothing, then pushbuttons larger than the recommended minimum of 15 mm are required.

People living in colder climates will be accustomed to seeing gloves being removed to press doorbells during the winter.

Foot operated pushbuttons are usually only indicated for use when the hands are occupied and when a very definite on–off switch is needed, the effect of which is continuously monitored by the operator. In most other settings pedal controls are to be preferred. Where foot operated pushbuttons are used, they should be operated by the ball of the foot or toes, not by the heel which is fatiguing. Murrell suggests a minimum diameter of 15–20 mm to avoid too much pressure on the foot, and this is important if operators are barefoot or wear footwear like flexible rubber soled thongs because of hot conditions. Maximum movement is constrained by the range of ankle movement to be around 50 mm, and feedback, either in the form of an audible click or sudden change in pressure, should be used to indicate the button has been operated. A comfortable required force is 20 N (corresponding to a mass of 2 kg), unless the foot rests on the button continuously when 50 N (corresponding to a mass of 5 kg) is widely recommended. This is the same as the minimum resistance given for continuously operated pedals.

While less common outside industrial premises, it seems worthwhile to include levers, pedals, etc., in this section since a great deal of information has been amassed on these controls.

5.4.7. Levers

Like many other aspects of ergonomics the main point about levers is obvious when thought about, but, in practice, what is suitable in one context is sometimes transferred to other settings where it is unacceptable. The point is that the muscles used to operate levers depend upon factors such as distance from the lever, and whether the operator is standing or seated, and the direction of the movement. Murrell (1971), notes that for seated operators, maximum horizontal force of about 525 N can be exerted if a vertical lever is located about 750–900 mm forward of the back of the seat, and the handle is about 300 mm above the height of the seat. This rapidly drops to around 200 N if the lever is brought closer to the chair and located some 550 mm in front of the back of the seat.

For horizontal levers to be pulled vertically, maximum force, assuming the lever is at hand height for a standing individual, is 475 N but is only 270 N if the lever is 250 mm above the normal position of the hand. Similarly, using a lever horizontally across the front of the body, the further the lever is away from the operator, the less is the force which can be applied. As a rough guide, levers to be used in this manner should not be more than 450 mm from the front of the body.

A practical exercise in working out which muscles are involved when operating levers in various ways, is the best way of demonstrating the muscles used and the maximum forces for the group under test. The maximum values above are to be avoided if a lever is to be used by a large number of people since variations in strength, height, arm length and so on will ensure that some individuals are incapable of achieving the required force.

Other features of levers which concern the ergonomist include the handgrip design, and the range of movement of the lever. On the handgrip, diameters of 25 mm to 75 mm are usually acceptable. Shaping the handle to fit the hand is often less important than providing a textured surface that allows the handle to be gripped firmly. Estimates of how far the lever should move vary; Morgan *et al.* (1963) cite 350 mm as the maximum fore and aft movement, though, for convenient use 150 mm as cited by other writers (e.g. Murrell, 1971), is a more appropriate recommendation. Similarly, the 970 mm maximum sideways movement given by the former, should be treated as the *maximum* it was intended to be. In general, 45° is a comfortable pulling distance for levers moving parallel to the front of the body for a very wide range of lever lengths, but this increases to 90° or even more from the vertical for pushing movements. This principle, that from a vertical position, pushing actions can be sustained over much longer distances than can pulling movements, particularly where, as in seated operations, the individual's other movements are constrained, applies to fore and aft movements also, and is one of the more general principles to be borne in mind in designing levers.

5.4.8. Pedals

Pedals are such widely used control devices that they have been heavily researched. They can be categorised by their function for on–off use or continuous adjustment, or according to the force required to operate them. Size, angle and separation between different pedals, are other important features for ease of operation. The human leg can be regarded as a series of levers consisting of the foot hinged at the anklejoint, the lower leg hinged at the knee, and the thigh which articulates with the pelvis at the hip-joint. These levers can bring greater or lesser forces to bear on pedals depending on the muscle groups involved. For maximum strength it is necessary to provide a fairly rigid backrest, to angle the pedal so that the foot is not doing all the work, and to allow the leg to be almost straightened. Murrell (1971) suggests a knee angle of 160°. However, most pedal operations are not designed for maximum strength performance and knee angles are more usually between 90–130°. At 90°, backrests are much less effective, and less force can be expected. The resistance for leg-operated pedals needs to be greater than the weight of the leg resting on it, and Orlansky (1948) made an early recommendation of a 45 N minimum, and an operating range between 35–270 N. However, it is undesirable to require an operator to have to hold his leg in the air because the pedal cannot bear the weight of the leg, and Murrell's suggestion that the return pressure of leg-operated pedals should be 80–89 N allows a reasonable margin of safety for a standing operator.

For the more common foot-operated pedal, the length of the foot determines the angle of the foot when operating a pedal. Ideally, the angle of the foot should be close to 90° when resting on the pedal, and the pedal should not travel through more than about 30°, otherwise one may come close to the limit of foot flexion in a downward direction. For the same reasons pedal height is optimal around 50–75 mm and a resistance of 10–15 N is required to support the weight of the foot, and Dupuis (1958), cited by Morgan *et al.* (1963) suggests 45 N as the maximum permissible resistance.

Pedal size is more important than shape and, normally, pedals should approximate the width of an operator's footwear. In some circumstances, however, to allow adequate spacing between pedals, it may be better to trade some pedal width for space between pedals. What is adequate spacing is affected by the nature of the footwear of the users, as well as other constraints such as the need to move the foot rapidly from one pedal to another as in braking in a car. In such cases, some movements to reposition the foot are faster than others, and it has been shown that moving the foot sideways is faster than moving the foot to a higher pedal alongside (Davies and Watts, 1970), which is how one normally brakes a motor vehicle. The resistance of emergency pedals is a compromise between speed of operation, risk of accidental operation, and the effect of too rapid operation—as in skidding in motor cycles, as well as the factors discussed above.

5.4.9. Handwheels

Handwheels are used for many different types of machinery, and are most effective when the rate of turn required is not very rapid, and when the amount of adjustment produced is relatively small. Where rapid rates of turn are indicated, or large adjustments, e.g. of the position of a cutting or marking head, are required, a handle or crank on the handwheel will allow much faster operation. Other ergonomic properties of handwheels which need to be considered are size, the ratio of adjustment produced to the amount of turn, location, which is affected by whether the handwheel is to be used continuously or only infrequently for resetting, and by whether the operator is seated or standing.

Considerations of size depend upon how important it is to make readjustments quickly, and on the effect handwheel size has on the ratio of adjustment to the distance moved. We probably could drive cars with steering wheels of 100 mm in diameter, but the accuracy of our steering would depend on the ability to make small very fine movements. Moreover, it is easy to 'lose the place' if the handwheel is turned through more than one complete turn. Too large handwheels, on the other hand, require unnecessarily large movements which take more time. The location of handwheels depends on how they are to be operated, whether by one hand or two, seated or standing. Where only partial turns are required, a seated operator requires a horizontal wheel to be lower and closer than a tilted or vertical handwheel. This may appear to conflict with Murrell's suggestion that vertical wheels should be 300–350 mm in diameter, with the wheel centre 500 mm above the top of the seat, and the wheel 350 mm from the back of the seat, while horizontal wheels should be 225–300 mm above the seat, and centred around a point 550–700 mm from the seatback. However, the only point of real disagreement is that 350 mm from the seatback is too close for vertical wheels. Depending upon arm length, the elbows are more or less tightly bent and arm movement is very restricted. It can be important to rest the arms to avoid fatigue, but with proper arm rests even as much as 550–700 mm in front of the seatback is a comfortable distance for most people, and allows much less constrained arm movements. In general, to obtain greater movement, handwheels are tilted when intended for continuous use. Various other recommendations are made concerning the thickness, 20–50 mm, moulding or texturing the surface to allow a firm grip, and, in general, using handwheels of greater diameter as torque increases, and only in exceptional circumstances positioning vertical handwheels parallel to the frontal plane of the operator but at his side. Even this unusual location may be admissible if great force is required to move the wheel, or as in a small boat's skipper operating the ship's wheel while leaning out of the wheelhouse, particular information is needed which can only be obtained in this way.

5.4.10. *Control–Display Relationships*

The final principle offered at the start of this section was that the relationship between control and display needs to be studied in addition to studying the design of the control and the display separately. The importance of this cannot be overstressed because people build up expectations of what effects will be created by particular responses. These expectations *govern*, indeed *are* the ways that we interpret information and understand what responses we should make. So much so, that it is easy to produce a perceptual illusion or confusion by contradicting strong expectations. A rapidly inflating balloon moving away from the perceiver can be made to look stationary if the size of the image on the retina remains constant. Psychological laboratories throughout the world contain demonstrations, such as the Ames' demonstrations, of illusions which are compelling in the way they make us see what we know cannot be correct. Less entertaining but just as interesting are the effects upon performance of the human operator's expectations and interpretations with various control–display relationships. While it is not possible to consider in turn all possible relationships between all controls and displays likely to be used together, one example from the writer's research with his colleagues in Adelaide may serve to illustrate one of the most general ergonomic principles of control–display relations. This superordinate principle is that all principles (or expectations) should operate in concordance with one another, and facilitate the same response.

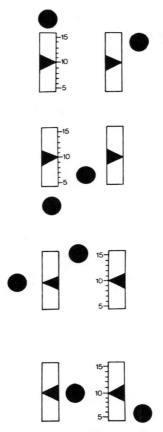

Fig. 5.4.1. Examples of control–display relationships for rotary controls and linear displays.

As in many situations, what is an important statement can seem self-evident, and, where many different factors interplay, it is often easier to ignore this complexity' in favour of a simple-minded interpretation. How wrong this can be is seen where rotary controls are used in conjunction with linear displays (see Fig. 5.4.1). At least four principles operate in settings like this where round knobs control indicators on straight displays. Where any principle is widely accepted throughout a community it is sometimes referred to as 'population stereotype'. There are obvious advantages for safety and ease of operation in designing control–display relationships which fit with population stereotypes. However, where more than one principle operates within the same situation, the possibility exists that different principles may tend to result in different responses, thereby opposing one another and destroying any population stereotype of what effects will be produced by different responses.

In the rotary knob and linear display set up, we can describe four principles which govern people's expectations of what they have to do to make the pointer move one way or the other. For simplicity's sake we shall limit the discussion to the various arrangements shown in Fig. 5.4.1. The four principles are given below.

'Clockwise for anything'

So much equipment throughout the world is turned on by a clockwise movement that there is a very widespread tendency for people to try turning a round knob in a clockwise direction whenever there is any ambiguity in the situation. This learned tendency is reinforced by the fact that, if the right hand is used, a much longer movement can be sustained in a clockwise direction than in an anticlockwise direction. By adopting unusual starting points for the movement, as in turning the wrist as far as it will go before grasping the knob, the difference in the amount of movement possible in either direction can be overcome, but people do not typically do this unless they know from experience that a particularly long turning movement will be needed. This built-in advantage would seem to be the reason why Verhaegen *et al.* (1975) were able to confirm the 'clockwise for anything' principle in a cross-cultural study of stereotyped expectations. The clockwise move depends on the assumption that the right hand is used, but the fact that left handed people, using the left hand, show a natural tendency to make anticlockwise movements (Bradley, 1959), supports the view that the longer movement is the more natural choice.

'Clockwise for increase'

There is evidence that when asked to produce an increase in intensity, or a higher indicated value on a scale, the majority of people also make clockwise movements (Bradley, 1959). This is not unrelated to the point above, and is again partly due to experience with so much equipment where a clockwise movement turns the unit on, and a continuation of the movement increases volume or gain. There are, however, some interesting exceptions which are firmly learned and equally widespread. Wherever the person confronts a situation in which he or she believes (even without being conscious of the inference they have brought with them to it), that turning the knob will release a force, then the natural tendency is for an anticlockwise movement. The commonest example of this is turning a tap to release water. Here, clockwise movements restrain the flow, anticlockwise movements release the force. Other examples exist in everyday situations and some ambiguous cases can also be seen in some gas appliances, but, generally, gas appliances should be turned on anticlockwise and electric ones clockwise.

Warrick's Principle

Based on research he carried out in a military context soon after the end of World War II, Warrick (1947) derived one of the longest lasting principles for control–display relations. As it applies to the variations shown in Fig. 5.4.1, Warrick's Principle can be most simply stated as 'the indicator/pointer will be expected to move in the same direction as that portion of the control knob which is closest to it'. Note that this principle cannot apply where the control knob is located at the top or bottom end of the display. This is unfortunate since, quite apart from the fact that Warrick's Principle is a strong one where it does apply, there are often good practical reasons for providing banks of vertical displays with their associated controls directly under them. Placing the control above the display is to be avoided outside experimental laboratories, since the display is obscured by the arm when operating the control. Similar considerations apply when horizontal rather than vertical displays are employed.

'Scale-side/pointer-side principle'

With the preceding consideration in mind, the writer has attempted to create a 'dominant' side of the rotary control so that, even in the top and bottom positions, the operator would tend to expect the indicator/pointer to move in the same direction as either the left or right half of the control knob. (For horizontal displays it would be the top or bottom half of the knob, but this has not yet been tested.) The method of doing this was simple. Some expectations are learned, others are more 'natural' in the sense that they are reinforced by easier response tendencies, or by a very powerful influence in our perception of an interaction with the physical environment—the inherent tendency to code and store information economically. The Gestalt theory school of psychology in the 1920s produced many examples of this, both in perceptual and in motor performance

	(a)		(b)
	O O O O O O O O O O		O X O X O X O X O X
	X X X X X X X X X X		O X O X O X O X O X
	O O O O O O O O O O		O X O X O X O X O X
	X X X X X X X X X X		O X O X O X O X O X
	O O O O O O O O O O		O X O X O X O X O X
	X X X X X X X X X X		O X O X O X O X O X
	O O O O O O O O O O		O X O X O X O X O X
	X X X X X X X X X X		O X O X O X O X O X
	O O O O O O O O O O		O X O X O X O X O X
	X X X X X X X X X X		O X O X O X O X O X

Fig. 5.4.2. The Gestalt principle of grouping by similarity.

(Koffka, 1935; Buytendijk, 1931). Amongst the best known is the principle of similarity, which states that similar items will be perceived as a unity or group, so that in Fig. 5.4.2(a), we see rows rather than columns; in Fig. 5.4.2(b), we see columns rather than rows. Utilising this principle, we can invoke a spatial or 'side' similarity, using the location of the scale markings on left or right of the display, or the direction indicated by a pointer, to impose a 'dominant' left or right side of the control knob. We should note that we cannot talk about focusing the operator's attention on one side of the knob rather than the other, because the operator is rarely aware of the process, but rather approaches the task with 'unconscious inferences' just as the great 19th century German psychologist Helmholtz described. This 'scale/pointer-side' principle predicts that the indicator/pointer is expected to move in the same direction as that portion of the control knob which is on the same side as the scale or pointer direction. That is, in Fig. 5.4.3(a), the pointer should move up or down as the right side of the knob does so, but in Fig. 5.4.3(b), the indicator would be expected to move in the same way as the left side of the control knob.

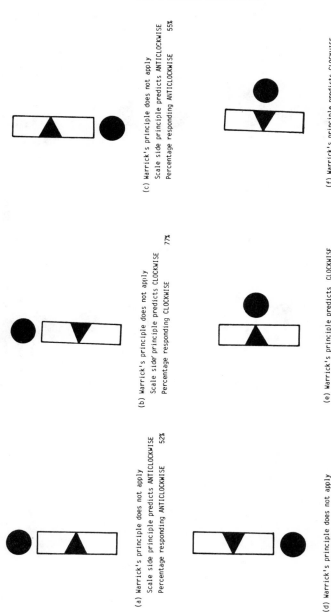

(a) Warrick's principle does not apply
Scale side principle predicts ANTICLOCKWISE
Percentage responding ANTICLOCKWISE   52%

(b) Warrick's principle does not apply
Scale side principle predicts CLOCKWISE
Percentage responding CLOCKWISE   77%

(c) Warrick's principle does not apply
Scale side principle predicts ANTICLOCKWISE
Percentage responding ANTICLOCKWISE   55%

(d) Warrick's principle does not apply
Scale side principle predicts CLOCKWISE
Percentage responding CLOCKWISE   72%

(e) Warrick's principle predicts CLOCKWISE
Scale side principle predicts ANTICLOCKWISE
Percentage responding CLOCKWISE   57%

(f) Warrick's principle predicts CLOCKWISE
Scale side principle predicts CLOCKWISE
Percentage responding CLOCKWISE   85%

Fig. 5.4.3. Some results obtained when the principles are in conflict with one another, or are in concordance.

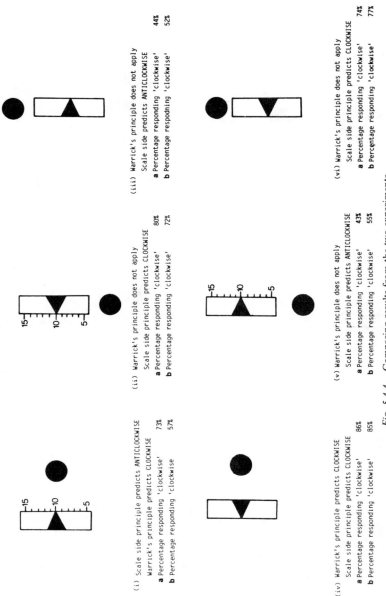

Fig. 5.4.4. Comparing results from the two experiments.

Given these four principles all operating in what may have seemed a very simple control–display setting, all sorts of different behaviour can be produced. In two studies, which between them tested several hundred subjects, the first using a paper and pencil test and visitors to our laboratory during an 'Open Day' (Brebner and Sandow, 1976), the second employing a computerised on-line test with a real rotary control to be turned clockwise or anticlockwise (Petropoulos and Brebner, 1980), results for some of the possible arrangements were ascertained. In the data presented here, subjects were always instructed to increase the setting or move to the scale marking of '15'. Figure 5.4.4, (a) results, gives the results of the Brebner and Sandow (1976) study. Figure 5.4.4, (b) results, shows the closely similar data obtained in subsequent work by Petropoulos and Brebner. What is most noticeable is that, in both studies, whether subjects turn the control clockwise or anticlockwise, varies from close to chance levels with the worst arrangements, up to high levels of agreement with the best. Whether an arrangement is good or bad depends on whether the principles above all tend to evoke the same clockwise or anti-clockwise response, or whether they conflict with one another and successfully inhibit any particular response tendency from over-coming others.

Figure 5.4.4 gives the varying proportions responding in the expected ways.

These results indicate very clearly that it is how the several principles combine that determines the workability of the various arrangements. Some shown here would give rise to continued error-making; in others, relatively simple adjustments produce a high level of concordance in the samples of people tested. The twin dangers of oversimplifying control–display relations, or relying on any one principle alone to produce the desired result, are demonstrated by these two laboratory studies.

5.5. SEATING

This section outlines different seating functions and comments on appropriate designs. The most common forms of seating are of the types found in lounge and kitchen/dining room suites, in motor cars, and in indoor and outdoor entertainment or recreational settings. Most other types, such as a typist's chair, can be treated as a modification of one of these, although there are other specific seat designs such as bicycle saddles, which provide exceptions.

Few people consider that sitting is behaving actively although sitting still for more than very brief periods requires training. Nevertheless, sitting is an activity we all engage in for greater or lesser periods, and it is possible to sit in ways which do not stress the body or to have such poor seating or sitting habits that serious and irreversible damage is done to the spine or to the blood circulation. Ergonomically, a few very important features are required of any chair, regardless of its type, to allow the opportunity to sit correctly. Before treating these, it is worth noting that sitting is far more than posture. Like eating, sitting is a social activity for most people and, just as eating habits often alter when a person who is usually a member of a social group of family or friends, finds him/herself temporarily alone in a different environment, people sit in different ways in different social situations. Body language or expressive gesture continues when seated for the human being and is even shared to some extent with other species who also sit. Thus, cocking the ear when standing may tend to imply hunting or checking on some puzzling or possibly threatening stimulus. When seated, cocking the head tends to lose the first connotation and becomes associated with widening of the eyes into the sort of 'Oh, really!' response to new information. To my knowledge no behavioural scientist has compared expressive gesture when standing, and when seated, to show how the meanings of gestures alter. But, how one sits communicates information, and asking visitors to be seated, or not, is a social as well as a physical act.

Returning to more traditional ergonomic features of seating, we can list nine features of sitting which are as generally accepted as anything ever is by ergonomists throughout the chair-using world. All but one of the main points are included in the unusually informative British Standard 3044 '*Ergonomic aspects of furniture design*', prepared by Floyd and Roberts (1958).

(1) *Changing posture delays fatigue*. This is a point made by most writers on seating. Any posture requires particular muscle groups, and unless you allow posture to be changed from time to time, it

rapidly becomes tiring to rely on the same muscles all the time. Therefore, seats which require the sitter to maintain one sitting position must be avoided except, say, in the case of disabled people with physical deformities, where there is no alternative. In such cases, often little voluntary control of posture is possible, and tailor-made seats for deformed spines have been proved to be useful (Seeger and Stern, 1980).

(2) *Two parts of the body have adapted to withstand pressure for reasonably long periods:* the feet and the part of the buttock under the ischial tuberosity when seated. The former is obvious, and provided that the policeman's traditional rocking off the heels is used to allow good circulation of the blood, one can stand relatively still for quite long periods. The latter will become obvious if the fingers are inserted underneath the buttock when seated, to feel the bony protuberance, or ischial tuberosity which supports the weight of the trunk. On standing up, the muscle and other tissue of the buttock moves in to cover the bony part; on sitting down the tissue moves to the side and is not compressed by the seated weight of the person. In addition, the epidermis is thickened in this area in the same way, though to a lesser degree than on the sole of the foot. Finally, there are no main blood vessels which are seriously compressed in a correctly seated position, and the blood supply to the skin under the ischial tuberosities is capable of longer periods of pressure than is true in other parts of the body.

(3) Thirdly, it is usual to find that some weight is borne by the thighs when seated. *If too much weight is taken by the thighs, the tissue surrounding the femur has to be greatly compressed before the femur takes the load.* At worst this is tantamount to putting a tourniquet on the underside of the thigh, and can not only prevent blood circulation or cause damage to blood vessels, but may also affect muscles and nerve fibres. Two common faults with chairs which produce these problems are the front of the seat being too high and, as is most obvious when the supporting material of the seat has lost its strength, the weight being taken on the narrow bar of wood or metal which forms the front of the seat. In sitting positions where weight can be taken on the feet and forearms as well as the ischial tuberosities, the seat may slope slightly forward. This is a special case, however, which is unlikely to be widely acceptable or generally appropriate, and it is

usual for a chair seat to slope down to the back slightly to help counteract slipping forward off the seat.

(4) Fourthly, *the appropriate height for the top of the front edge of the seat is not less than the popliteal height—the knee to heel measurement of the individual.* Consideration may be given to the effect of footwear on popliteal height, as well as the rigidity of the seat, or the provision of footrests or footstools to raise the thighs. The alternative of lowering the height of the seat under the thighs is found in the sort of seat with a slight pommel. Such seats seem to be found in agricultural machinery like tractors, or some heavy machinery and, while they can be acceptable if the space for the thighs is wide enough and the pommeling is only slight, and especially if the weight can be taken on the feet, this design seems to owe more to its hint of still being a saddle, than to comfort, or the need to be mobile while in the seat.

(5) *Any seat needs to be sufficiently wide to allow for movement while seated,* and various seats, from plastic mouldings to bean bags, if they attempt to define very closely the shape of the bottom, are liable to compress the tissue of the buttocks and thighs which becomes uncomfortable in quite a short time. Insufficiently wide seats create the same problems at the sides of the seat as occur with seats with too high front edges. Movement is also necessary to prevent overheating if sitting for prolonged periods. This point is not usually discussed by writers on seating, but any medical practitioner working in a warm climate will confirm that, for the millions of women in the seated workforces of the world, the combination of plastic upholstery, bifurcated nether garments made of nylon, and prolonged sitting, is excellent for the production, or continuation, of urino–genitary infections.

(6) The sixth point is that *seats should be easy to sit down in and stand up from.* Too low chairs can cause the person to fall back into them as the centre of gravity shifts backward. Rising from a chair normally occurs in one of two ways. Where there is space under the front of the chair, the heels are first drawn back under the thighs, then the trunk is leaned forwards, moving the centre of gravity over the feet until the thigh and leg muscles can be used to straighten the legs and stand upright. To allow this action, BS 3044: 1958, suggests that space under the seat is necessary. Some chairs, particularly armchairs, have a straight front edge reaching to the floor, necessitating the side

to side wriggle forward to the edge of the seat to gain the correct relation of trunk to feet. But it is also usual to use leverage by the arms as the second way of standing up or sitting down. By practising standing up from a seated position with the feet forward or under the chair, and from varying heights, the amount of weight to be lifted by the arms can be found, and it can be ascertained whether an individual or group has the requisite strength to use chairs of particular design. It is not uncommon to see elderly or heavy people struggling in or out of chairs, and cost and appearance really should not outweigh the ergonomic aspects of seating for most people, although they tend to do so because many people are unaware of design features which would help them choose more usable types of chair.

(7) The *backrest of the chair is just as important as the seat itself* unless the weight is taken on feet and possibly forearms and elbows, as in sitting at a desk writing. The four most important features of the backrest are: (i) that it should permit movement while seated for the sorts of reasons mentioned above: (ii) to avoid stressing the spine, the backrest should be shaped to maintain a slightly concave lumbar region for the sitter. Sitting with the lower portion of the back in a rounded position is a commonplace bad sitting habit; (iii) the height of the backrest varies with the chair's function but, if the backrest is too low, the effect is to push the individual forward, and if it is too high, it can produce pressure on the bones of the shoulder blade which are close to the surface of the skin. Generally, slightly curved backrests meet the requirement of support without pressure; (iv) the provision for resting the head is important for many types of chair, and the angle of the headrest should take the weight on the back of the head and maintain the chin in a slightly raised position. Garden chairs typically do not have headrests, although a few designs which have the seat low off the ground have backrests high enough to permit one item to serve as a chair or as a lounger.

(8) Probably the largest category of chair of all, is that intended to be used in conjunction with some table top. The height of the work surface may depend upon what the person is to do, but in general terms, *table tops which are too far below or above the elbow height are less comfortable than those at elbow height.* Note that the common 750 mm desk and 450 mm chair are regarded as too high (Murrell, 1971; Bennett, 1977; BS 3044: 1958) for most people. As a general

guide, 710–740 mm is a preferable desk height, but it depends on the height of the chair and the worst arrangements are to have low chairs with high desks or *vice versa*. Recommendations about the height of the underside of the table or desk above the thigh, are made in many texts on ergonomics, with little apparent impact on designers, and whether it is possible to cross one's legs while sitting at a desk, still depends on whether there is a central desk drawer effectively lowering the height of the underside. If the leg space at a desk is less than a 650 mm cube, some constraints on leg movements will be experienced by most people, and in many cases larger spaces will be required for comfort. The common practice of using desk size to indicate status, is ergonomically less sound than marrying the dimensions of the desk to the size of the user. Distances between people sitting alongside one another, can also be important when more than one person is seated at a table. For very many functions a minimum distance of 300 mm between chairs will be acceptable.

(9) A feature of some chair designs is that, in the interests of economy, some or all of the points above are often satisfied if the sitter uses the chair in a particular way. Plastic mouldings which are cheap to purchase may, for instance, be intended to be sat in with the bottom pushed far back into the seat and the sitter leaning forward, as found in some lecture theatres. Unfortunately, people rarely follow very precise dictates of design even if they fully understand them, and it is a general principle of good seating that *the requirements above should still be met when the person sits in a variety of postures*. Having said that, one must sympathise with designers, in that people are extremely creative when it comes to adopting bad sitting postures in perfectly well designed chairs.

This brief discussion of seating in no way exhausts the subject but only introduces the major requirements of seating. If sitting now seems a more important, even somewhat hazardous activity if undertaken wrongly, enough will have been achieved.

5.6.   DESIGNING FOR SPECIFIC FUNCTIONS

When this consideration of ergonomics in and around buildings was in its early stages, it seemed important to include a section which dealt with some fairly specific situations to show how some of the principles and guidelines of ergonomics could be applied. The area which offered itself most naturally for this purpose was some aspects of office computerisation. There now exists a huge array of office equipment unknown before recent technological advances in silicon chip and computer technology and photo reproductive processes. What has most obviously remained the same in offices is the use, while seated, of the standard QWERTY keyboard by mainly female staff, while the most obvious changes are the widespread use of cathode ray tubes to display information, and the increased speed of access and retrieval of data. This process will not stop at the office and, in the not too distant future, it will be possible to use the television set in the home to communicate directly with data bases and organisations outside the home. For these reasons it seems worthwhile to apply some of what has been stated elsewhere in the text, as well as additional information, to the use of cathode ray tubes as visual display units (VDUs). Almost fifteen years ago Singleton (1966) advocated research into human problems of computer design, much of which has crystallised into problems with VDUs.

The health and safety aspects of regularly using VDUs for prolonged periods, has been a matter of concern by management and trade union groups alike in recent years, and a number of conferences with titles like 'Are computers a health hazard?' have been held in countries around the world. In some cases comprehensive prospective studies have monitored the health of those using VDUs not as alphanumeric devices, but, e.g. Rose *et al.* (1978), as radar screens used by air traffic controllers. The importance of good design for air traffic controllers is acknowledged, but there are more and more tasks which involve the use of VDUs, making them a matter of general concern. A comprehensive account of health factors is given in '*Visual display terminals*' by Cakir *et al.* (1980), including the various types of radiation emitted by VDUs most of which are typically more threatening psychologically than physically harmful. Handbooks in languages other than English also exist, e.g. Östberg's (1976) '*Designing CRT workplaces: A handbook*', which is in Swedish.

Most considerations of VDUs look at four aspects of the total situation separately, namely, the task, the workstation, the larger workplace containing the workstation, and the operators themselves. Here, a slightly different approach is taken, making use of the general model for human information processing and performance.

The basic tasks for most operators are:

(1) data entry by keyboard which need not involve looking at the visual display except for checking purposes, but often requires the operator to work from some document which shows the data to be entered; and

(2) using the keyboard to access and interact with information already stored within the computer system. This requires attention to the visual display even if documents are also used during the interaction, so that some of the problems with the visual display may be most severe in this sort of task. Also, because such interactions do not resemble typing as much as simple data entry, the need for typing skills is not so great.

Recalling the model for human information processing from Chapter 3, gives us a framework within which to locate the sources of difficulties and the nature of their effects on performance. It should again be emphasised that the different functions are unified into coherent patterns of skilled activity so that the model acts as a whole. But we can try to locate where difficulties occur within the system.

Starting with the receptor surface, the most frequent problem areas are in the ambient conditions of the working environment, particularly in illumination levels, and in some features of the visual task being performed. The issue of seating could be raised also but has been treated separately.

The physical working environment may affect performance as we have seen earlier. Temperature and humidity may be slightly more important since VDUs themselves generate heat and unlike, say, photocopiers or word processors, many VDUs may be in operation in one room.

Noise may be distracting where it is unexpected, or just irritating by being continuous. Aerodynamic noise produced by the cooling fan within a VDU or air conditioners is difficult to eliminate, but can usually be contained to acceptable levels. Loud noises from equipment which may be part of the total system, e.g. high speed line printers, is totally unacceptable and such equipment needs to be housed elsewhere. The main problem, however, is the visual environment. This is because the operator has conflicting demands for a dim background light to make the VDU display provide relatively stronger signals, and for higher illumination levels to read documents and to work at the keyboard. Recommendations vary from 100 lux through the 300–500 lux suggested in Cakir *et al.* (1980), up to 1000 lux. The higher readings usually place more emphasis on documents and keyboard, and may assume that some sort of hood is present on the VDU to shut out light from windows or luminaires. Hoods can provide a solution if they are properly designed but, unless the VDUs are properly sited in relation to windows and other sources of light, the operator will be working against veiling reflections on the screen and specular reflections from the keyboard. It is not enough to make the VDU face inwards leaving the operators facing bright windows since other problems result from this. Glare from the window may affect performance and the operators may take time to adjust to the dimmer screen.

Transparent mesh material placed in front of the screen has sometimes been used to reduce reflection. This approach may have some success where conditions are particularly bad, but it is important that the graininess of the material or its pattern should not produce a different type of problem for viewing.

The information displayed on the screen suffers from several possible defects which affect sensory performance as distinct from perceptual organisation. To begin with the size of alphanumeric characters needs to be large enough to distinguish individual letters easily; Cakir *et al.* (1980) suggest the optimum size of letters would occupy about 20 minutes of arc and would have a width about three-quarters of the height. This accords reasonably well with the suggestion earlier of a two-thirds ratio (US Military Standard AND 10400, 1957); and the Peters and Adams (1959) formula, referred to earlier, could be applied to VDU displays.

Discriminability is affected by the brightness and stability of characters as well as their size, and VDUs can be very inferior to printed material in these respects. The problem starts with the fact that VDU letters are composed of a set of illuminated dots which limits the amount of curve that can be used for any given size of letter. Poor discriminability can lead to an effort to compensate for this with increased brightness which can itself prove fatiguing. Worse, the dots are not uniformly illuminated and may appear to jump about on the screen. The rate at which the brightness of the dots is refreshed will, if it is too slow, produce a horizontal moving line which goes from top to bottom of the display at regular intervals. This is due to the difference in brightness of the dots most recently refreshed and those about to be, and it can interfere with discriminability. Working under these conditions for prolonged periods can be very much more fatiguing and place greater demands on the operator's visual system than occurs in dealing with printed matter for comparable times. VDU operators do suffer from eyestrain more frequently and complain of headaches more often. The changes in vision which occur with ageing such as loss of acuity led Kryzhanovskaya and Navakatikayan (1970) to make the suggestion that people over 50–55 years of age should not be employed as VDU operators. This suggestion would not be acceptable in all countries, but there are fewer older VDU operators than there are typists, and a high proportion of VDU operators wear spectacles; Devos-Petiprez (1973) found 66 % in a survey he performed.

Turning to perceptual organisation, although psychologists always have trouble in laying down any absolute line between sensation and perception, we can draw our line at the level of meaning. Perceptual organisation of the visual stimuli into a meaningful pattern by the operator is part of practically all VDU uses, and again VDUs are often more difficult to read than printed information. Some minor difficulties may exist, e.g. distortions of letters at the edges of screens, or with spacing between lines of alphanumeric characters, but these are typically simple to deal with by not writing close to edges or corners, and by having control of line spacing as on a normal typewriter. However, the biggest difficulty for perceptual organisation concerns the moving nature of the display. For data entry where the operator controls the rate of change of the display, just as in typing, there is no serious problem. But when interacting with a computer's memory banks, the computer writes information from left to right, adds new lines at the bottom of the display, and does so at its own timing. The result is that some operators find themselves not only reading lines as they are written which accords with most Western reading habits, but faced with a display which continually jumps upward as new lines are added at the bottom of the display. This jerky running up of the display is completely counter to our habitual reading practice and, since to all intents and purposes we cannot read while our eyes are moving at any speed, or the material itself is, the operator may be faced with the need for continued refixation on the same lines. Where this happens, the task is fatiguing and creates visual strain as well as reducing the operator's performance level. Although one can see the logic of adding new lines at the bottom, some types of interactions with a computer would be greatly facilitated if material was displayed in units of 'pages' instead of letters on lines. However, it would probably be critically necessary for the operator to control when a new 'page' appeared or not, to avoid the initiation of unexpected flashes in front of unprepared eyes. In practice, another solution has been sought by some manufacturers whose displays can be controlled to roll upward slowly enough to be read and move smoothly without apparent jerkiness. The reader can reproduce the effect described by having someone else draw this text away in a series of steps while he is trying to read it, and compare this with a slow, smooth movement of the text.

Short-term memory difficulties may derive from two main sources, overload and distraction. Overload will occur if too many items or rules have to be stored at the same time. Situations with the complexity similar to 'On this page cross out every second "a", every third "b", every fifth "c" unless it is preceded by a vowel, and every eighth "e",' are to be avoided. Most codes and instructions are not so complicated as to be unworkable, even though many of the interactions with computers require them. Overload is more common when the operator is working from source material and dealing with such a long sequence of items that it is sometimes necessary to check back on earlier entries in order to decide what next instruction is appropriate. But, given the STM function's vulnerability to new information overwriting what was being held in store, distraction and interruptions may be the most common cause of information dropping out of STM among VDU operators.

Consideration of the long-term memory implies that, wherever possible, what has already been stored should be used rather than requiring new relationships to be learned, and that what is already stored should not be contradicted. Standardisation, as in the use of the QWERTY keyboard or common words and terms instead of code names and letters which require translation, can improve operators' efficiency although if in continual use code names gain the familiarity of ordinary words. Problems arising from the LTM are not frequently mentioned by VDU operators but, if members of the general public are required to use a keyboard to interact with a computer, a host of problems are immediately evident. These range from uncertainty about how to use the keyboard, or where particular letters or symbols are, through typing errors and not understanding the meaning of information displayed, to being unable to find information the person is requested to enter whether from a source document or from memory.

Computer systems are more efficient when experienced operators classify and code information and perform the functions necessary for a required outcome. In the future it seems likely that more people will become accustomed to keyboard interaction with computers and that standard ways of achieving successful outcomes will be developed. If so, many more people will have stored relevant facts and relationships in their LTM and the current difference between keyboard operators and laymen in such tasks will be reduced.

The central process of motor co-ordination involves the selection and integration into a unified, skilled activity of sets of component programs which are capable of being run separately. Obviously some integrations are more effective than others, but much of being highly skilled seems to depend on requiring smaller samples of data in order to organise an appropriate response. There is considerable evidence that people have a high capacity to deal with multiple, successive inputs at the level of perceptual organisation. However, ever since Vince (1948), evidence has been amassing from psychological research that once the central organisation of a response has started it is protected from being interrupted by subsequent stimuli which would evoke competing responses. The significance of this is obvious, if different responses require the same central programs or processes, they would interfere with one another, producing sets of interacting, disorganised responses and prevent the central organisation of some entirely. Such an arrangement would be very maladaptive. Rather, while the complexity of responses can be great, and co-ordination of separate response elements into concurrent activities can be achieved with practice, once the central organisation of a response begins it cannot be immediately modified by new stimulus information. The response may be disrupted, but it is not even possible to stop it in response to a signal not to respond, once the organisation of a response has begun (Hick and Bates, 1950). At the level of perceptual analysis people can fail to perceive signals, or fail to hold them in store, but this usually happens under serious overload conditions involving far more information than is required to produce a simple response. As far as VDU operation is concerned the keyboard responses required are, by nature, sequential and with the QWERTY keyboard the design tends to inhibit 'chord striking' responses so that speed is traded for accuracy. But, as mentioned earlier, specialised non-standard keyboards are for specialised circumstances and relatively few difficulties are mentioned.

Possible sources of keyboard problems are the height and angle of the keyboard and at least one study (Yllö, 1962), not of VDUs but of card punching machines, resulted in lowering the keyboards and tilting the whole machine. This had the effect of reducing the incidence of muscle pains among the operators which was the reason for the study.

The height of the VDU in relation to the operator's line of sight is a frequent source of difficulties. Usually this is because the VDU is placed on whatever tables or benches already exist, but sometimes the VDU is deliberately placed so that the operator has to tilt his head to look up at it. If he happens to wear bi-focals, the wear and tear on the neck may well prove a source of trouble. Both too high or too low positions are liable to cause strain, and the best position is about 30–40° below the horizontal.

Poor working posture has been related through electro-myographic studies to the increase in the incidence of upper back ailments which follows the computerisation of offices (Carlsöö, 1976). This is not an inherent feature of computerisation, and attention to the ergonomics of seating and reading from the seated position can prevent this becoming another specific occupational health risk.

5.7. BUILDINGS AND THE DISABLED

In recent years very much more interest has been shown in providing access for disabled people to buildings used by the general public. The climate of opinion in which this has taken place has been affected by the publicity given to many unnecessary difficulties for the disabled, which are the result of lack of consideration of their problems rather than anything else. Along with this, the therapeutic milieu has become one in which the disabled person's self-image and self-esteem is recognised as a key factor in leading as normal a life as possible. Self-esteem is affected by the ability to participate in activities independently and successfully, and the clinical professions have added their weight to improving the accessibility of buildings. The number of people benefited by the improved access is very difficult to assess with any accuracy because not all disabled people will take advantage of the improvement, and others, who would not usually be classed as disabled, may find some of the facilities for the disabled useful for themselves. However, from surveys carried out in 1968 and 1974 by the Australian Bureau of Statistics, it is estimated that as many as 9% of the population has some permanent impairment of mobility and activity, so that in Australia alone we could be dealing with around one and a quarter million people, making it clear that the lives of very many people are affected.

The nature of the facilities provided obviously must reflect the abilities the individual can call upon, so that, for example, there is a case for emergency warnings of fire being both visual for deaf and auditory for blind people. The trend to pedestrian mall shopping areas has in some instances included braille maps and identifications. These need to be in easily located places, but in one shopping area of Nottingham, UK, putting them on the regularly spaced supporting pillars seemed to be effective. Probably the main advantage is that of opening up unfamiliar places to blind people. Travel between places is also relevant and a variety of pocket booklets with relief maps have been produced for use by blind people. How widespread the use of these will be is not yet certain, and probably depends on how readable the relief maps are, and how easy it is to find an identification in the environment of where one is.

Most of the problems of access are experienced by people with loss of mobility who depend upon some artificial aid either to walk, or to propel themselves. The range of such aids varies from the walking stick, through crutches and calipers (or the more recent polypropylene substitute for calipers, which is vacuum formed over a cast of the lower leg so that it moulds to the shape of the leg and can be worn inside a knee length sock (Seeger and Stern, 1980), to artificial legs and wheelchairs of different types.

The solutions to loss of mobility depend upon a few cardinal rules. All of them are critically necessary in designing for people in wheelchairs. These rules are as follows.

(1) Reserved parking and vehicular access to buildings, preferably covered for protection from the weather, must be provided. This means ensuring that there are no steps or other barriers at one entrance (at least) which is also clearly signposted for use by the disabled. Additionally, the surface of pathways should be suitable for wheelchairs.

(2) Seated rather than standing height is the basic anthropometric datum. From this follows considerations of reach in the restricted, seated position for everyday activities like opening doors, hanging up coats, or taking books from bookshelves. Approximately 600–750 mm can be reached from the chair. The degree of mobility in the upper half of the body may also be impaired, and this indicates against locating items further from the wheelchair, or placing them where the wheelchair user cannot operate them in the same fashion as the ambulant person.

(3) With loss or serious impairment to the use of the legs, and because of the seated position, wheelchair users are limited in the strength they can bring to bear in movements like lifting, pulling or pushing. This militates for handles and handrails in positions where they can be used to allow leverage and arm-supported movement, and for one-hand operation of all necessary mechanisms.

(4) Wheelchair users require more space to manoeuvre, and may, in some cases, require space to be available for another person whose assistance is needed. Doorways, toilets, telephone boxes, and lifts are the main sources of problems in the past. Those which remain are steps such as are on buses, steep gradients, too high shelving, some types of terrain, and sometimes too high windows. Despite recent advances, the built environment still affords disabled people plenty of trouble, and the natural environment is almost totally closed to them without help from other people or devices.

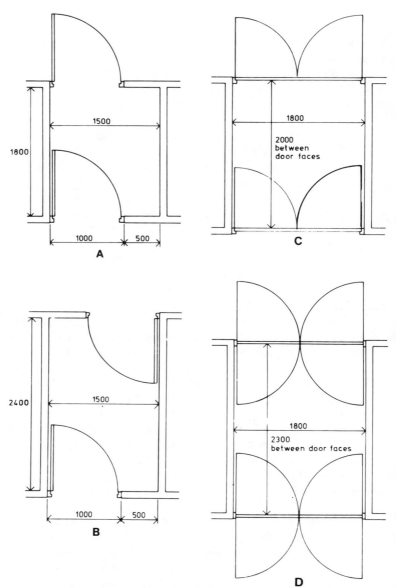

Fig. 5.7.1. Recommended dimensions for entrance lobbies. British Standard 5810:1979. Dimensions are in millimetres. Note: for variants A and B dimensions are taken to structural faces of walls; for variant C where automatic sliding doors are used, lobby length should be 2100 mm; where automatic side-hung doors are used, lobby length should be 2500 mm.

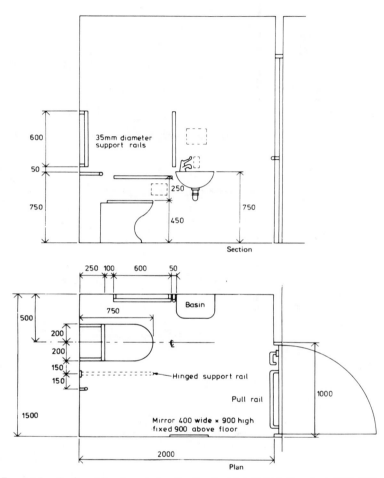

Fig. 5.7.2. Preferred lavatory design for the disabled. British Standard 5810:1979. Dimensions are in millimetres. Note: (1) 'clear' dimensions are shown; (2) positions for paper holder, soap dispenser and tower dispenser are shown dotted. A disposal bin should be provided.

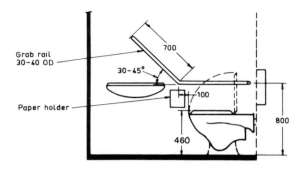

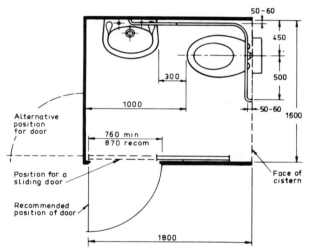

Fig. 5.7.3. A WC compartment for the disabled. Australian Standard 1428-1977. Dimensions are in millimetres. Note: where a mirror is placed above the handbasin the length of the sloping section of grab rail may be reduced to 300 mm.

There are a number of volumes directed at designing for specific functions for the disabled such as the Canadian CMHC's '*Housing the Handicapped*' (1974) which treats residential alternatives; or Walter's (1971) '*Sports Centres and Swimming Pools*' which deals with the subject of recreational access and usage of facilities by the disabled. However, as a set of general guidelines to dimensions, portions of the

British Standard (BS 5810: 1979) are reproduced here by kind permission of the British Standards Institution.

BS 5810: 1979 gives design recommendations for the approach and internal planning of buildings, lavatories, general design recommendations, and signs indicating facilities for the disabled. The actual minimum dimensions of entrance lobbies with single and double doors are given in Fig. 5.7.1. Other lobbies and passageways are recommended to be not less than 1200 mm wide, with some designs offering broader corridors of 1500 mm.

The standard preferred lavatory facility is shown in Fig. 5.7.2 and takes into account the fact that, for people in wheelchairs, mirrors above washbasins at standing height are inappropriate.

The relevant Australian Standard 1428-1977 provides similar dimensions for a WC compartment (see Fig. 5.7.3), and includes a recommendation for modifying existing toilets (Fig. 5.7.4).

Lifts are recommended to have an internal depth no less than 1400 mm with a minimum width of 1100 mm, and a door opening of 800 mm or more. A clear space 1500 mm × 1500 mm should be in

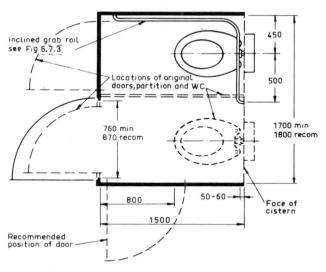

Fig. 5.7.4. Modifying existing toilet facilities for the disabled. Australian Standard 1428-1977. Dimensions are in millimetres.

front of lift doors. Controls and telephones should not be more than 1400 mm above floor level so they can be used by disabled people.

These are only some of the recommendations of the British Standard BS 5810: 1979, for more detail the Standard itself should be consulted. Similarly, the Australian 1428-1977 '*Design Rules for Access by the Disabled*', also offers further information including lighting and signals and warnings, making it well worth consulting in the interests of the disabled.

Chapter 6

Spatial Arrangements for Interpersonal Interaction

6.1. ERGONOMICS AND ENVIRONMENTAL PSYCHOLOGY

It is not easy, without grossly oversimplifying, to comment in general but meaningful terms on the huge portion of human behaviour made up of all the types of interpersonal interactions which take place in buildings. However, there are regularities, and Garfinkel (1964) observed recurring patterns of spatial behaviour, and suggested that departing from routine creates problems in interpersonal interaction. This is an area where ergonomics and environmental psychology merge, and the interaction between people needs to be borne in mind as well as the arrangement of objects and spaces. Ergonomics may be the sharp end of environmental science, which includes psychology, though it is necessarily interdisciplinary in nature, but, sometimes it is a fine line between ergonomics and environmental psychology. For example, a number of subtle effects have been illustrated in studies of environmental psychology which may affect the workability of specific interactions. Bloom *et al.* (1977), for example, set up two different types of psychotherapist's office, one a formal setting with office furniture, and professional diplomas framed on the walls, the other furnished informally, including posters replacing diplomas. The clients were then asked to describe their psychotherapist. Curiously, the answers depended on the therapist's sex. Females were judged less credible in the informal setting, males more credible in it than in the formalised office. If credibility plays a role in the effectiveness of therapy, as would seem to be inevitable, there must be more to effective design than tables and chairs. Much of the research literature is made up of specific results like this, but some fairly general statements can be made on the basis of research results.

First, obviously, buildings and their parts are designed for particular functions, and they reflect the understanding of those functions and socio-cultural attitudes to them. Thus, since the turn of the century, attitudes to mental hospitals, and the patients in them, have altered so much that few patients are now condemned to remote fortresses to ensure their confinement behind bars and high walls. Advances in psychotherapeutic techniques and medicines, such as the modern tranquilliser (the original tranquilliser used in France some hundreds of years ago was a metal skull cap that could be tightened to compress and even crush the cranium), are only partly responsible for the improvement in conditions for mental patients. The understanding of mental illness determines both treatment and conditions. When the mentally ill were possessed by evil spirits, some had to be drowned or burned at the stake with the holiest of motives—to drive out the demon and allow the person entry into heaven. Even now the process of identifying the nature of, and effective treatment for particular conditions continues, and some psychologists like Bandura (1963), reject any medical condition or illness as the underlying cause of much abnormal behaviour, relying instead on psychological techniques of behaviour modification such as desensitisation and counter-conditioning. Our buildings express our knowledge of, and our attitudes to, their functions. If these are wrongly based, the buildings themselves may act against the people in them, helping, in the case of mental patients, to foster withdrawal and alienation, and creating the apathetic, institutionalised personality who, deprived of adequate stimulation from the environment and social interaction, loses the skills used in dealing with those, becomes unable to cope with the world outside, and is then totally dependent on the institution.

Sommer in his book '*Tight Spaces*' (1974*b*) cites the aggressive reaction of prisoners to very hard environments, describing how, when Eastern-style or 'hole in the floor' lavatories are introduced to save the costs and inconvenience of replacing smashed ones of the usual Western types, this challenges the prisoners' ingenuity to find other ways of expressing aggression. As Sommer notes, 'By law the California authorities are required to provide even strip-cell inmates with their own Bibles. The result is that the Bible becomes a weapon in a manner unintended by the most ardent missionary. Inmates stuff the pages into the ventilator shaft and use the covers to stop up the hole in the floor toilet'.

The extent to which the environment provokes violence, or simply is the arena for it, is unanswerable in our present state of knowledge. But many studies, whether of vandalism, littering, or use of recreational areas, support the obvious truth that people behave protectively to what they value, and we may not need to know the answer to that question in order to reduce aggressive behaviour.

The prisons and mental hospitals mentioned are good examples of buildings whose nature is determined by society's attitudes to what their essential function should be, and what range of social interactions is permissible within them. This in turn affects spatial arrangements and raises the question of how far secondary functions should be accommodated. Provision for visitors has improved in both prisons and hospitals, to the extent that conjugal visits are sometimes permitted, and parents of hospitalised children may stay with their child, but Ronco's (1972) observation that hospital design is aimed at accommodating the functions of staff, rather than the secondary needs of patients, is still true though the two need not always conflict.

6.2. SOCIOFUGAL AND SOCIOPETAL SPACES

It was Osmond (1957) who described settings as tending to bring people to them and promote their interaction (sociopetal), or having the opposite effect of isolating people who are in them from one another (sociofugal). Which is appropriate depends upon the function served by the space. Serried ranks of chairs or benches which, by denying eye contact through seating people side by side, may serve a useful sociofugal function in large public waiting areas (Sommer, 1974a), allowing many people to use the same space without intruding upon one another. Eye contact seems to be the action by which we signal and initiate our intention to interact with others (Argyle and Dean, 1965). Where eye contact is not possible within a physical setting, it is very unusual for socialisation to occur. Similarly, where it is denied, any attempt to socialise more usually peters out rather than persists. Provision for eye contact, therefore, militates against straight lines for sociopetal areas. However, there are some suggestions that being face to face is a less sociable arrangement than being offset at an angle. Sommer (1959), for example, noted that patients and visitors tended to seat themselves on either side of a corner at the tables in the hospital cafeteria. The face to face confrontation may be adopted in competitive situations (Argyle, 1967; Sommer, 1965), but the evidence is less reliable in the opposite direction—that competitive behaviour will necessarily be evoked if people are forced into face to face positions, though the unwavering stare means hostility and provokes aggression or flight. There is by now a considerable literature on mutual looking behaviour, some of which is relevant to buildings in that the placement of people operating through behavioural variables such as eye contact, non-verbal communication and expressive gesture, and spatial variables such as orientation, distance and relative height, makes spaces sociofugal or sociopetal.

In 1974 (see Lang *et al.*, 1974, p. 93) the analysis of human spatial behaviour was argued to involve two units, 'activity systems' (Chapin, 1965) concerned with the sequence of activities in a given setting, and 'behaviour settings' where the layout of the setting tends to produce a 'standing pattern' of behaviour (Barker, 1968). These units remain with us because of their utility, but the influence of architectural studies, and research into more molar aspects of behaviour, tends to review behaviour within spaces or settings classified by their main function (Bell *et al.*, 1978). This approach is more easily linked to some other research fields such as ergonomics, but there remains a divide between design criteria and ergonomic recommendations, even though they may both emphasise ambient conditions, spatial arrangements and other similar areas. In part, this is because the more, or less, detailed recommendations are made from different sources of information, but also because it is still unusual outside ergonomics to perform detailed studies which try to pinpoint the nature of any critical factor by identifying all of the activities and assessing how well they can be performed. Checklist approaches which attempt to do this, rating, e.g. speech intelligibility, weight of lifted objects and the height lifted to, or walking distances and times, and other specific functions have remained the province of ergonomics. The value of such checklists has been appraised by Easterby (1967*a*). In the same way, the many models of the design process itself which have been offered, nearly all of them being very useful (Altman, 1975; Zeisel, 1975), tend to produce dialogue between environmental psychologists and architects and designers, but not ergonomists.

Why does the great interdisciplinary divide persist? Perhaps the main reason is simply that, because of codes, standards, and other practices leading to standardisation, most design tasks either do not, or seem not to, need ergonomic assessment. In its absence, the effectiveness of the design is accepted for what it is without questioning whether it would have been capable of improvement, and any problems which do arise are treated in an *ad hoc* manner. It is also true that if serious enough problems occur, there may be no simple ergonomic answer in contexts which have already been created. This, in itself, may serve to devalue the utility of ergonomics in the eyes of others.

Yet another reason is that communication between disciplines decreases as each person, with their own role to play, is forced back to their own training and methods in order to make their contribution. The most serious conflicts are usually created by economic pressures, sometimes by speed stress. But, in all spheres of human activity, not just in matters to do with the built environment, the sciences and social sciences have developed to a point where there is useful information to be applied.

What is not always acknowledged in texts like this, however, is that good designers outnumber good ergonomists. Moreover, one should not overplay the value of research any more than one should undervalue it. All of our information about our environment does not depend upon research. We know when cultural norms are being broken, and what personal space invasions feel like, without necessarily knowing the distances Hall observed. The research literature on interpersonal distances is a fascinating contribution to our understanding of human behaviour but, as Sommer (1974*b*) says: 'I do not believe that the personal space bubble is a logical unit in architectural design. It may be an interesting and useful concept for architects to have around for conceptualising interaction spaces, but I would not like to see buildings designed with personal space used as some kind of standard or unit of measurement'.

In some circumstances the research findings may indicate acceptable minimum distances, but their main value may lie in reminding the designer to take distances between people into account for successful interactions within a particular setting as he conceives it. Since there is more behaviour experienced by us than is researched, one cannot totally disregard intuition or common sense, though the approach advocated in the opening chapter, of using these to review the applicability of research findings, rather than ignoring research, seems the best procedure.

The use of interdisciplinary design teams instead of architects, to be employed for the design of expensive public buildings does not seem likely to be discontinued. But there does not seem to be much in the way of *evidence*, either from user satisfaction studies, or comparative studies of difficulties, or any other data, to prove the superiority of the interdisciplinary approach. And, in any case, even where an eminent architect or firm is contracted for a building, that does not imply that they do not consult people with other expertise. But it is, in principle, possible to compare, in many different ways, the effectiveness of designs of groups which include behavioural scientists, and others which do not. Similarly, the value of user consultation at various stages of design could be investigated using a number of different criteria for the 'performance' of the eventual building. Finally, the importance of the approaches used and information which was taken into account, or possibly not taken into account, could also be assessed. Research into approaches to design and building performance, as well as straightforward user satisfaction studies, could prove to be informative if there really are reliable differences to be found.

Sommer (1974*b*) also stressed the needs for flexibility, and to allow for personalisation, so that sociopetal or sociofugal spaces can be created by the users. This involves more than the manipulation of spatial factors, of course, but distances have their significance. Joiner (1976) studied the positioning of desks in one-person offices in terms of whether the desk was used as a physical barrier between the occupant and visitors. This is one aspect of personalisation. As might be expected from the nature of their jobs, a higher proportion of academics sat in positions from which they could not see the door than did commercial or government employed people. Joiner suggests that being able to see the door from one's workingplace implies readiness for interaction. Since most academics interact with colleagues and students many times a day, it is difficult to know whether these spatial arrangements reflect less frequent interactions for academics, or the desire on their part to spend their time with the subject matter of their area, rather than other people. Since, in the commercial and government groups, the majority of more senior people sat facing the door, whereas the more junior ones sat with the door visible, but not facing it, status may be involved. It may be that academics advertise their status in other ways, or that they prefer less formal interactions in their offices. Many explanations are possible but, however accurate and general this sort of observation is, to uncover the causal mechanisms requires that we learn how to manipulate the phenomenon rather than just showing it to be a general one. In general, this has not yet been done, though some research has been performed. Campbell and Herren (1978), for instance, have shown that, in interviews between undergraduates and professors, whether the desk was between them or against the wall made no difference to the ratings given, or to the duration of interviews. So, although there are attempts to view the office as a projection of the occupant's personality (Sherven, 1978), it may be that their decoration and arrangement signal the nature of preferred, or expected, interactions, but say nothing about their outcomes. This would seem likely to the extent that any outcome depends on the basis of information exchanged within rules or constraints which affect the outcome. This is the case for many office-based interactions.

In some other settings, however, social behaviour has been shown to be influenced by design features. Generally, the frequency with which relative strangers meet each other, and the conditions under which they do so, affects the probability of their conversing together. Crowded conditions tend to inhibit social behaviour except in settings given over to leisure pursuits. One example of this is the finding (Fairbanks, 1977) that psychiatric patients were more likely to engage in conversation when there were only two people in the room, though as one would expect, the presence of a member of the staff contributed to social interaction. Eye contact was mentioned earlier, and it may be that this is more acceptable in some leisure settings, allowing people to interact within them. But, having common ground for discussion, as spectators at sporting events do, marks bounded areas for interaction within the infinite universe of possible communications, even though the supporters of rival teams' interpretations of events may differ.

There is a very sizeable literature on crowding, from which we can draw the generalisation that, outside leisure settings, perceived crowding, as well as high numbers of people per unit, reduces social activity. That social groupings develop more rapidly in smaller spaces, as witnessed by Baum *et al.* (1978*b*), who showed this happened more readily in a dormitory with short corridors than in another with long corridors, is probably a function of the number of people involved. Moreover, Baum *et al.* (1978*a*) managed to chart the time-course of the effect of the greater number of people in long-corridor dormitories. Testing their subjects after 1, 3, and 7 weeks of residence, they showed that, while more competitive and reactive after 1 or 3 weeks, long-corridor residents were more withdrawn, less involved, and exhibited signs of helplessness, when compared with those living in a short-corridor design. Evidently, we can easily overestimate people's ability to cope with living among many others.

Other factors of design, like the placement of doors, which is known to facilitate or inhibit interaction (Merton, 1947; Festinger *et al.*, 1950) does not seem relevant here, although it is possible that the same result as the Festinger study of housing, namely, that distance between doors was an important variable for the development of friendships, could have emerged had that aspect been investigated. Vertical isolation has also been demonstrated in high-rise buildings. Zalot and Adams-Webber (1977) showed that people living in single family dwellings both interacted more frequently with their neighbours than high-rise dwellers did with theirs, and, perhaps because of this, gave more complex descriptions of their neighbours. This, in itself, need not imply that high-rise building residents are less happy with their social existence, but in a study of high-rise student housing, Holahan *et al.* (1978) found an inverse relationship between floor level and satisfaction with social participation. Satisfaction with privacy was greatest for those living on the middle floors, but again lowest on higher floors. The number of friendships which were based within a dormitory was also greatest on the lower floors. Similarly, among the variables which accounted for satisfaction with housing, living in single-family rather than multi-family units, emerged as an important one in Rent and Rent's (1978) study of more than 250 occupants of low-income housing units. Even where, in contrast to many studies, residents generally express satisfaction with public housing schemes, the findings of Mullins and Robb (1977) in New

Zealand, suggest that satisfaction will be higher if dwellings do not have densities greater than one family. The manner in which this is achieved may be that, within the family, it may be easier to set up spaces for particular functions, even if only temporarily. Within the home, Lennard and Lennard (1977) have reviewed the effects of territories and boundaries on the·mode of functioning; and the manner in which roles are taken on, or prevented from being assumed, is part of one line of argument that lack of available space within the home can produce conflict between those with different roles to play.

Results like those of Holahan *et al.* (1978) may reflect a pyramidal structure of accidental social encounter when entering the building, with those on the pinnacle being isolated when they reach it, and remaining so while they remain there. The contrary effect, that since more people inhabit high-rise structures, residents should come in contact with more people in the public spaces of their building, is often true, but it does not lead to more socialisation. McCarthy and Saegart (1978) showed this, comparing three-storey with 14-storey apartment buildings. Their interview data supported the interpretation that there were more problems with social relationships, more alienation, and less satisfaction with the environment, among the 14-storey residents, who also were less active socially outside their building. Baldassare (1978*a*) suggests that rather than withdrawing from primary social relationships, by which he means family, friends and social networks, it is the secondary relationships which are reduced, or avoided. Reactions to relative strangers, involvement with those living close by, and meeting new people, are the sorts of secondary relationships whose frequency decreases.

These points are worth bearing in mind since some earlier writers (Jacobs, 1961; Newman, 1972; Freedman, 1975) have taken the line that making people have contact with others, perhaps by sharing communal facilities, will produce socialisation. They are not necessarily wrong in this, but, along with the nature of the forced contact, and its duration, the numbers of people present at the time must come into the reckoning. While spaces can be so small that they produce defensive withdrawal from social interaction, so that few friendships begin in lifts, the evidence is accumulating that spaces can also be too large. The mediating variable appears to be the inhibitory effect that too many people has upon pairs of people interacting, even in settings where such interactions are intended to be possible. There is no universal number for how many is too many. Nor are these effects necessarily due to individuals feeling crowded, though perceived crowding itself varies with design features and the nature of activity taking place (Desor, 1972; Dabbs *et al.*, 1973; Stokols *et al.*, 1973). Specific settings have also been considered though not always from the point of view of the implications of these researches. Field (1973), for example, considers design implications in health care systems. Promoting the development of social networks through design seems to demand that, some of the time, people should come into contact in pairs. The more frequently that happens, the greater is the likelihood of interaction. The duration of the contact is also relevant, and transient meetings in lifts and corridors, for example, are too short to allow sufficient exchange and appraisal of information for acquaintance to result. Distance (Willis, 1966) has also been shown to be relevant, and reliable differences observed in the distances at which conversation begins for people differing in age, sex or race. Sharing facilities is noted by some writers (Freedman, 1975) as a way of reducing isolation. The most obviously effective approach through design, however, is the provision of areas for group leisure or recreation. Possibilities range from children's playgrounds to saunas, and their appropriateness is determined by social and cultural factors as well as by age and interest, but where appropriate spaces are provided, fewer instances of social isolation will be found.

There is research at both levels, room and house, showing some of the environmental effects on social behaviour. Sommer's emphasis on flexibility of rooms is backed up by research on student rooms in a residential college (High and Sundstrom, 1977), which found that the extent to which the furniture could be moved around was related to the frequency of visitors. Most visits were made to the rooms of female students, but those with the most flexible rooms attracted more visitors. There is the perennial 'chicken and egg' problem here, however, and it may be that more sociable people seek flexible spaces to accommodate their various social activities. Certainly, Moos (1978) found, in groups of university students, that where the proportion of single-occupant rooms was higher, more stress was placed on academic achievement, and less on social interactions. There is also an argument along the lines that good habits of studying are built up by conditioning oneself to work in the same space, so that being in that place evokes the responses related to studying. This is achieved by actually working whenever in that place, rather than conditioning oneself to daydream in it, or to clean out drawers, sharpen pencils, doodle, or any of the other escape behaviours which are easily adopted. The reinforcing effect of a successful period of study is diminished by such competing activity, and the conditioning weakened. On this argument, maintaining a constant context in which to study is important since it aids in evoking the appropriate response. If correct, then perhaps flexibility can aid the learning process, with rooms being ordered in one way which is reserved for periods of academic work, but changed for other activities. In practice, this does not happen because of the effort of rearrangement, and because those most sociable students may not realise that, if they use the same environment for work and social activities, they may be instilling in themselves competing response tendencies which are evoked by being in that place.

There are other studies of academic performance which implicate perceiving oneself as living in crowded conditions as a factor related to lowering academic performance (Stokols *et al.*, 1978; Baldassare, 1978*a*). Still others point to animosity between students, which arises from being crowded (Baron *et al.*, 1976) as a key factor in poor academic performance. Gradually, the picture which is emerging from research in this area is reasonably similar to that found for noise. Indeed, crowding can be dealt with as an ambient condition of a person's environment, though it normally is not in the literature on ergonomics.

Crowding not only reduces interactions, unless measures are taken to promote social intercourse, but, as was found for noise, the adaptations people make are such as to reduce pro-social behaviour. In one study Bickman *et al.* (1973) dropped stamped-addressed letters around dormitories which were of low-, medium- or high-density of residents. The 'lost-letter' technique is used to measure the frequency with which people will make the pro-social gesture of posting on the letter to its destination. From the high-density student dormitories, 58 % of the letters were returned; from the medium-density, 79 %

came back; and 88 % were sent back by people living in low-density accommodation.

Other minor acts of pro-social behaviour have usually been shown to be inhibited by population density, with less helping behaviour the more people there are. On the pretext of having obtained a wrong number, and having no more money, help was requested from the person called who was asked to call the number that should have been obtained (Milgram, 1970). People living in small towns acceded to this request more often than residents of Chicago, New York or Philadelphia. This result was replicated by Korte and Kerr (1975) who compared the response in small towns in Massachusetts with that in Boston. Requests for other assistance, such as seeking permission to use someone's telephone, were also shown to be more frequently allowed in small towns (72 %) than cities (27 %) (Milgram, 1970).

In commercial transactions, overpayments made by customers were more frequently corrected, and some money returned to them, in small towns (80 %) than in cities (55 %) (Korte and Kerr, 1975). And this despite the fact, reported by Lowin *et al.* (1971), that city bank clerks tended to check how much money customers were paying in, more often than small town bank clerks did. Finally, shoplifting was less frequently reported by urbanites (Gelfand *et al.*, 1973).

Not all studies have found differences of this sort, but there does seem to be some quite reliable evidence showing the urbanite is more likely to ignore or refuse appeals for assistance. 'Bystander apathy' is a phenomenon of very large cities so that, as Rosenthal (1964) in his book '*38 Witnesses*' indicates, many people saw the murder of Kitty Genovese in New York and none went to her aid. Fear of being attacked is one factor, but it is hard to explain the behaviour as reported in the press, of people who urge those contemplating suicide to jump from high buildings; or find funny the plight of a man struggling to climb back on to a railway platform, from which he had fallen, as a train approaches, and eventually crushes him to death.

It is possible that aggression is a key factor, but research findings in this direction are inconsistent. More likely, the most important feature is alienation, not necessarily from everyone, but from stigmatised groups of others. This view, that aggression is permissible against alienated groups, would at least help unify the observations of 'bystander apathy' with those of mob behaviour. As far back as 1895,

Le Bon in his book '*The Crowd*' (reprinted 1968), described the loss of identity and relaxing of behavioural constraints which followed identification of oneself as part of a crowd.

Another factor which mediates, and gives direction to the effects of crowding, which is frequently mentioned, is the degree of perceived control, or the perceived negative effects of crowding (Stokols *et al.*, 1978). Inescapable noise generally has worse effects than noise under the person's control (Kryter, 1970), and, similarly, lack of perceived control of crowding is associated with more adverse effects (Rodin, 1976). The nature of the effects of noise and crowding, though not identical, appear to be more closely similar than is the case for some other ambient conditions, presumably because the latter are mediated by particular physiological effects.

In drawing a parallel between exposure to noise and crowding, it is possible to consider the effects crowding has on specific performances. At some stage also it needs to be acknowledged that crowded situations are often noisier than less crowded ones, so that outside the laboratory the two probably interact. The effects of crowding on performance tend to be grouped into invasions of personal space, stimulus overload in which crowding is often only one aspect, and the long-term effects of living in high densities. There are also specific results, like the observation that the speed at which pedestrians walk is positively related to city size (Bornstein and Bornstein, 1976), which may be due to architectural features like higher buildings, but may equally reflect the press of other people, or walking with different intentions.

These areas have been, and still are being heavily researched, but a few examples will illustrate the degree of similarity in the findings. First, on personal space, some indications that cognitive performance is affected by the proximity of other people emerged from an experiment by Rawls *et al.* (1972) on arithmetical calculation. But only those people who had previously been shown to prefer larger distances between themselves and others showed impaired performance under crowding, both in terms of the number of problems attempted, and the number of errors made. Another group of people who were low on personal space demands actually improved their performance in the crowded condition. This lends credence to individual differences in spatial sensitivity.

The complexity of the personality factors involved should, however, not be underestimated. Too simply drawn hypotheses are liable to be disproved. Some support for the view that one combination of personality features which leads to performance decrements is the mixture of extraversion and emotionality exists in data from Katsikitis and Brebner (1980). The hypothesis from the Brebner–Cooper model of extraversion (Brebner and Cooper, 1978), that increasing the demand for stimulus-analysis, as opposed to increasing the rate at which responses are organised and emitted, would adversely affect the performance of extraverts more than introverts under crowded conditions, was confirmed. The view that the degree of emotional lability of the person would determine whether his performance worsened, also gained some support from these results. The tasks used were a simple and a more complex letter-cancellation task in which the subject searched for, and checked, either the letter 'a', or the letters 'w', 'm', 'n', and 'c'. For the introverted group, while their performance was worse at the more difficult task, being crowded had less effect on them in that condition than in the easy one. The opposite was true for the extraverts, whose performance was better than that of the introverts in the easy condition, but markedly worse than theirs at the crowded, difficult task.

The obvious possibility that the mechanism for such a result is extraverts trading accuracy for speed when crowded, does not fit the results. While emotionally labile extraverts did speed up in the difficult, crowded condition, stable extraverts slowed down slightly, but their performance was still poorer and they missed more of the target letters. Perhaps the increase in information from the proximity of other people, and in this experiment being crowded meant touching the knees of the person opposite and the sides of those next to the subject, overloaded the capacity of the system, so that tactile information was processed rather than the visual symbols.

Another point which needs to be made is that laboratory studies are often designed to pinpoint changes in performance far more accurately than everyday activities, so that any appearance, outside the laboratory, of no effect of crowding, may belie the reality. The more complex the task, the more likely it is that a decrement in performance will emerge, a point made indirectly by Bell *et al.* (1978).

Those writers quote Aiello *et al.* (1975) as showing a crowding in dormitories, and note the adverse effects of high spatial, and high social density on solving complex mazes.

These results shade into the stimulus overload aspects of crowding. The notion of stimulus overload has been around for a long time in environmental psychology, but the specific information processing functions which are affected tend not to be stated very precisely. Yet, extrapolating from laboratory studies aimed at measuring the amount of information we can process (e.g. Miller, 1956; Vickers, 1980), there is good evidence that the limits of human information processing can be easily surpassed, and that some decisions take a very long time. However, it is not the general, familiar and stable aspects of the environment which overload us, no matter how elaborate it is; the long-term memory has stored enough to deal with that. But dealing with new environments can produce fatigue. It is the multitude of new and specific features, which we treat each as a unitary percept or action, and which are changing all round us, that is the source of overload. Part of the reason we do not recall every specific event or action of, say, going to work each day, is just the sheer volume of information which we process, in greater rather than lesser amounts, before pigeon-holing them only as of this category or that category.

Dealing with overloading of the sort deriving from other people has been the subject of research into the behavioural changes that this induces. Milgram (1970), comparing urban and rural dwellers, found urbanites tended to deal with one another in more impersonal ways, and in more formal, compartmentalised interactions, and that there was a greater screening out and selectivity under urban overload, and possibly some flattening of affective responses. The question is open, however, as to whether these become permanent features of the individual. Bystander apathy and aloofness may be readily witnessed in the centres of large cities, but these may only represent strategies designed to cope with overload, which the individual shrugs off on his homeward journey. The particular tactics adopted by the overloaded urbanite, which are given by Milgram, include reduced time spent on any input, ignoring inputs of low priority, shifting the onus of responsibility to other people, using screening methods (e.g. having to go to a secretary to gain access to his or her employer), and having institutions within the urban community which perform more specialised functions than in the rural communities in order to reduce the number of people attending them. Some of these tactics can produce stress, and further overload, on other people.

Saegart (1976) includes in her analysis of the stress-inducing qualities of the environment, attentional overload which may be sheer stimulation; informational or decision-making overload; the frustration or interruption of activities directed at some goal or other; the psychological and social meaning of a person's environment; and underloading stresses of too little physical or social stimulation.

Cohen (1977) makes the point that the greater the intensity, and the less the predictability of an input, or the control the person has over it, then the greater is the attention which needs to be paid to it. Moreover, after prolonged periods of intense demands, the attentional capacities may be reduced and more easily overloaded by further stimulation. Overload is most frequently detected by the need for more time to deal with an input, increased error rates, and particularly missed signals, increased variability of performance, loss of capacity to perform secondary tasks simultaneously, and stated feelings of fatigue and irritability. All of these are observed in laboratory studies of human performance, and it seems unlikely that, if similar overload conditions are present in the urban environment, any defence mechanisms other than selectivity, avoidance and escape, are available to the overloaded individual.

Both withdrawal and aggressive behaviour are reported in the literature under crowded conditions (Hutt and Vaizey, 1966), although there is some evidence to suggest that it is only when people are forced into competition that this turns into conflict (Rohe and Patterson, 1974). These studies were carried out using children as subjects and it is questionable how far such findings should be regarded as typifying human behaviour. Nevertheless, Milgram (1970) did cite competition for scarce resources as one of the characteristics of urban living, and irritation, if not aggression, born of frustration, is a daily experience in many large cities. Arguments that crowding is a matter of adaptation, and that in parts of India or Asia being crowded is not stressful, do have some force and it is possible to distinguish between crowding and density. But even in those settings, where there is competition for space the usual stress effects have been found (Mitchell, 1971).

Long-term effects of living under crowded conditions have been studied for many years, and from many different angles. Health aspects have been researched (Wilner *et al.*, 1962), behaviour and personality disorders have been shown to be more frequent among the residents of poor housing areas near city centres, and sometimes mental disorders have been found to be as much as 15 times more frequent in such areas as in better residential areas (Faris and Dunham, 1939). Caution needs to be exercised in laying results like this at the door of crowding as the only relevant variable. The 'downward drift' hypothesis, for example, would suggest that people who are in the process of breakdown, like alcoholics, gravitate to such areas bringing their disorders with them, rather than producing them in response to their environment. Still other factors are also recognised to operate and Dayton (1940), in a study of almost 90 000 people, found mental illness to be significantly more common among non-naturalised immigrants to America than among those who had become naturalised, showing that the degree of adaptation, identification and affiliation may reflect the mental status of the person. But, while accepting that many variables operate, crowding does seem to be one which is involved in long-term effects on people's behaviour. The approach adopted by Gallé *et al.* (1972) in Chicago, which analysed density as the number of persons per room of the dwelling, the number of rooms per dwelling, the number of dwellings per structure, and, finally, the number of structures per acre, was able to show that the highest correlations between psychopathological behaviour and these density measures were found with the number of persons per room.

The resources which are present in the environment have also been shown to contribute to social behaviour, and, more than that, may promote functions which are therapeutic for the individual, or at least stave off a decline in their capacities. Comparing an enriched setting with a deprived one, Tognoli *et al.* (1978) recorded the ratings professional staff made of the activities of mentally retarded men. There were marked differences in behaviour in the two settings, with the enriched one producing better and more active behaviour. Miller

(1978) also showed that the introduction of new materials, some of which were of the arts and crafts types, others were games, into the environment of severely retarded young men, led to them becoming significantly more active and socially involved. Nor is this restricted to people. Yanofsky and Markowitz report that when a discrimination apparatus was introduced into the cage of a pair of mandrills in a zoo, stereotyped behaviour was reduced as the space-usage and general activity levels of both animals were increased. By reducing inactivity and isolation, resources can serve a therapeutic function.

The limitations of the people being studied are a critical factor in experiments on flexibility, so that when Peterson *et al.* (1977) looked at a wide range of the behaviour produced by geriatric patients under three different furniture arrangements, the only one which showed any systematic change was talking.

Looking at the wider environment, Kalt and Zalkind (1976) quote Newman (1972), who surveyed 165 public housing projects, stressing the importance of defensible space for the quality of life and social behaviour in these projects. According to Newman, defensible space is a product of three design features. First, the spaces outside the houses should be perceived by the residents as their own territory, rather than being seen as impersonal space. Where this happens, the areas outside the houses tend to become an area for social interaction, and Ottensmann (1978) found there was more 'street life' in high-density and working class districts than in middle class areas. Middle class people, defined by their income grouping, tend more to use their homes, or their own gardens, when meeting their friends. As a pure speculation, in the absence of evidence, one relevant factor could simply be cost. Entertaining friends in their homes among the middle class implies providing things like food and drink for guests, while socialising on the street among the working class does not.

The second feature noted by Newman involves visibility. Providing opportunities to observe all the public, or semi-private spaces, means that antisocial behaviour will be witnessed. Discouraging vandalism, hooliganism, and even littering, obviously improves the experienced quality of the environment, and making such actions visible is one way of doing this.

Finally, Newman suggests that designing public housing which is not readily differentiated from the rest of the built environment, or seen to have an institutional identity, can prevent the stigmatisation of such projects. Alienation and depersonalisation foster the sort of behaviour which Newman's three factors are intended to counter. But also, as shown by Wilner *et al.* (1962) in their review of the effects of housing, the social adjustment and the health of residents are adversely affected by poor housing conditions. Defensible spaces, by improving the quality of the residential environment, may serve to improve the self-concept, and self-esteem of those living in them. Feedback from others living outside these areas also plays an important role in maintaining the psychological status and well-being of residents. The often cited, ill-fated Pruitt–Igoe housing project in St Louis, which created a ghetto-like environment, failed, in that people with any choice would not live there, and the project was largely demolished in 1972.

Physical health areas which are affected by housing conditions, tend to be those associated with overcrowding, multiple usage of water and sanitary facilities, and inadequate heating and ventilation systems, according to Wilner *et al.* (1962). Hence, respiratory tract infections, children's diseases, digestive tract diseases, and skin conditions, are all more frequently met in very poor housing. But another aspect needs to be included to complete the list. Accidents, in and around the house, are more frequent and tend to be more serious in slum conditions. They derive in the main from dilapidation, inadequate lighting, and electrical faults, so that, in addition to exposure to the health risks, people living under such conditions are more prone to falls, fires and even electrocution. There have, of course, been marked improvements over the last half century, but a large part of the world's population still lives with some of these hazards and no prospect of escaping them.

Even if free of these particular threats, there remain other problems which affect particular sub-groups of the population. Old people are a good example. In a study of how mobile the elderly living in San Antonio, Texas, or San Francisco were, Carp (1980) showed that old San Franciscans walked far more than those living in San Antonio. This was ascribed to the fact that residential lots are smaller in San Francisco, so that homes tend to be closer together, and to the relatively fewer corner shops in San Antonio which tends to have major shopping centres which are reached by car. Social visiting was almost twice as frequent among the old in San Francisco where 61 % visited friends at least once a week, while the comparable figure for San Antonio was 35 %. At the lowest end of social visiting, 42 % of the San Antonio old 'never' went to see friends, in comparison with only 14 % of those living in San Francisco. Longer trips made to other cities for entertainment were rare among the San Antonio sample, 81 % stating they 'never' made such journeys, but common among San Franciscans, only 20 % of whom 'never' took this sort of trip. It is possible that these gross differences reflect styles of behaviour which begin as adaptations to the immediate environment, walking to local shops or not, and so on, but then generalise to other spheres of activity, like social visiting and inter-city travel. We cannot be certain this is the case, but these results do seem to fit this sort of explanation. If it is correct, the design implications are clear, the social skills of the elderly may decay, and their interaction with others decrease to a greater extent, if their residential setting makes demands upon their mobility which they cannot meet.

Similarly, elderly people who retain the ability to live in their own homes, even though in many cases they will depend on help from relatives, social services, friends and neighbours, to be able to continue to do so, may be more active and independent, and have more positive approaches and adaptations, as well as being less routinised in their lives. Without attempting any review of environments specifically for the aged, the results of Marcoen and Houben (1975) support this standpoint. However, just as one would expect, when old people know that they would improve the quality of their lives by living communally, rather than individually, perhaps because none of the support systems above remain, but are necessary, then an equal amount of research proves that this does happen (e.g. Carp, 1976). But, for this to happen, architectural design and the resources provided therein, have their part to play, and while there is certainly no very simple rule about what should be done, the disciplines can come together, behavioural and social scientists can explain what functional losses have been found to occur with ageing, those with environmental interests can describe many of the factors which create sociofugal and communicofugal places, any clinical aspects can be treated in perspective, rather than dominating to the extent that they create more problems than they solve, and the very particular needs of any elderly group can be considered. All this tends to rest on the shoulders of those actually making decisions about the environment of the aged. If the information which exists in reliable form is ignored, then, the sort of situation as it was in some of the worst areas of Great Britain in the 1960s will continue. There, the old who were condemned by poverty to be housed in old people's homes, were often segregated by sex into dormitory accommodation which they shared with people who were of the same sex, but who might be incontinent, insomniac, retarded, or sometimes moribund. Dining rooms were only for eating in, lounge accommodation could, at worst, consist of bentwood chairs, backs to the four walls of a room whose hard and sterile appearance was dictated by problems like enuresis, and there was nowhere else for married people to be together. These are not just images, but memories of a three-year study of ageing, and they are ameliorated by the fact that people do temper the environment, not just for themselves, but for others; and only one of the old people's homes visited had all of these features. Even there, the matron had made a heroine's effort to organise a garden with private nooks and benches, and four old married couples had staked their claim to particular territories which others did not seem to dispute. Nevertheless, given the variability of weather conditions throughout the country, this was only a seasonal solution, and it depended upon a matron modifying an environment which had been purchased rather than designed. It is possible to do very much better, and nowadays that is the norm rather than the exception, but the contribution of those trying to fathom the rules which govern social behaviour in architectural settings, and those dealing with all the many other problems of producing workable settings, needs to be overseen and reviewed to implement change where that is indicated, whether for the old or any other sub-group of society.

6.3   SOME PROCEDURES AND MODELS

Various procedures have been devised with the aim of including ergonomics in the design process of the building (Easterby and Lawson, 1971; Szokolay, 1979). Szokolay's approach requires the designer to consider six attributes of the designed environment,

namely, space, light, sound, heat, resources (i.e. matter and energy)
and some aspects of human ecology, at three different levels which
may be described as:

(1) the physical effects on the users,
(2) the control of those effects exerted by the design of the
     building, and
(3) the control of those effects through special installations which
     can be brought into use if needed.

This approach includes the consideration of space and the interaction
of people, and can derive some support from studies done by
psychologists. Canter (1977) describes some of the approaches used
to find how people evaluate places, in particular a very simple form of
analysing ratings of places into those which go together, directly or
indirectly, to form related clusters of judgements. One such approach
is outlined by Rump (1974) and may be used to find the 'dimensions'
of people's judgements of particular spaces. Basically, the place is
rated on a five- or seven-point scale in terms of a number of possible
descriptions, e.g. beautiful, calm, busy, clean, airy, etc., and the
correlation coefficients between pairs of items for a group of
respondents are calculated and formed into a matrix. Then, using the
highest coefficient in the matrix first, those items which correlate most
highly with it are extracted, then those which correlate with them are
taken out in their turn. Once that grouping has been exhausted, the
procedure can start again to find the second grouping or cluster of
items. This sort of approach was used to provide the data on hospital
noise in Chapter 4 (Ambient Conditions), and produced clear clusters
of items.

There are always pitfalls for any method. In the one outlined it is
important not to duplicate the same item, otherwise a large cluster of
descriptions will emerge which really only means, say, 'pleasing', but
these methods have advantages. First, language is the normal mode of
communicating and it can be used with great subtlety. At the same
time, rating procedures may reduce the risk of the respondents taking
their cue from the stated or tacit view of an interviewer, or of their
responding in a 'socially acceptable' way. But most useful is just the
clear picture of which items are related, whether the evaluation is
positive or negative.

Other more complicated approaches can also be used. Canter (1972) again furnishes a useful example of this. Using more complex procedures he studied the conceptualisation of a ward in a children's hospital, using items to describe what nursing staff felt about parts of the ward as well as how easy or difficult they were to work in. His results showed that people tended to conceive the ward as three distinguishable spaces comprising the area with beds and play space, the preparation and treatment areas, and the offices and cubicles used by the staff. Interestingly, the nursing station was seen as the psychological focus of the ward linking other parts of it. Given the function of a nurses' station, it is not difficult to accept that this is so, but it need not be, depending upon the design. Moreover, the internalised representation of a building such as a hospital, differs for different groups of people, and Canter's study revealed good agreement between domestic and nursing staff in their positive evaluation of an older children's hospital, while medical staff evaluated a more modern hospital with more sophisticated equipment more highly.

Such methods are increasing the reliability of information about the psychological effects buildings have upon people. Many studies use techniques somewhat similar to these to identify the psychological dimensions of living rooms (Honikman, 1973), shopping centres (Stringer, 1974), or landmarks (Harrison and Sarre, 1974), and even to compare the mental representation of environments of those professionally involved with environments and the general public (Leff and Deutsch, 1973; Sanoff, 1974). Moreover, within social psychology, these methods are widely used to monitor changes in attitudes and judgements to, say, other ethnic groups, before and after acquaintance with them. In principle, there is no reason why these techniques should not be applied in environmental studies to discover what clusters of items are obtained before the design process begins, and at various stages as the product unfolds. It is a moot question whether better communication between users and designers would result, but it is possible that through knowing the *pattern* and *strength* of relationships between various items, and especially by seeing how these change with experience of the design, the designer would obtain a far more reliable picture of what the users really want of their environments.

One other possible advantage to be derived from these departures from the usual question and answer discussion of user needs, lies in avoiding the simplest design solution which presents itself. Lawson (1970) found some evidence among architects for a tendency to work within a narrower range of possible solutions than is necessary, in a laboratory study of problem solving. Perhaps related to this is the finding by Thomas *et al.* (1977) that students, given extensive background data for a complex design problem, namely, to design a restaurant in a former church, showed a negative correlation between the rated practicality and originality of the design.

However, whether these methods are to be successful will depend on their correct application and there are many pitfalls. What you get out depends on what you put in with such approaches, and the first step, which has not yet been taken, will be to produce standardised lists for the person to make his ratings. These lists will have to have been demonstrated to provide reliable information. That is simply to say that we need to have some idea of how well the technique works before we start having faith in it. Trust has to be earned through research and, as things stand today, that research is only just beginning.

Turning to other approaches, Akin (1973) suggests the basic functions of built environments to be four in number, namely, the modification of climate, activity, culture and resources. Any one of these will influence interpersonal interaction so that, not only will the resources largely specify the types of behaviour which can occur, but as noted above, it has also been shown (Rohe and Patterson, 1974) that where there is competition for resources then more aggressive behaviour occurs.

Hillier *et al.*'s (1972) four-function model is rather similar, emphasising the modification of climate, activity, culture and symbolic significance, and resources. This illustrates the degree of agreement in this area, but it is only at a very general level and Beck (1967), for example, argues that for the individual it is his internalised, subjective space which matters and this 'immanent' space incorporates the person's own spatial styles which express their individuality. Again, some research data can be invoked in support of this idea, and people who score high on the dominance end of submissiveness–dominance scales have been shown to use space in ways different from people with lower scores. Esser *et al.* (1965) report that, in a study of behaviour in a hospital ward, dominant people roam widely and freely in their environment, defending no space as belonging to themselves. Lower scorers tended to use more secluded areas as their particular territories.

The range of possible behaviours which can, or may, take place in any setting, may be constrained by the personal or public nature of the place. Thus, personal spaces allow a wider range of behaviours (Taylor and Stough, 1978), while places with highly structured cultural significance, such as art galleries, churches, hospital waiting areas, and so on, produce stereotyped actions which we learn as children are acceptable in these places. There is an (individual, subjective)–(group, shared) dimension to the meaning of places, and the two types of meaning given by Hershberger (1970, 1974) seem to be related to this. His *representational* meaning is, very broadly, the perception of the objective properties of the environment, but his *responsive* meaning covers the feelings and emotions which determine for us as individuals how we react.

Another term, 'congruence', has been used to describe different forms of relationship between the form of, and activity type of, different places (Steinitz, 1968). If we accept Hershberger's distinction which, in broad terms, must surely be unexceptionable, congruence may be perceived as one thing for other people but not necessarily shared by an individual. The extent to which this known group interpretation, even when not shared by the individual, still modifies the individual's behaviour, and the direction of that modification, seems to depend upon the individual's extent of identification or alienation from the social group. Pickpockets may view race meetings or Petticoat Lane markets as excellent business opportunities, or even places to exercise different techniques, like trying the effectiveness of a false arm in a sling while the operating hand remains free under the jacket, but they rarely show the degree of alienation from the group as does the calculating vandal. While Krau (1977) is undoubtedly right that the meaning attributed to situations determines behaviour, it is the ongoing task of psychology and other social disciplines to understand the factors which govern the individual's interpretation and significance.

Adapting to the environment involves processes of selective

interpretation which means that much of the information in familiar places ceases to be processed, being replaced with smaller samples which confirm the properties of that environment, not only in recalling it but even in recognising it. This may underlie the point made by Moore (1979) that, in the main, buildings are remembered in terms of their functional significance rather than their architectural features. The same is true of the natural environment, and we tend to store only general representations of the world though there are individual differences in this and some people have eidetic imagery or 'photographic memories'. It would, however, be wrong to conclude that the building as a setting for activities, is more important to people than its architectural features. The latter must first be processed before the general picture of the environment can be built up and stored, and, since this demands the particular features, they are critical in determining the nature of the general representation which is stored. For this reason architecture plays an important role in governing our perception and behaviour, including social inter-actions, within our built environment, even though, if Moore (1979) is correct, we may more readily store activity possibilities than buildings' specific architectural features. Studies of recognition memory for buildings shown on colour slides have confirmed that recognition is far from perfect, and seems to depend to some extent on factors like the building's spatial position (Sadalla and Burroughs, 1978).

Certainly, Moore's idea is compatible with Ittelson's (1978) division of environmental experiences into four major categories of external objects, self-representations, embodiments of value and arenas for action, as well as with notions of congruence, and stereotyping of behaviour in public places.

The selective interpretation of environments, which is based on the abstraction of general features through sets of transactions between the person and his environment, means that everyone builds up a cognitive pattern of place-identity (see Proshansky, 1978), and although this is personal and internalised, a common scheme of place-identity is shared by people to the extent that they have gone through similar transactions. Because people process information in the same basic ways, there is more communality of place-identity than there is idiosyncrasy. This is not to deny idiosyncrasies exist, but simply to note that they depend upon the uniqueness of person–environment transactions and not on the uniqueness of the person. Functioning in the same ways, and on sets of stimuli which, while they vary from time to time, like the appearance of a building in wet or dry weather, are all transformations of a common referent, leads us to internalise the referent for long-term use. This internalisation is not restricted to any one type of information, visual, auditory or whatever, but is the complex relational network of all available information for that referent. This not only includes all sensory information, but also mood, status and emotional information, in fact anything which can be related to the particular referent. The variations are individually experienced, but the common referent is shared.

These two aspects of human information processing, the storing of activity possibilities and common referents, underlie the development of similar conceptions of our environment, and similar ways of behaving within it. For people to have different conceptions means having different experiences or, like a blind person, an extremely retarded individual, functioning in a different manner. But, to the extent that blind and sighted people have the same auditory or other non-visual experiences, there will be some communality of conception and of place-identity. It is only in some pathological conditions such as extreme autism where there appears to be little or no shared experience of the world around us. In extreme autism the individual is almost totally withdrawn and uncommunicative, avoids looking at other people's faces, makes repetitious movements, and is confused and often angry if anything in the environment changes. At the risk of oversimplifying a very complex condition, this is the sort of behaviour one would expect if there was impairment of the capacity to abstract and, consequently, inability to generalise. The existence of such abnormal conditions may make us realise that functioning in the same way makes people respond in similar ways to their environments, whether conceptualising it or interacting in it. Seen from this perspective, individual differences not due to functional abnormalities are a matter of degree and of one's past experiences. This makes improving people's experiences where environmental conditions are bad more than a way of improving the people, but also an instrument for social unification.

Chapter 7

Ergonomics of Aesthetics

7.1. Aesthetics, Human Information Processing, and 'Dimensions' of Aesthetic Experience

The appreciation of beauty is a peculiarly human characteristic, even though a very great deal of animal social behaviour is triggered and maintained by features of physical appearance or specific behaviour such as courtship dances which we, as humans, may regard as beautiful. The attempt to study the variables which influence our aesthetic experience is one of the oldest areas of experimental psychology, dating back to Fechner's '*Vorschule der Aesthetik*' written in 1876. However, for all Fechner's early attention to the problems and methods of studying aesthetics, progress has been even slower than in areas such as learning, memory or motor skills. Berlyne's books, '*Aesthetics and Psychobiology*' (1971) and '*Studies in the New Experimental Aesthetics*' (1974), attempt to describe mechanisms which may underlie our aesthetic appreciation of the things around us, linking the novelty and complexity of input to the arousal level of the individual. But because of the lack of any well structured theoretical model for aesthetic judgements, most of the experimental findings on aesthetic experience are of limited generality. The age-old golden section, for example, where a space is divided into two parts, A and B, in such a manner that the ratio A:B is the same as the ratio B:A + B, has received experimental attention by, among many others, Berlyne (1969) himself, who managed to show that, if asked to show the major subdivisions in a series of paintings, people tended to divide the pictures close to the golden section. How far this should be attributed to the artists' training rather than the viewers', however, is not clear from this study. But, the results of a more recent empirical investigation (Piehl, 1978), in which varying proportions were rated for their pleasingness, found that the most preferred proportion was the golden section. The golden section or golden mean has, of course, a very long history, and has been the

154

subject of an enormous amount of speculation and analysis. Psychologically, however, it is suggested that, accepting that novelty and a degree of complexity are relevant, the basis of aesthetic preference and tastes is the set of abstracted relationships or schemata described in Chapter 3. This view is shared with Lee (1976), who specifically includes affective properties in his description of socio-spatial schemata which he was researching in the 1950s, making him one of the genuine pioneers of environmental psychology (Lee, 1954).

If this schematic approach is correct then it would be expected that some rapprochement should be possible between artistic and psychological analyses of aesthetic experience. That this is possible can be shown briefly by using some of the Gestalt principles of psychology. These principles refer to some of the ways in which we integrate parts of our perceptual experience. The figure–ground principle allows that by shape, location, colour, contrast, relative size, and so on, features of the environment will be seen either as figure or ground. These are also some of the ways in which artists control the effects their work gives rise to, though few would operate in quite the manner of Fig. 7.1.1 which is produced using random numbers. Similarity, another Gestalt principle is used by artists and architects to unify various parts of their pictures or buildings, most often using colour, though similarity of form and repeated features are common. The principle of 'common fate' can be related to 'line' in paintings and, as in painting, interruption of line may be overcome using the principle of similarity. 'Goodness' of figure, which depends upon factors like symmetry and closure, which are themselves Gestalt principles, is involved in controlling the salience of different parts of a picture, although if the principles create too 'good' a figure it tends to become aesthetically neutral like circles and squares. Finally, perspective or spatial interpretation is produced in painting by utilising the same two-dimensional cues to depth and distance which operate in the geometric illusions or the perceptual constancies, e.g. angles, or the size of the image on the retina, and both of these to produce the relationship between various components of a picture. There is no simple formula for a work of art, but these are a few of the ways we process information which are involved in aesthetically pleasing percepts. Whether one describes them as artistic or psychological principles is irrelevant. For aesthetic experience what

Fig. 7.1.1.   The figure–ground principle.

matters is how they affect our perception, rather than how we
understand these principles.

Various other suggestions have been made and tested. Berlyne,
among others, has theorised that patterns of muscle tensions are
related to our perception of tilt and balance, and this can be taken
further to mediate our perception of disconnection, inharmonious-
ness or even incongruities which can be unpleasant. Sometimes these
are even humorous, as in cases of comedy duos where one long thin
person is contrasted with another short fat one. However, no single
factor, psychological or physiological, can be invoked to account for
the whole range of aesthetic experience, or has been found necessarily
to be involved in all types of aesthetic preferences. Rather, our
judgements of beauty seem to be rooted in our comprehension of the
world, and in our ability to deal with the information presented to us.
The psychology of aesthetics is, therefore, part of the psychology of

Fig. 7.1.2. The 'ghost' transverse lines noted by a number of different people with an interest in vision.

human information processing. This is clearly seen in the borderlines between art, geometric illusions, and what visual scientists would regard as perceptual effects.

An interesting example of the degree of overlap which exists was drawn to my attention by my colleague Michael White of the University of Adelaide. Four illustrations were all produced quite independently even though on inspection they all show the 'ghost' transverse lines running through the junctions between lines (shown in Fig. 7.1.2). In order, this effect was published by Preyer (1897) and Prandtl (1927) studying perception, created by Escher in 1945 as a wood engraving (see Locher, 1974), and noticed on the tiles of his bathroom floor by the ophthalmologist Ronald Schachar whose 'pincushion grid' illusion (Schachar, 1976) was featured on the cover of '*Science*'. Such interesting optical effects can be demonstrated in objects of beauty, but they can also be studied for what they tell us about how we process visual information.

Viewed in information processing terms, aesthetic judgements depend mainly on the ability to integrate the sensory information into a unified structure, and upon the significance of that structure. Thus, for example, people differ in the degree of abstractness or lack of significance which they find acceptable, as well as in the range of distortions of perspective or objects which remain pleasing. Perhaps the main function of the great artist, whether musician, painter, sculptor, architect or whatever, is to educate us to experience the world in new ways. That is, by exposure to their works, to restructure our LTM so that we increase the range of possible integrations of information which we find aesthetically pleasing. Saying that, we must not beg the question of what makes particular integrations pleasing or not, even though any comment must be highly guarded and made very tentatively. Even though aesthetic judgement is an area where there will be little acceptance of any attempt to produce a theoretical understanding, it is not enough to avoid the issue by invoking individual differences between people. There are individual differences in intelligence, personality or special abilities, and we measure these reliably and in ways which are valid for specific purposes, and our predictions made on the basis of tests can (and must) themselves be evaluated against performance. Aesthetic appreciation is, at present, less easily measured because the two standard ways of seeking the truth, counting heads or consulting the wise, have not yet yielded a sufficiently simple interpretation to spread into the social sciences. Counting heads is not uninformative. Depending on what they have been exposed to, communities share certain criteria of acceptability and limitations of ability to interpret an artist's symbolism. Just as Freud originally suggested that particular symbols in dreams would be likely to have similar significances for individuals who shared a common cultural heritage, to the same extent, shared past experiences control our capacity for present aesthetic judgement.

Consulting the wise can, however, be more illuminating and texts like Arnheim's '*Art and Visual Perception*' (1969) can really open eyes which, though previously closed, were almost ready to see and comprehend the work, of, say, Henry Moore.

An understanding of aesthetic judgement is essential for designing pleasing environments, and it is not necessary to assume that some people just inherently possess good taste while others do not. Rather, because our LTM stores relationships, good taste should be viewed much more in terms of an educational advantage which has been derived from interacting with various symbolic representations of the physical or psychological world. This view can be important ergonomically in so far as environments can be designed for use by people whose tastes and judgements are predictable.

For the ergonomist, aesthetics is an interaction of cognitive and emotional processes. Using the simple model of information processing once more, aesthetic judgement is learned as the sets of relationships abstracted from experiences of different environments and objects in them which generalise to new or subsequent environments, becoming the rules and principles by which sensory information is integrated into our perception and understanding of the world around us. Similarly, in large measure our emotional responses stem from our interpretation of the world. Particular patterns of physiological effects can be evoked by fairly specific stimulation such as the startle response which occurs if one is unexpectedly dropped in space. But even that effect owes a great deal to our expectations about the stability of the world and usually does not happen if we have anticipated the event.

Part of our understanding consists of an evaluation, which is not necessarily made consciously, of the environment we live in compared to others. The implications of this evaluation can be so much part of the 'given' of an individual's everyday life that very general features of their self-concept are affected by them, perhaps even controlled by them, without the implications ever being consciously stated. Precisely how strong this effect can be is not well understood, but many studies suggest it is a powerful influence. Taylor, for example, reported that patients in a mental hospital responded positively to the introduction of carpeting on previously bare floors, regarding this as an indication that society still cared about them. However, before considering specific findings it is worth mentioning some of the 'dimensions' of aesthetic experience which have been suggested. Broadly, these fall into two categories depending whether physical or psychological factors are given greater emphasis. Some approaches, e.g. Leopold (1972) attempt to analyse environments in terms of physical factors, biological and water quality factors, and human use and interest factors. Very many questionnaire studies have been performed in the field of environmental aesthetics along broadly similar lines trying to pick out the relevant factors which affect the perception of the environment. To give two examples, Gregory *et al.* (1978) produced a scale to measure the 'benevolence' or 'malevolence' of the environment. This scale is one of many which exist but are not widely used. On the other hand, tests based on measurable aspects of the environment, such as noise levels, have been created for assessing the perceived quality of landscapes, recreation facilities, work environments and many other settings (Craik and Zube, 1976). The Perceived Environmental Quality Index is representative of the group of more frequently used tests.

Other approaches have used ratings of large numbers of slides depicting the environment to analyse the dimensions of preference (Kaplan, 1974). This method produced a number of important factors which can be described as coherence, familiarity, complexity, amount visible, texture and mystery. Mystery seems to be something like the degree to which further information is implied to be available but requires further exploration to be obtained. Climbing the brow of a hill to see what is on the other side, may be motivated by the same properties of the viewed environment which gave rise to the mystery factor. These factors were obtained using the quantitative methods of statistics, although many dimensional models which have been put forward rely on the qualitative judgement of the individual who suggests them. Cupchik (1974) suggested that paintings can be considered in terms of four bipolar dimensions: (1) linear v. painterly; (2) abstract v. representational; (3) multiplicity v. unity; and (4) sombre totality v. bright colour; and experimental evidence (see Berlyne, 1974) been adduced by him which provided four factors which he then terms Classicism, Subjectivism, Complexity, and Expressionism.

For spatial settings Beck (1967) suggested a typology using five dimensions: (1) diffuse v. dense; (2) open v. delineated; (3) vertical v. horizontal; (4) left v. right; and (5) up v. down; which again makes everything rest on the physical environment: whereas Hooper (1978) stresses that people respond to the built environment with *perceptual* responses rooted in cognitive processes, with *evaluative* responses rooted in affective processes, and with *inferential* responses rooted in their symbolic interpretation; which probably underplays physical factors.

Sandhal (1972) also emphasises psychological aspects in expressing the view that an individual's conception of the environment will be a function of prior experience, the social context of the person–environment interaction, and the needs, objectives and relationships of the individual as he understands them within the situation. It is usually only a matter of emphasis, but those writers who place more equal weightings on physical and psychological factors tend to give a prime place to the effect of environments on self-concept and self-esteem. Steele (1970) discusses spatial problem-solving behaviour, with self-esteem determining the acceptability of many environments or the need to change them. The adaptations people make as they try to develop and maintain a sense of competence, self-esteem and identity within whole environments, are noted by Perin (1974), and in a very interesting discussion Sandhal describes how the prescriptions for certain roles are learned and, once internalised, become an integral part of the person. Sandhal also stresses that in building up the person's store of roles, a very important part is played by the environment itself. The adoption of particular roles and self-concept interact, but the point most writers make is that the environment itself partly defines for an individual the functions he or she must perform, in the context of the value others place on those functions, with some abilities and capacities being fostered and sustained by performing those functions, while others disintegrate through disuse or are inimical to the functions which must be performed. In these ways and others like them, the individual is defined, in part, by the environment.

Proshansky (1978) identifies three dimensions of place-identity: (1) cognitive–descriptive; (2) affective–evaluative; (3) role-related; but he stresses that self-identity also depends upon the readiness to shift from one setting to another, and on how adequately the individual uses physical settings. The view expressed at the start of this section would suggest that how well physical settings can be used by an individual is related to the person's capacity to perceive relationships and, if necessary, educe correlates for novel situations on the basis of past experience. But the unfortunate difficulty exists that the higher, and more sensitive, those capacities are, the less satisfactory or acceptable inappropriate environments will be, and the more damaging the effect on self-concept will be unless the individual can move to better environmental settings.

But it is not only self-concept that can be affected by environmental influences. Ertel (1973) reported that giving intelligence tests to children in colourful rooms which were liked by the children, produced IQs which were higher by some 12 points. Since, for properly standardised intelligence tests the mean is 100 and the standard deviation around 15 points, this would appear to be a large difference. When the tests were taken in black, white or brown coloured rooms, which the children are reported not to have liked, IQ scores dropped by 14 points. Without any understanding of the psychological processes mediating this effect it is easy to dismiss results like this, or at least to regard them as of doubtful generality. But if, for argument's sake, the children in the drab rooms were anxious to escape from them, their poor performance could reflect a lack of proper motivation and show that these children were trading accuracy for speed of performance. Since Srivastava and Peel (1968) found adults who were looking at the same set of Japanese paintings spent 30 % more time in the display room if the walls were painted a beige colour than if they were coloured dark brown, it is conceivable that adult intelligence test scores could also reflect the desire to move out of an unpleasing room which could attenuate motivation to perform as well as possible on the test.

Another result reported by Ertel, that over a six month period kindergarten children using beautifully coloured building blocks in an aesthetically pleasing setting had IQs 15 points higher than children in a more conventional kindergarten, is again easy to criticise. It could be argued that parents who chose to allow their children into the less conventional setting were more intelligent anyway. Or that IQs of children under 7 or 8 years are not as reliable as we would need for this sort of research. But equally it could be said that if colour formed an additional dimension for one group, then their practice at manipulating more variables (say number of, pattern or structure of, and colour of the building blocks) then they would be better at tasks involving three dimensions, and many children's tests of intellectual ability require the child to make specific patterns with a fixed number of blocks of different colours. Perhaps the most important point is that until we comprehend *how* aesthetic considerations affect levels of human performance or the sorts of behaviour people choose to engage in, aesthetic considerations will continue to be easily outweighed by factors of convenience and economy, and their possible advantages lost.

Psychologists have made suggestions about the functions of aesthetic experience for us. Berlyne (1971) discusses the commonly accepted ways in which art serves people and lists the four main ones.

1. Providing pleasure, or hedonic tone to use his term, which may among other things determine whether we value an environment and behave protectively towards it or not. Sommer (1974*b*) in his book '*Tight Spaces*' notes the challenge which many forms of hard architectural environments provide for people alienated by them to mutilate or destroy them, and cites subway spray-can artistry as an attempt to soften a hard environment. Vandalism and delinquency are far too complex to be simply explained, but environments which are not valued and regarded as pleasurable, seem to trigger behaviour which is interpreted as aggressive in its motivation and destructive in its effects. Opposite effects are created by objects and environments which are experienced as aesthetically pleasing, as noted in the previous chapter, so that, ergonomically, a degree of control over mood, tension and behaviour can be exercised through the design of an environment and its artefacts. This is taken up again below.

2. Informing us about ways in which we can reshape, transform, translate or symbolise the world.

3. Exercising our information processing capacities. One of the prerequisites for aesthetically pleasing design is that it loads our information processing capacity to some extent. Because we tend to code and store sensory data in the most economical ways we can often reinterpret our experiences into simpler forms. We can see this tendency, e.g. in recalling and reproducing visual material where we make it more symmetrical, more regular than it really was, and we tend to close figures which were open and, in retrospect, to give identity to, or confer a meaning upon figures, which they did not originally have. For examples of these see Birren (1961). Those most simply and economically coded and stored figures which are regular and completely symmetrical, such as circles, squares and so on do not

usually give rise to any experience of an aesthetic nature unless some other dimension, say the relationship between the colour of the figure and the background, adds more sensory information. Similarly, where by repeated experience we are very familiar with an environment, objects in it, like paintings, cease to be sources of information in their own right, and we become aware virtually only of their presence or absence because there is no new information for us to process. At the other end of the spectrum it is easy to create environments or to produce artefacts which cannot be organised into a unified perceptual construct, either by their being too many different elements, or by subsets of them requiring perceptual organisations which conflict with one another. Satisfying aesthetic experiences can only result when, after some perceptual effort or inspection, integration into a unified percept occurs. That is, some degree of complexity which places a loading on our information processing capacities is a *sine qua non* for aesthetic experience. Even in its simplest form, the golden section invokes so many more varied relationships than equally bisected spaces that it evokes an aesthetic response while they do not.

4. Defining our personality or sense of identity. Some comment has already been made on the role of the environment in the development of self-concept but it needs to be added here that environments can also affect people's identification with particular groups and their aims and ideals, as well as promoting their own sense of individuality. The range of such effects is very great and can vary from evoking identification with a nation's history and tradition or its current aspirations, to identifying with small subgroups in society. A trivial example of this occurred in an English city when young couples started buying homes among a neighbourhood of terraced houses which were owned for the most part by elderly people who had lived there for many years. To brighten their surroundings many of the young people painted their front door a bright and vivid colour, and the area was soon altered from a set of uniform green doors to a multiplicity of yellows, blues, reds and oranges. By this simple expedient a change in the character of the neighbourhood was announced and a subgroup of the population was formed. Moreover, the young people's less conservative tastes were advertised. From this information many inferences could be made, influencing further

young couples' perception of the neighbourhood as a possible one to live in.

Finally, Bruner, in his essay '*Art as a mode of knowing*' in his '*On Knowing: Essays for the Left Hand*' (1979), looked at four aspects of aesthetic experience:

(1) connecting experience, which act of comprehension is inherently rewarding,
(2) the requirement for human effort,
(3) the conversion of impulses in emotional effects of beauty, and
(4) generality in aesthetically pleasing experiences.

There can be no substitute for reading Bruner in the original, but the points he makes in his analysis are so compelling that it is worth examining some of the most important.

Discussing the connecting of experience, which I understand as another way of describing what has been termed the integration of information in this text, Bruner suggests two bridges which allow this communication and interpretation, first the making of not *a* but what is in its own context *the* 'tautly economical symbol'.

Second, the 'exploitation of the category of possibility'. Here, Bruner would perhaps agree that schemata built up through experience exist to effect a successfully 'taut' integration of past and present information into a new experience. Bruner's 'category of possibility', or the search for *novelty which is knowable* may well be one of our strong motivations for cognitive experience, although trumped in real-life situations by our need for a world of known and predictable stability, and the primacy of the rules which underpin that. The perceptual constancies can be used to create illusions in psychological laboratories, but they work very well in everyday man–environment interactions to provide correct non-illusory information, so well, in fact, that most people believe the relationships controlling their perception of the world are stable, exact, and derive from the immediate physical world. That it may take the poet, or artist, or perceptual scientist to show we have the capacity for more than our stored experience, is another point we can derive from Bruner's essay. So too is the role of experience at one remove from reality. Novelty which is knowable is safer and more acceptable in *representations* of reality than in the world we live in, and so is exploring the 'category of possibility'.

When he talks of 'effort' Bruner (1979, p. 66) quotes an example in which Gombrich (1954) improved the aesthetic pleasingness of a 'very ordinary academic painting by Bonnencontre' by making it be viewed through unevenly rolled glass. The effort to integrate all that is present, the effort after meaning, is certainly there playing a critical role in aesthetic judgement. But the eventual meaning and accompanying experience achieved is what determines the aesthetic outcome. Would Bonnencontre agree that his painting had become more beautiful by being seen through rolled glass? One cannot be sure, but it seems likely that the artist himself would prefer the stylised beauty of the three graces as he represented them. That is to say, through his eyes, sufficient effort was required by his representation without the use of rolled glass.

On the conversion of impulse, Bruner argues that works of art arouse desires and impulses and afford ways of containing them. Some experiences of beauty may, as in some nude studies, be mediated by sexual arousal which never reaches consciousness in that form, but is reduced in strength and converted from the physical desire to a mental experience, not of sexuality, but of aesthetic satisfaction. Other forms of impulse may also underlie our enjoyment of a work of art. Lautrec's lithograph 'Le Jockey', for example, evokes speed, movement and energy for the viewer, who shares the horse's world rather more than the jockey's.

Bruner's point on generality is like Freud's approach to the symbolic content of dreams mentioned above. Given that individuals are all different, not only from each other, but from their former selves as experiences alter them, nevertheless there is enough constancy and communality in experience to provide us with a shared 'grammar of metaphor'. It may be amusing or irritating to be told that white horses are sexual symbols in dreams, or that spiders may symbolise women, but whatever the reaction one can see some connection between them.

Freud's own view on art was not well or frequently expressed but as a psycho-analyst he leaned heavily on the use of symbols to express the prohibited, and to give some rein to repressed desires. Ernest Jones (1957), Freud's biographer, records Roger Fry's criticism of Freud's views, arguing that rhythm of line, sense of mass and space,

Fig. 7.1.3. The role of shadows.

light and shade and colour, create the experience of aesthetic pleasure by their balance and harmony. From an information processing standpoint both are right, and the only real difference is that we tend to take meaning for granted and fail to recognise it. For example, a circle within a rectangle may have some aesthetic possibilities, whether it does or not, we usually see the circle as *lying in front* of the black rectangle not behind it. Even lines, shapes, light and shadow and colour, are processed by us into meaningful experiences. Take shadows, their placement dictates the meaning of what we are looking at, Fig. 7.1.3 gives examples of this. The truly meaningless is unattainable. The fractionally meaningful, the fragmentation into unconnected meanings, and the ambiguous, bear witness to the human capacity to organise information according to the rules of our experience. Some of these, such as the size of the image on the retina being a cue to depth and distance, even in two dimensions, are so powerful that parallel lines do converge with distance, and, knowing that they do not, alters our stable and comfortable perception of a straight road disappearing into the distance not one jot. That rule is universal for normally sighted people, and it is no accident that, in art, generality derives from the rules of information processing as well as from symbols which are less well abstracted. The meaning of symbols change and the strength, vigour and national unity widely evoked by the swastika in Germany in the 1930s became a threatening and rejected mark of ruthlessness, cruelty and immorality for almost every German in the 1940s. The rules of organisation of our experience change very much less readily and, in that sense, the sort of argument put forward by Fry is correct. But we bring all our store of experience to bear on every situation we encounter, and that includes what Bruner called the 'grammar of metaphor'. Aesthetic experience does not have to be easily put into words to have meaning, or for symbols to have a shared interpretation. Non-verbal metaphors exist and identity and relationships can be implied with lines, shapes and spaces, light and shade and colour. Beautiful or ugly, stable or unstable, worlds can be depicted and emotions can be aroused without the requirement that their identity can be mediated by verbal processes.

It is tempting to suggest that where artists employ symbols or metaphors of too common currency, or where, in Bruner's terms, too little effort is required, or no emotional impulse is generated, then aesthetic judgement will go against the object. But the history of art of all forms shows none of these is true; great innovators can make use of the commonplace, can reduce the amount of effort needed until it seems not to exist, and can act on the individual at cognitive levels so far from any expression of emotion that to suggest any specific emotion would be to invent it. The range of aesthetic experience, through the 'category of possibility', contains rules for organising information which can be derived from the store of abstracted relationships, but which have never been put into operation before, and truly great artists may sense these intuitively and put them to work on us.

If it is true that, in its informative function, art is safer (at least in its more extreme forms of bringing new rules into operation), and more acceptable when at one remove from reality, this implies a distinction between aesthetic objects and aesthetic environments. The poet or painter is constrained by fewer requirements for stability and predictability than the architect, and is more free to explore the principles by which we organise our knowledge of the world. This puts practical limits on the acceptability of 'novelty which is knowable'.

7.2. THE USE OF SPACE AND OBJECTS TO CONTROL BEHAVIOURS

If we accept the foregoing account of the basis of aesthetic judgement, it follows that we can try to control behaviour through aesthetic properties of environments and artefacts in them. Even at the physiological level, the level of arousal of individuals can be increased by factors like the presence of music, the use of angular shapes, or intense primary or secondary colours. At what we might call the pseudo-physiological level, the use of warm looking colours like reds, pinks and oranges may make people believe their environment to be warmer than it really is, and could be used in an attempt to cut heating costs, even though Bennett and Rey (1972) report that this effect is only a belief which does not have much effect on comfort. At the psychological level there are now many examples of people using objects to mark out their territory as well as their dominance (Bell *et al.*, 1978). It is agreed that status can be advertised through objects, providing their significance is agreed upon. But, restricting this discussion to the aesthetic properties of objects, the importance of this has emerged in psychological studies by Canter (1968) and Maslow and Mintz (1956) as well as Berlyne's work mentioned above. Canter's study of the environmental factors which affect us, produced four main dimensions which can be described as 'pleasantness', 'comfort', 'friendliness' and 'coherence'; the last one deriving from responses indicating that the environment should be stable, harmonious and so on. He then tried to determine what specific features affected judgements of pleasantness and the other dimensions, comparing the stated importance of lighting, heating, furniture, noise and other features. The relevance of these as contextual factors for aesthetic appreciation is undoubted.

The effect of the aesthetic nature of the environmental context was shown in 1956 by Maslow and Mintz to affect judgements of the 'energy' and 'wellbeing' of people judged from photographs of their faces. Students acted as experimenters, testing others in one of three rooms. One was an untidy, ugly room with torn, dirty shades and curtains, which had the general appearance of a 'janitor's storeroom in a dishevelled condition'. Another was an 'average' academic office. And the third room was beautiful and well furnished with an attractive rug and paintings and sculptures. Significantly higher ratings were made by students tested in the aesthetically pleasing room. Evidently there is experimental evidence that we can improve others' judgements of ourselves through the environmental appeal of the setting in which they meet us. But what about the effect on ourselves? In a neat way, Maslow and Mintz checked on that too. Each of the student examiners began each day with a 'practice' session of 15 min in which they acted as subjects, ostensibly to familiarise themselves with the procedures once more, but in reality their own scores were compared across rooms. The result of the 'examiners' acting as subjects confirmed the main results, they gave higher ratings in the most attractive room. Mintz (1977) found similar results when his subjects were asked to judge the expressions on faces using photographic negatives. Two rooms, ugly and beautiful, were the settings in which judgements were made. Less favourable responses were made in the ugly room. Some of the subjects in the experiment, when interviewed, appeared to be aware that the aesthetic quality of the room was responsible for the judgements they made.

A different approach adopted by Canter *et al.* (1974) bears on the same issue of context. Photographs of people were superimposed on different backgrounds. Ratings of the same individual differed with the context. It is likely that the complementary effect, where judgements of the background will be affected by the perceived evaluation of the people in them, will also be obtained.

The effect of representing environments negatively was found (Sherrod *et al.*, 1977) to decrease the amount of help their subjects provided when their assistance was sought. Using three variants of the experiment, those subjects who previously had listed more pleasant aspects of their residential environments, spent significantly longer in helping, than those listing more negative aspects. Similarly, viewing slides of attractive or unattractive outdoor environments, created a differential effect upon the time spent helping, and so did focusing more pointedly on the positive or negative aspects of the slides.

Sometimes the influence of environmental features upon behaviour comes as a surprise, and the fact that, more than changes of degree, the direction of judgements, from good to bad, pleasant to unpleasant, can be altered, makes them very important. Sometimes, on the other hand, experimental data simply confirm what is commonly believed to be the case, though they may suggest why it is so. Thus, it is easy to accept that ceilings in many rooms are lower than people would like them to be (Baird *et al.*, 1978), or that the presence of plants tends to create more pleasant environments (Thayer and Atwood, 1978), or that socio-economic and educational factors play a role in determining preferences so that there tends to be agreement within groups but differences between them (Verderber and Moore, 1977). But it may be somewhat disconcerting to discover, as Cunningham (1977) did, that when shown floor plans of apartments, the group tested showed a strong tendency to select those plans on which the living room was situated in the far right, as against the far left, corner. How strongly such an effect would be related to actual choices of apartments, and even differences in satisfaction between people in the two types of accommodation, could be found out, but the reason for such a finding is not obvious. It could be linked to the right-turning tendency mentioned in Chapter 5, and perhaps even to the dominant side of the body being more often the right than the left, but we do not know this, and one could just as easily invoke a left-to-right scanning hypothesis based on reading habits.

The need to load, but not overload, our information processing capacities, and to be able to achieve an integration of the environmental stimuli acting upon us, demands that our environments should not be too cluttered or too complex, and a number of research findings, following Berlyne's lead, relate this to the aesthetic quality of our environment. One point which follows from this is that, because in most natural environments there is little 'clutter', they are less demanding. 'Clutter' is used to mean the sort of multiplicity of different objects, colours, edges and so on which conflict with each other and compete for attention to make themselves figure and the others background. In contrast to this, there are many leaves on a tree, but we group them effortlessly through their similarity, proximity and their significance, and perceive a unitary tree. Compare this to the arrays of styles, objects, signs and symbols which assail us in many urban contexts. It is a recurrent finding that people who seek wilderness areas for recreational purposes are, in general, of higher educational level than the general population (Don, 1978). This may reflect the need to escape from stimulus overload being particularly strong in people whose throughput of verbal information is above average. Just as the speed of jet transport is now so fast that it exceeds the reaction times of pilots who, if they detect a collision course with another aircraft by seeing it, are already too late to avert the crash; in the same way, increases in the rate at which verbal material can be produced, means that input has, for many people, already surpassed their capacity to process it. This may be one factor in the pattern of use of the natural environment.

Scale is also an aspect of the natural environment which reduces 'clutter'. Although, compared to mountains, even small hills do not exactly dash around the environment very busily, moving through them, or past them, gives a similar perceptual effect that watching a light aircraft coming in to land does. The smaller aircraft seems to be travelling much faster than larger passenger aircraft, though the reverse is true. The rate at which classes of salient features alter in the natural environment is also usually slower than in most man-made environments, i.e. vegetation and physical features tend to be similar rather than altering every few metres. This again reduces the 'clutter' overload. While there is some evidence supporting the desire for an 'action-oriented' environment in some roadside settings (Winkel *et al.*, 1969; Brebner *et al.*, 1976), this is more applicable to situations already seriously affected by human intervention. It is the degree of intrusion as well as the nature of the alterations wrought, which affects the perceived quality of the environment. As the impact of potential land development along the roadside was varied from 'sympathetic', i.e. low intrusion, to 'unsympathetic', in a study of a designated highway which was photographically represented (Evans and Wood, 1980), people tended to judge the highway more worthless, useless, cluttered, unpleasant, ugly and drab. These results were obtained by asking for ratings of the low and high intrusions. It is always possible to argue that such results would not be found in real environments, or that 'unsympathetic' alterations can be made acceptable by other benefits accruing from them, like submerging most cities under a spaghetti-like clump of light and power wires to reduce costs. And, in that latter case, because of previous decisions, the costs of altering the situation would often be so enormous, that people prefer the cheaper, intrusive alternatives. But hypothetical arguments that research findings will not apply outside the laboratory are often countered on the grounds that, in the absence of evidence, ignorance is no grounds for inference.

The opposite end of the scale from 'clutter' overload is the sort of bareness deficit which exists in hard and uniform environments which are inflexible and tend to depersonalise those living and working in them.

Wohlwill (1976) notes that Berlyne's 'complexity' is the most frequently invoked in considerations of environmental aesthetics, and gains empirical support from studies like Schwarz and Werbik's (1971) experiment using motion pictures of scaled down model streets. This study found that too little and too much complexity were unfavourably regarded. Complexity was controlled by varying combinations of three different distances of houses from the street, and four possible angles to the street. Two studies by Wohlwill himself, using colour slides, support the relationship between complexity and what Berlyne called 'hedonic tone' (Wohlwill, 1968, 1975), and show that it holds for children as well as adults.

Not all studies support the curvilinear relationship which Berlyne's model between complexity and pleasingness implies, where too little or too much stimulation alike are aversive. However, the point made by Wohlwill (1976), and many other psychologists, cannot be repeated too often: if a relationship is curvilinear, rather than linear, then correlation coefficients will be low and there will appear (rightly) to be no (linear) relationship. This may be why some studies fail to confirm Berlyne's view. If, as suggested here, the natural environment more rarely overloads the perceiver than the urban environment does, then a linear relationship between liking and complexity should be demonstrable for natural settings, but not obtained for built environments if they include the 'clutter' overload aspects of urbanisation. The need to distinguish between natural and urban settings which was stressed by Kaplan *et al.* (1972), is reinforced by these considerations. Fitting neatly into this picture, Schellekens (1978) in making the attempt to identify the general qualities of attractiveness of streets, suggests that both some variety in architecture and the presence of trees produces the best effects without under- or overloading perceptual capacities.

The conclusion that Berlyne's 'complexity' and hedonic tone are related, thus, gains general support from a number of studies other than those of Berlyne, though he and his co-workers did produce experimental evidence, again using slides, that architectural preferences are related to hedonic tone and familiarity, e.g. Oostendorp and Berlyne (1978).

Beyond showing that people react positively to aesthetically pleasing environments, the studies above also suggest that judgements of other individuals may be affected by the aesthetic quality of the environment in which they are encountered.

7.3.   COLOUR—SOME PSYCHOLOGICAL EFFECTS

Within psychology, colour vision is very well understood and many perceived colour effects can be manipulated by controlling the variables which give rise to them. Behavioural effects other than perceptual ones are not well understood, however, and in the experimental literature which exists, studies are sparse and disconnected. There is a strong tendency to regard colour as being determined by the physical attributes of the light which produces the three subjective features of a colour which are, hue, saturation and brightness. It is recognised that colours interact so that the relationships between different colours determine the colours which are perceived. Facts like these are sometimes applied using coloured mortar to change the apparent colour of buildings built in brick, but more often the effects are accidental, or *ad hoc* rather than controlled, even though the rule that 'lighter colours lighten, darker colours darken' is a simple one.

The role which our past experience plays in determining the perceived colour of things around us tends to go unnoticed outside experimental psychology. Yet, knowing that white swans are white makes them still look white on a colour slide even if it is projected through a coloured filter. If a blue filter is used, the usual perception is of white swans bathed in, or surrounded by, blue light. The fact that the swans remain white is due to one of our perceptual constancies, in this case colour constancy; but we also tend to perceive people as being of the same size regardless of how far away they are, and, therefore, compensate for the actual size of the image they cast on the retinae of our eyes, this is size constancy. Shape constancy means that if we know a table top is square, we perceive it to be of that shape, not as trapezoidal which, from many viewing points, is the true sensory impression. These perceptual constancies derive from our experience and include colour.

Texts exist which include some of the effects on behaviour other than the purely perceptual. Birren (1969), for example, mentions a number of research results including Goldstein's (1942) that red excites, and may be connected in some circumstances with aggression. Green operates in the contrary, quieting fashion. But Goldstein was very careful not to claim any simple or inevitable effect, and he noted that red was not always disturbing, though it might stimulate activity. There is a folklore about colours so that even books about colour put out by paint companies (e.g. Walpamur Co. Ltd's '*Colour in Buildings*') includes a statement that pink suggests 'well-being'. Sometimes cultural conventions can imbue colours with meaning, but they tend to be situation specific, like black at funerals or during periods of mourning.

It has been suggested that colours derive their general meanings from the natural environment, so that blue skies, which are that colour because some of the longer reddish wavelengths are filtered out by the earth's atmosphere, are distant and cool. Possibly green, being the predominant colour of vegetation, is more often a context for activities, rather than a stimulus for them. Lüscher (1970) has taken a line that relates the passive connotations of blue to the reduction of activity by primitive man as night fell, and the active significance of yellows and reds to the rising sun heralding the beginning of daily activities. His colour test, which is supposed to reveal features of personality, depends upon some idiosyncratic assumptions, e.g. that blue, green, red and yellow are the 'basic' colours, or again that preferences for brown, grey or black imply a negative attitude to life. Nevertheless, the test is used in some quarters and some success is claimed for it.

There are other attempts linking personality to colour pre-ferences, but in most cases the theoretical basis on which personality differences in colour preferences stands is questionable. Guilford's

(1933) finding that brighter colours are judged to be more pleasant is qualified by Götz and Götz (1975) who showed this to be untrue for introverted people. Their preferences were for quieter, earthy colours rather than the primary colours. Given the wealth of studies showing introverts have low sensory thresholds, these particular results seem to make sense. Preferences for particular colours have often been obtained, so much so that Eysenck (1941) was able to amass over 20 000 such judgements. For what it is worth the general preference went from the most preferred blue, through red, green, violet and orange, and ended with yellow.

However, just as personality factors have been found to correlate with preferences for Romantic or Classical styles of architecture (Juhasz and Paxson, 1978), it seems more likely that personality factors may emerge as relevant when colours are being considered for specific purposes. Certainly, the specific style of domestic interior—Modern, Georgian or Art Nouveau—gave rise to differences in the rank order of colours judged for their appropriateness (Whitfield and Slatter, 1978), and the same authors showed that their subjects' views on what were appropriate colours, varied when they were considering colours for a lounge room or a bedroom (Slatter and Whitfield, 1977). Individual differences in preferred colour intensity and variety would seem to fit the general picture of differences in thresholds, and this together with their past experience of various colour arrangements, seems more likely to underlie people's preferences than any commitment to particular hues. This may be why Pederson *et al.* (1978) found few effects of differing room colours when ratings were taken using a wide range of adjectives, in actual settings of different colour. Nevertheless, research along these lines continues to search for the determinants of preference, just as specific psychological effects are claimed for particular hues (Birren, 1973). The expected word associations with various colours have been found (Odbert *et al.*, 1942), with red being more often 'exciting' and green 'leisurely'; and, given descriptions of various moods, Wexner (1954) showed that her subjects tended to agree in choosing the same colour for many of the moods. Thus, red was once more selected for 'exciting, stimulating', blue for 'secure, comfortable', orange for 'distressed, disturbed, upset', blue and green for 'tender, soothing', black or brown for 'despondent, dejected, unhappy, melancholy', blue and green for 'calm, peaceful, serene', purple and black for 'dignified, stately', yellow and to a lesser extent red for 'cheerful, jovial, joyful', and black, and again red to a lesser extent, for 'powerful, strong, masterful'. From these experiments it appears that people may share general verbal associations for particular colours, but that tested in the manner of Pederson *et al.* (1978), coloured settings do not so reliably produce similar associations.

Colour is also a cue to other attributes, so that objects made of colours which advance toward the viewer, rather than receding, tend to appear heavier than if they recede. While many variables can interfere with the effect colour has on the perceived weight of objects, the heaviest colour is red, followed by blue, purple, orange, green and yellow (see Porter and Mikellides, 1976, p. 99). In the same text it is noted that in warm colours time is overestimated, but in cool coloured settings time is underestimated, and the suggestion is made that cool colours are more suitable where routine or monotonous tasks are to be performed. The basis of these effects is not clear, though one could hazard a guess that, if the warm colouring crowded the individual, time spent in such places would seem longer. As well as time, size (not volume) is also affected by colour so that things in warm colours seem larger than they do in cool colours. Most of these effects are easily observed even if some of them are less readily explained and, along with the relative amounts and intensities of different colours, make colour one of the most influential variables in creating an aesthetically pleasing environment.

7.4. A Last Word

This book was written with the aim of providing those who are most involved in creating and modifying our built environment, not so much with sets of precise dictates and prescriptions, or a compendium of all psychological knowledge, but a more general acquaintance with psychological and ergonomic factors which research has shown to affect the transactions people have with their environments. Having been written by a psychologist primarily for people in other disciplines, there are two ways in which it is hoped this might be of some value, by drawing attention to psychological variables which were not previously known, or realised to be so strong in their effects; and by promoting interactions between people from different disciplines which they find helpful. Since the book is largely about workability, it is appropriate that it stands or falls by whether it serves these functions.

Glossary of Terms and Abbreviations

Amacrine cells:	cells connecting with bi-polar cells which modify their signals.
Anthropometry:	measurement of the body and portions of it.
Aqueous humour:	transparent fluid in the space between the lens of the eye and the cornea.
Basilar membrane:	membrane in the cochlea on which lies the organ of Corti.
Bi-polar cells:	cells connecting with cells on the retina.
Caprylic:	faint, unpleasant odour associated with fatty substances.
Ciliary muscles:	muscles attached to the lens of the eye which vary the focal length of the eye.
Circadian rhythm:	occurring with a frequency about once a day.
Cochlea:	spiral shaped part of the inner ear containing the end organs for hearing.
Cornea:	transparent covering of iris and pupil of the eye.
CRT:	cathode ray tube.
Electromyography:	measurement of electrical activity in muscles.
Ergonomics:	usually the study of people and their work environment. Here used in the broadest sense to mean the study of the workability of built environments.
Extraversion:	personality characteristic of being outgoing and sociable.
Fovea:	small depression on the retina containing many of the elements (cones) involved in pattern vision.
Infradian rhythm:	occurring with a frequency less than once a day.
Introversion:	personality characteristic of being quiet in company and reflective rather than impulsive.

Ischial tuberosity:	bone at the base of the pelvis capable of bearing the weight of the trunk when seated.
LTM:	long-term memory.
Nystagmus:	rapid oscillation of the eyeball.
Organ of Corti:	structure in the inner ear containing hair cells whose movement generates electrophysiological impulses involved in hearing.
Popliteal height:	distance between the heel and the back of the knee. Used in determining seat heights.
Retina:	inner layer of the eye which contains the receptors for vision.
Schema:	set of relationships abstracted from experience which functions as a rule for the translation or interpretation of sensory information.
Sclerotic membrane:	tough, white outer part of the eyeball.
STM:	short-term memory.
TTS:	temporary threshold shift.
Ultradian rhythm:	occurring with a frequency more than once a day.
VDT:	visual display terminal.
VDU:	visual display unit.
Vestibular system:	neural mechanism which receives auditory sense data and adjusts balance.
Vitreous humour:	transparent substance inside the eyeball.

Appendix 2

Conversion Tables

A2.1. METRIC SI UNITS TO BRITISH UNITS AND TO NON-SI METRIC UNITS

Length: 1 millimetre (mm) = 0·039 37 inches (in)
Mass: 1 kilogram (kg) = 2·204 62 pounds (lb)
Force or weight: 1 newton (N) = 0·224 809 pounds-force (lbf)
$$= 0·101\,972 \text{ kilograms-force (kgf)}$$
$$= 100\,000 \text{ dynes}$$
Pressure: 1 pascal (Pa) = 1 newton per square metre (N m^{-2})
$$= 0·020\,885 \text{ pounds-force per square foot (lbf ft}^{-2})$$
$$= 0·010\,197 \text{ kilograms-force per square metre (kgf m}^{-2})$$
$$= 10 \text{ dynes per square centimetre.}$$

A2.2. BRITISH UNITS AND NON-SI METRIC UNITS TO SI METRIC UNITS

Length: 1 inch (in) = 25·4 millimetres (mm)
1 centimetre (cm) = 10 millimetres (mm)
Mass: 1 pound (lb) = 0·453 592 kilograms (kg)
Force or weight: 1 pound-force (lbf) = 4·448 22 newtons (N)
1 kilogram-force (kgf) = 9·806 65 newtons (N)
1 dyne = 0·000 01 newtons (N)
Pressure: 1 pound-force per square foot (lbf ft^{-2})
$$= 47·880 \text{ pascals (Pa)}$$
$$= 47·880 \text{ N m}^{-2}$$
1 kilogram-force per square metre (kgf m^{-2})
$$= 9·806\,65 \text{ pascals (Pa)}$$
$$= 9·806\,65 \text{ N m}^{-2}$$
1 dyne per square centimetre
$$= 0·1 \text{ pascal (Pa)}$$
$$= 0·1 \text{ N m}^{-2}.$$

References

AIELLO, J. R., EPSTEIN, Y. M. and KARLIN, R. A. (1975) Field experimental research in human crowding. *Paper read to Eastern Psychological Association, USA.*

AKIN, O. (1973) Contextual fittingness of everyday activity encounters. In: *EDRA 4*, 1. Ed. Preiser, W. F. E. Dowden, Hutchinson and Ross: Stroudsburg, Pa.

ALLEN, F. and SCHWARTZ, M. (1940) The effect of stimulation of the senses of vision, hearing, taste and smell upon the sensibility of the organs of vision. *J. Gen. Physiol.*, **24**, 105.

ALTMAN, I. (1975) Some perspectives on the study of man–environment phenomena. *Representative Res. Soc. Psychol.*, **4**, 109–26.

ALTMAN, I. and WOHLWILL, J. F. (Eds.) (1976) *Human Behavior and Environment, Vol. 1.* Plenum: New York.

AMERICAN NATIONAL HEALTH SURVEY (1965).

ANGEVINE, O. L. (1975) Individual differences in the annoyance of noise. *Sound and Vibration*, **9**, 40–2.

ARGYLE, M. (1967) *The Psychology of Interpersonal Behaviour.* Penguin Books: London.

ARGYLE, M. and DEAN, J. (1965) Eye contact, distance and affiliation. *Sociometry*, **28**, 289–304.

ARNHEIM, R. (1969) *Art and Visual Perception: A Psychology of the Creative Eye.* University of California Press: Berkeley, California.

ASHRAE: American Society of Heating, Refrigerating and Air-Conditioning Engineers (1960) *Heating Ventilating Air Conditioning Guide, Vol. 38*, 431–3.

AUSTRALIAN STANDARD 1428-1977. *Design rules for access by the disabled.* Standards Association of Australia.

AVERILL, J. R. (1973) Personal control over aversive stimuli and its relationship to stress. *Psycholog. Bull.*, **80**, 286–303.

BACH, L. M., SPERRY, C. J. and RAY, J. T. (1956) *Studies of the Effects of Flickering Light on Human Subjects.* Toulard University: New Orleans.

BAIN, A. (1868) *The Senses and the Intellect.* 3rd edn. Longmans, Green & Co.: London.

BAIRD, J. C., CASSIDY, B. and KURR, J. (1978) Room preference as a function of architectural features and user activities. *J. Appl. Psychol.*, **63**, 719–27.

BALDASSARE, M. (1978*a*) Human spatial behavior. *Am. Rev. Sociol.*, **4**, 29–56.

BALDASSARE, M. (1978*b*) *Residential Crowding in Urban America.* University of California Press: Berkeley, California.

BANDURA, A. (1963) *Behavioristic Psychotherapy.* Holt: New York.

BARKER, R. G. (1968) *Ecological Psychology.* Stanford University Press: Stanford, California.

BARKLA, D. (1961) The estimation of body measurements of British population in relation to seat design. *Ergonomics*, **4**, 123.

BARNETT, S. A. (1976) *The Rat.* Revised edn. ANU Press: Canberra.

BARON, R., MANDEL, D., ADAM, C. and GRIFFEN, L. (1976) Effects of social density on university students. *J. Personality and Social Psychol.*, **34**, 434–6.

BAUM, A., AIELLO, J. R. and CALESNICK, L. E. (1978a) Crowding and personal control: Social density and the development of learned helplessness. *J. Personality and Social Psychol.*, **36**, 1000–11.

BAUM, A., MAPP, K. and DAVIS, G. E. (1978b) Determinants of residential group development and social control. *Environmental Psychol. and Nonverbal Behavior*, **2**, 145–60.

BECK, R. (1967) Spatial meaning of the properties of the environment. In: *Environmental Perception and Behavior*. Ed. Lowenthal, D. Dept. of Geography Research Paper No. 109: University of Chicago.

BELL, P. A., FISHER, J. D. and LOOMIS, R. J. (1978) *Environmental Psychology*. W. B. Saunders: Philadelphia.

BENEDEK, T. and RUBINSTEIN, B. B. (1939) The correlations between ovarian activity and psychodynamic processes: 1. The ovulation phase. *Psychosomatic Medicine*, **1**, 245–70.

BENNETT, C. (1977) *Spaces for People—Human Factors in Design*. Prentice-Hall Inc.: Englewood Cliffs, N.J.

BENNETT, C. A. and REY, P. (1972) What's so hot about red? *Human Factors*, **14**, 149–54.

BERGER, C. (1944) Stroke width, form and horizontal spacing of numerals as determinants of the threshold of recognition. *J. Appl. Psychol.*, **28**, 208–31.

BERGLUND, B., BERGLUND, U., EUGEN, T. and LINDVALL, T. (1971) The effect of adaption on odor detection. *Perception and Psychophysics*, **9**, 435–8.

BERLYNE, D. E. (1969) La section d'or et la composition picturale occidentale et orientale. *Sciences de l'Art*, **6**, 1–5.

BERLYNE, D. E. (1971) *Aesthetics and Psychobiology*. Appleton-Century-Crofts: New York.

BERLYNE, D. E. (Ed.) (1974) *Studies in the New Experimental Aesthetics*. Hemisphere Publishing Corp.: Washington, D.C.

BERRY, C. A. (1969) Preliminary clinical report of the medical aspects of Apollos 7 and 8. *NASA Tech. Memo.* X-58027.

BICKMAN, L., TEGER, A., GABRIELE, T., McLAUGHLIN, C., BERGER, M. and SUNADAY, E. (1973) Dormitory density and helping behavior. *Environment and Behavior*, **5**, 465–90.

BIRREN, F. (1961) *Colour, Form and Space*. Reinhold Publishing Corporation: New York.

BIRREN, F. (1969) *Light, Colour and Environment*. Van Nostrand Reinhold Co.: New York.

BIRREN, F. (1973) A colorful environment for the mentally disturbed. *Art Psychotherapy*, **1**, 255–9.

BJERNER, B., HOLM, A. and SWENSSON, A. (1955) Diurnal variation in mental performance. *Brit. J. Industrial Medicine*, **12**, 103–10.

BLACKWELL, H. R. (1959) Specification of interior illumination. *Illum. Eng.*, **54**, 317.

BLAKE, M. J. F. (1967a) Relationship between circadian rhythm of body temperature and introversion–extraversion. *Nature*, **215**, No. 5103, 896–7.

BLAKE, M. J. F. (1967b) Time of day effects on performance in a range of tasks. *Psychonomic Science*, **9**, 349–50.

BLOOM, L., WEIGEL, R. and TRAUTT, G. (1977) Therapeugenic factors in psychotherapy. Office orientation, sex of therapist, and sex of subject and their effects on therapist-credibility. *J. Consulting and Clinical Psychol.*, **45**, 867–73.

BORNSTEIN, M. and BORNSTEIN, H. (1976) The pace of life. *Nature*, **259**, 557–76.

BRADLEY, T. V. (1959) Direction of knob-turn stereotypes. *J. Appl. Psychol.*, **43**, 21–4.

BREBNER, J. and COOPER, C. (1978) Stimulus- or response-induced excitation: a comparison of the behavior of introverts and extraverts. *J. Res. Personality*, **12**, 306–11.

BREBNER, J., RUMP, E. E. and DELIN, P. (1976) A cross-cultural replication of attitudes to the physical environment. *Internat. J. Psychol.*, **11**, 111–18.

BREBNER, J. and SANDOW, B. (1976) The effect of scale side on population stereotypes. *Ergonomics*, **19**, 571–80.

BRECKENRIDGE, J. R. and GOLDMAN, R. F. (1971) Solar heat load in man. *J. Appl. Physiol.*, **31**, 659–63.

BRITISH STANDARD 3044:1958. *Ergonomic aspects of furniture design.*

BRITISH STANDARD 5810:1979. *Access for the disabled to buildings.*

BRUNER, J. (1979) *On Knowing: Essays for the Left Hand. New edn.* Harvard University Press: Cambridge, Mass.

BUETTNER, K. J. K. (1962) Human aspects of bioclimatological classification. In: *Biometeorology: Proc. Second Internat. Bioclimatological Congr.* Ed. Tromp, S. W. Pergamon Press: Oxford.

BULLOCK, M. I. (1978) The measurement of pull forces for parachute ripcord release. In: *Human factors and contemporary society: Proc. 15th Ann. Conf. Ergonomics Soc. Australia and New Zealand.* Ed. Triggs, T. J. Printed at Monash University: Melbourne.

BULLOCK, M. I. and STEINBERG, M. A. (1975) An anthropometric survey of Australian civilian male and female pilots. *Control*, **2**, 29–43.

BURNS, W. (1968) *Noise and Man.* W. Clowes and Son Ltd: London.

BURTON, A. C. and EDHOLM, O. G. (1955) *Man in a Cold Environment: Physiological and Pathological Effects of Exposure to Low Temperatures.* Edward Arnold: London.

BUSKIRK, E. R. and BASS, D. E. (1957) *Climate and exercise.* Report EP-61, US Army Quartermaster Research and Development Center, Natick, Mass.

BUYTENDIJK, F. J. J. (1931) *Reaktionzeit und Schlagfertigkeit.* Rudolph and Neister: Kassell.

CAIRNEY, P. C. (1979) Testing public information signs. In: *Human factors and the quality of life: Proc. 16th Ann. Conf. Ergonomics Soc. Australia and New Zealand.* Ed. Devereaux, G. Printed at the University of Queensland: Brisbane.

CAKIR, A., HART, D. J. and STEWART, T. F. M. (1980) *Visual Display Terminals.* Wiley: London.

CAMPBELL, D. E. and HERREN, K. A. (1978) Interior arrangement of the faculty office. *Psycholog. Reports*, **43**, 234.

CANTER, D. (1968) Office size: an example of psychological research in architecture. *Architects J.*, **147**, 881–8.

CANTER, D. (1972) Royal Hospital for Sick Children: A psychological analysis. *Architects J.*, **156**, 214–38.

CANTER, D. (1977) *The Psychology of Place.* Architectural Press Ltd: London.

CANTER, D., WEST, S. and WOOLS, R. (1974) Judgements of people and their rooms. *Brit. J. Social and Clinical Psychol.*, **13**, 113–18.

CARLSON, L. D. and HSIEH, A. C. L. (1974) Temperature and humidity. In: *Environmental Physiology.* Ed. Slonin, N. B. C. V. Mosby Co.: St. Louis.

CARLSÖÖ, S. (1976) People with stiff backs should not perform keying tasks. *Arbetsmiljö*, **7**, 23–5.

CARP, F. M. (1976) User evaluation of housing for the elderly. *Gerontologist*, **16**, 102–11.

CARP, F. M. (1980) Environmental effects upon the mobility of older people. *Environment and Behavior*, **12**, 139–56.

CARPENTER, A. (1958) The effects of noise on work. *Am. Occupational Hygiene*, **1**, 42–54.

CATHCART, E., BEDALE, E. M., BLAIR, C., MACLEOD, K. and WEATHERHEAD, E. (1927) The physique of women in industry. IFRB Report No. 44, HMSO: London.

CHAPANIS, A. (1972) Design of controls. In: *Human Engineering Guide to Equipment Design*. Revised edn. Eds. Van Cott, H. P. and Kincade, R. G. US Government Printing Office: Washington, D.C.

CHAPIN, S. F. (1965) The study of urban activity patterns. In: *Urban Land Use Planning*, 2nd edn. University of Illinois Press: Urbana, Illinois.

CHEYNE, J. A. and EFAN, M. G. (1972) The effect of spatial and interpersonal variables on the invasion of group-controlled territories. *Sociometry*, **35**, 477–89.

CHURCHILL, E., CHURCHILL, T., MCCONVILLE, J. T. and WHITE, R. M. (1977) *Anthropometry of women of the US Army*. Technical Report No. 2. The Basic Univariate Statistics. Webb Associates Inc.: Yellow Springs, Ohio.

CLEMENTS, E. M. B. and PICKETT, K. G. (1952) Stature of Scotsmen aged 18–40 years in 1941. *Brit. J. Social Medicine*, **6**, 245.

CMHC (1977) *Housing the handicapped*. Canadian Government Publication NHA 5076.

COERMAN, R. (1970) Mechanical vibrations. In: *Ergonomic and physical environment factors*. ILO: Geneva.

COHEN, S. (1977) Environmental load and the allocation of attention. In: *Advances in Environmental Research*. Eds. Baum, A., Singer, J. and Valins, S. Erlbaum: Norwood, N.J.

COHEN, S., EVANS, G. W., KRANTZ, D. S. and STOKOLS, D. (1980) Physiological, motivational, and cognitive effects of aircraft noise on children: Moving from the laboratory to the field. *Am. Psychologist*, **35**, 231–43.

COLE, C. S. and COYNE, J. C. (1977) Situational specificity of laboratory-induced learned helplessness. *J. Abnormal Psychol.*, **86**, 615–23.

COLLINS, J. B. and HOPKINSON, R. G. (1954) Flicker discomfort in relation to the lighting of buildings. *Trans. Illum. Eng. Soc.*, **19**, 135.

COLQUHOUN, W. P. (Ed.) (1971) *Biological Rhythms and Human Performance*. Academic Press: London.

COLQUHOUN, W. P. and CORCORAN, D. W. J. (1964) The effects of time of day and social isolation on the relationship between temperament and performance. *Brit. J. Social and Clinical Psychol.*, **3**, 226–31.

CONNAN, A. and CNOCKAERT, J. C. (1975) École normale supérieure d'education physique et sportive, Chatenay-Malabry, France. *Travail Humain*, **38**(2), 259–64.

CONRAD, R. and HULL, A. J. (1968) The preferred layout for numerical data-entry keysets. *Ergonomics*, **11**, 165–73.

CONRAD, R. and LONGMAN, D. J. A. (1965) Standard typewriter versus chord keyboard —an experimental comparison. *Ergonomics*, **8**, 77–88.

CONROY, R. T. W. and MILLS, J. N. (1970) *Human Circadian Rhythms*. J. & A. Churchill: London.

CRAIK, K. H. and ZUBE, E. H. (1976) *Perceiving Environmental Quality*. Plenum Press: New York.

CROCK, H. V. (1978) Orthopaedic aspects of workers' compensation with special reference to back injury. In: *Human factors and contemporary society: Proc. 15th Ann. Conf. Ergonomics Soc. Australia and New Zealand.* Ed. Triggs, T. J. Printed at Monash University: Melbourne.

CROUCH, C. L. (1958) A new method of determining illumination required for a task. *Illum. Eng.*, **53**, 416.

CUNNINGHAM, M. R. (1977) Notes on the psychological basis of environmental design: The right–left dimension in apartment floor plans. *Environment and Behavior*, **9**, 125–35.

CUPCHIK, G. C. (1974) An experimental investigation of perceptual and stylistic dimensions of paintings suggested by art history. In: *Studies in the New Experimental Aesthetics.* Ed. Berlyne, D. E. Hemisphere Publishing Corp.: Washington, D.C.

DABBS, J., FULLER, P. and CARR, S. (1973) Personal space when crowded: College students and prison inmates. *Paper read at the Montreal meeting of the American Psychological Association, USA.*

DALTON, K. (1964) *The Pre-Menstrual Syndrome.* Heinemann Medical Publishing Co.: London.

DAMON, A., STOUDT, H. W. and MCFARLAND, R. A. (1966) *The Human Body in Equipment Design.* Howard University Press: Cambridge, Mass.

DANHAUER, J. L., RASTATTER, M. P. and HERMAN, G. (1978) Distinctive features for short-term memory of consonants in noise. *J. Audio Res.*, **18**, 63–8.

DANIELS, G. S. (1952) *The 'Average' Man.* Aerospace Medical Research Laboratory, Wright-Patterson, AFB: Ohio.

DAVIES, B. T. and WATTS, J. M. (1970) Further investigations of movement time between brake and accelerator pedals in automobiles. *Human Factors*, **12**, 559–61.

DAYTON, N. A. (1940) *New Facts on Mental Disorders.* Chas. C. Thomas: Springfield, Illinois.

DELAUZUM, F. R. and GRIFFITHS, I. D. (1978) The problem of individual differences in sensitivity to traffic noise and the establishment of standards. *Internat. Rev. Appl. Psychol.*, **27**, 19–31.

DESOR, J. (1972) Toward a psychological theory of crowding. *J. Personality and Social Psychol.*, **21**, 79–83.

DEVOS-PETIPREZ, C. (1973) A propos des facteurs d'ambiance au poste de terminal d'ordinateur. *Unpublished dissertation.* Department of Occupational Medicine: Lille.

DIEHL, H. S. (1933) Height and weight of American college men. *Human Biol.*, **5**, 445.

DON, A. (1978) Forest recreation in the Adelaide hills. *Unpublished M. Env. Studies Dissertation.* University of Adelaide: South Australia.

DONNERSTEIN, E. and WILSON, D. W. (1976) The effects of noise and perceived control upon ongoing and subsequent aggressive behaviour. *J. Personality and Social Psychol.*, **34**, 774–83.

DREYFUS, H. (1972) *Symbol Sourcebook.* McGraw-Hill: New York.

DUPUIS, H. (1958) Some standards for the design of the tractor driver's workplace. *Paper given to American Society of Agricultural Engineers, Chicago.*

EASTERBY, R. S. (1964) Anthropometric data for machine tool designers. *Proc. 2nd IEA Congr., Dortmund.*

EASTERBY, R. S. (1967*a*) Ergonomics checklists: an appraisal. *Ergonomics*, **10**, 549–56.

EASTERBY, R. S. (1967*b*) Perceptual organization in static displays for man–machine systems. *Ergonomics*, **10**, 193–205.

EASTERBY, R. S. (1970) The perception of symbols for machine displays. *Ergonomics*, **13**, 149–58.

EASTERBY, R. S. and HAKIEL, S. R. (1977) Safety labelling and consumer products: Field studies of sign recognition. *AP Report 76*, Applied Psychology Department, University of Aston in Birmingham, UK.

EASTERBY, R. S. and LAWSON, B. R. (1971) Aids to problem solving in architectural design. *AP Note 27*, Applied Psychology Department, University of Aston in Birmingham, UK.

EASTERBY, R. S. and ZWAGA, H. J. G. (1976) Evaluation of public information symbols ISO tests: 1575 series. *AP Report 60*, Applied Psychology Department, University of Aston in Birmingham, UK.

EAYRS, J. T. and GLASS, A. (1962) *The Ovary.* Ed. Zuckermann, S. Academic Press: London.

ECKENRODE, R. T. and ABBOT, W. C. (1959) *The Response of Man to His Environment.* Dunlap and Associates: Stanford, Connecticut.

ERTEL, H. (1973) Blue is beautiful. *Time*, September.

ESSER, A. H., CHAMBERLAIN, A. S., CHAPPLE, E. D. and KLINE, N. S. (1965) Territoriality of patients in a research ward. *Recent Advances in Biolog. Psychiatry*, **7**, 36–44.

EVANS, G. W. and WOOD, K. W. (1980) Assessment of environmental aesthetics in scenic highway corridors. *Environment and Behavior*, **12**, 255–73.

EYSENCK, H. J. (1941) A critical and experimental study of color preferences. *Am. J. Psychol.*, **54**, 385–94.

FAIRBANKS, L. A. (1977) The ethological study of four psychiatric wards: Patients, staff and system behaviors. *J. Psychiatric Res.*, **13**, 193–209.

FALK, S. A. and WOODS, N. F. (1973) Hospital noise-levels and potential health hazards. *New England J. Medicine*, **289**, 774–80.

FARIS, R. E. L. and DUNHAM, H. W. (1939) *Mental Disorders in Urban Areas.* University of Chicago Press: Chicago.

FARRIMOND, T. (1959) Age differences in ability to use visual cues in auditory communication. *Language and Speech*, **2**, 179–92.

FECHNER, G. T. (1876) *Vorschule der Aesthetik.* Breitkopf & Härtel: Leipzig.

FESTINGER, L., SCHACHTER, S. and BACK, K. (1950) *Social Pressures in Informal Groups: A Study of Human Factors in Housing.* Stanford University Press: Stanford, California.

FIELD, H. H. (1973) Environmental design implications of a changing health care system. In: *Environment and Cognition.* Ed. Ittelson, W. H. Seminar Press: New York.

FIFE, D. and RAPPAPORT, E. (1976) Noise and hospital stay. *Am. J. Public Health*, **66**, 680–1.

FINKELMAN, J. M. and GLASS, D. C. (1974) A reappraisal of the relationship between noise and human performance by means of a subsidiary task measure. *J. Appl. Psychol.*, **54**, 211–13.

FISHER, M. B. and BIRREN, J. E. (1946) Standardization of a test of hand strength. *J. Appl. Psychol.*, **30**, 380–7.

FLOYD, W. F. and ROBERTS, D. F. (1958) Anatomical, physiological and anthropometric principles in the design of office chairs and tables. *British Standard No. 3044*, British Standards Institution: London.

FOLEY, P. J. (1956) Evaluation of angular digits and comparison with a conventional set. *J. Appl. Psychol.*, **40**, 178–80.

FOVEMAN, J. E. K., EMMERSON, M. A. and DICKINSON, S. M. (1974) Noise level—attitudinal surveys of London and Woodstock, Ontario. *Sound and Vibration*, **8**, 16–22.

FOWLER, C. J. and WILDING, J. (1979) Differential effects of noise and incentives on learning. *Brit. J. Psychol.*, **70**, 149–53.

FREEDMAN, J. L. (1975) *Crowding and Behaviour*. Freeman: San Francisco.

FRIED, M. (1963) Grieving for a lost home. In: *The Urban Conditions*. Ed. Duhl, L. J. Basic Books: New York.

GALLÉ, O. R., GOVE, W. R. and MCPHERSON, J. M. (1972) Population density and pathology: What are the relationships for man? *Science*, **176**, 23–30.

GARFINKEL, M. (1964) Studies in the routine grounds of everyday activities. *Social Problems*, **11**, 225–50.

GEEN, R. G. (1978) Effects of attack and uncontrollable noise on aggression. *J. Res. Personality*, **12**, 15–29.

GEISSLER, L. R. (1915) Sound localization under determined expectation. *Am. J. Psychol.*, **26**, 268.

GELFAND, D. M., HARTMAN, D. P., WALDER, P. and PAGE, B. (1973) Who reports shoplifters? *J. Personality and Social Psychol.*, **25**, 276–85.

GLANVILLE, A. D. and KREEZER, G. (1937) The maximum amplitude and velocity of joint movements in normal male human adults. *Human Biol.*, **9**, 197.

GLENCROSS, D. J. (1977) Learning to type. In: *Ergonomics in Australia, 1977: Proc. 14th Ann. Conf. Ergonomics Soc. Australia and New Zealand*. Ed. Brebner, J. University of Adelaide: South Australia.

GOLDMAN, D. E. (1948) A review of subjective responses to vibratory motion of the human body in the frequency range 1–70 cycles per second. *Report No. 1, Project NM-004-001*. US Navy Medical Research Institute: Bethesda, Maryland.

GOLDMAN, R. F. (1973) Clothing, its physiological effects, adequacy in extreme thermal environments, and possibility of future improvements. *Arch. Sci. Physiol.*, **27**, 137–47.

GOLDSTEIN, K. (1942) Some experimental observations concerning the influence of color on the function of the organism. *Occupational Therapy and Rehabilitation*, **21**, 147–51.

GOMBRICH, E. (1954) Psychoanalysis and the history of art. *Internat. J. Psychol.*, **35**, 401–11.

GÖTZ, K. O. and GÖTZ, K. (1975) Color preferences, extraversion, and neuroticism of art students. *Perceptual and Motor Skills*, **41**, 919–30.

GRANDJEAN, E. (1971) *Fitting the Task to the Man—An Ergonomic Approach*. Taylor and Francis Ltd: London.

GRANDJEAN, E. (1973) *Ergonomics of the Home*. Taylor and Francis Ltd: London.

GREENE, R. and DALTON, K. (1953) The premenstrual syndrome. *Brit. Medical J.*, **1**, 1007–14.

GREGORY, R. L. (1973) *Eye and Brain, 2nd edn.* Wiedenfeld and Nicolson: London.

GREGORY, W. L., BRENNAN, G. T., STEINER, I. D. and DETRICK, A. (1978) A scale to measure benevolent versus malevolent perceptions of the environment. *Catalogue of Selected Documents in Psychol.*, **8**, 36.

GRETHER, W. F. (1971) Vibration and human performance. *Human Factors*, **13**, 203–16.

GUIGNARD, J. C. and IRVING, A. (1960) Effects of low frequency vibration in man. *Engineering*, **190**, 364–7.

GUILFORD, J. P. (1933) The affective value of color as a function of hue, tint and chroma. *Psycholog. Bull.*, **30**, 679.

GUNN, W. J., SHIGEHISA, T. and SHEPHERD, W. T. (1977) Annoyance response to spectrally modified recorded aircraft noise during television-viewing. *J. Audio Res.*, **17**, 241–9.

HABER, R. N. and ERDELYI, M. H. (1967) Emergence and recovery of initially unavailable perceptual material. *J. Verbal Learning and Verbal Behavior*, **6**, 618–28.

HALBERG, F. (1964) Physiological rhythms. In: *Physiological Problems in Space Exploration.* Ed. Hardy, J. D. Chas. C. Thomas: Springfield, Illinois.

HALBERG, F. and AHLGREN, A. (1979) Chronobiology—1979. *Internat. J. Chronobiol.*, **6**, 145–62.

HALL, E. T. (1966) *The Hidden Dimension.* Doubleday: New York.

HANSEN, R. and CORNOG, D. Y. (1958) *Annotated bibliography of applied physical anthropology in human engineering.* USAF, WADD, TR 56-30.

HARRIS, C. S. and SOMMER, H. C. (1973) Interactive effects of intense noise and low-level vibration. *Aerospace Medicine*, **44**, 1013–16.

HARRISON, J. and SARRE, P. (1974) Personal construct theory and the measurement of environmental images. *Environment and Behavior*, **6**, 3–58.

HAUTY, G. T. and ADAMS, T. (1966) Phase shifts of the human circadian system and performance deficit during the periods of transition; I. East–West flight. *Aerospace Medicine*, **37**, 668–74. II. West–East flight. *Aerospace Medicine*, **37**, 1027–33.

HENDY, K. (1978) Australian Tri-Service Anthropometric Survey, 1977. In: *Human factors and contemporary society: Proc. 15th Ann. Conf. Ergonomics Soc. Australia and New Zealand.* Ed. Triggs, T. J. Printed at Monash University: Melbourne.

HERSHBERGER, R. G. (1970) A study of meaning and architecture. In: *EDRA 1.* Ed. Preiser, W. F. E. Dowden, Hutchinson and Ross: Stroudsburg, Pa.

HERSHBERGER, R. G. (1974) Predicting the meaning of architecture. In: *Designing for Human Behavior.* Eds. Lang, J. *et al.* Dowden, Hutchinson and Ross: Stroudsburg, Pa.

HERTZBERG, H. T. E. (1972) Engineering anthropology. In: *Human Engineering Guide to Equipment Design.* Eds. Van Cott, H. P. and Kincade, R. G. US Government Printing Office: Washington, D.C.

HERTZBERG, H. T. E., DANIELS, G. S. and CHURCHILL, E. (1954) *Anthropometry of flying personnel—1950.* USAF, WADC. TR 52-321.

HICK, W. E. and BATES, J. A. V. (1950) The human operator of control mechanisms. *Ministry of Supply, Res. and Development Monograph*, No. 17, 204.

HIGH, T. and SUNDSTROM, E. (1977) Room flexibility and space use in a dormitory. *Environment and Behavior*, **9**, 81–90.

HILLIER, B., MUSGRAVE, J. and O'SULLIVAN, P. (1972) Knowledge and design. In: *EDRA 3, Vol. II*, 129–30. Ed. Mitchell, W. J. University of California Press: Los Angeles.

HITT, W. D. (1961) An evaluation of five different coding methods. *Human Factors*, **3**, 120–30.

HOLAHAN, C. U., WILCOX, B. L., BURNAM, M. A. and CULLER, R. E. (1978) Social satisfaction and friendship formation as a function of floor level in high rise student housing. *J. Appl. Psychol.*, **63**, 529–31.

HONIKMAN, B. (1973) Personal construct theory and environmental evaluation. In: *EDRA 1*, 242–53. Ed. Preiser, W. F. E. Dowden, Hutchinson and Ross: Stroudsburg, Pa.

HOOD, W. B. *et al.* (1966) Cardiopulmonary effects of whole body vibration in man. *J. Appl. Physiol.*, **21**, 1725.

HOOPER, K. (1978) Perceptual aspects of architecture. In: *Handbook of Perception, Vol. 10*. Eds. Carterette, E. C. and Friedman, M. P. Academic Press: New York.

HOOTON, E. A. (1945) *A Survey in Seating*. Heywood-Wakefield Co.: Gardner, Mass.

HOOTON, E. A. and DUPERTUIS, C. W. (1951) Age changes and selective survival in Irish male. *Studies in Physical Anthropology, No. 2*. American Association of Physical Anthropology.

HORINO, S. (1977) Environmental factors and work performance of foundry workers. *J. Human Ergology*, **6**, 159–66.

HORNICK, R. J. (1962) Effects of whole-body vibration in three directions upon human performance. *J. Eng. Psychol.*, **1**, 93–101.

HUTT, C. and VAIZEY, M. J. (1966) Differential effects of group density on social behaviour. *Nature*, **209**, 1371–2.

INTERNATIONAL LABOUR OFFICE/ENTE NAZIONALE PREVENZIONI INFORTUNI (1970) *Proc. Symp. Rome 16–21 September, 1968*. ILO: Geneva.

INTERNATIONAL ORGANIZATION FOR STANDARDIZATION (1961) Rating noise with respect to hearing conservation, speech communication and annoyance. *Technical Committee 43, Acoustics, Secretariat-139*.

ISRAEL, H. (1938) Premenstrual tension. *J. Am. Medical Assoc.*, **110**, 1721–3.

ITTELSON, W. H. (1978) Environmental perception and urban experience. *Environment and Behavior*, **10**, 193–213.

JACKSON, C. (1953) Visual factors in auditory localization. *Quarterly J. Experimental Psychol.*, **5**, 52.

JACOBS, J. (1961) *The Death and Life of Great American Cities*. Random House: New York.

JAEGER, K. J. (1980) Hospital personnel: Annoyance by noise in the hospital and associated personality correlates. *Unpublished B.A.(Hons.) thesis*. University of Adelaide: South Australia.

JAKLE, J. A., BRUNN, S. and ROSEMAN, C. C. (1976) *Human Spatial Behaviour: A Social Geography*. Wadsworth Publishing Co. Inc.: California.

JAKOVLEV, P. A. (1940) The effect of sound on the limits of visual colour fields. *Vestn. Oftal.*, **17**, 459.

JENKINS, W. O. (1947) Tactual discrimination of shapes for coding aircraft-type controls. In: *Psychological Research on Equipment Design*. Ed. Fitts, P. M. US Government Printing Office: Washington, D.C.

JOHNSON, G. B. (1932) The effects of periodicity in learning to walk a tight wire. *J. Comparative Psychol.*, **13**, 133–41.

JOINER, D. (1976) Social ritual and architectural space. In: *Environmental Psychology: People and their Physical Settings, 2nd edn*. Eds. Proshansky, H. M., Ittelson, W. H. and Rivlin, L. G. Holt, Rinehart and Winston: New York.

JONES, E. (1957) *Sigmund Freud: Life and Work, Vol. 3*. The Hogarth Press: London.

JONES, J. W. (1978) Adverse emotional reactions of nonsmokers to secondary cigarette smoke. *Environmental Psychol. and Nonverbal Behavior*, **3**, 125–7.

JUHASZ, J. B. and PAXSON, L. (1978) Personality and preference for architectural style. *Perceptual and Motor Skills*, **47**, 241–2.

KALT, N. C. and ZALKIND, S. S. (1976) Effects of some publicly financed housing programs for the urban poor. *J. Communicating Psychol.*, **4**, 298–302.

KAPLAN, R. (1974) Some methods and strategies in the prediction of preference. In: *Landscape Assessment: Values, Perceptions and Resources*. Eds. Zube, E. H., Fabos, J. G. and Brush, R. O. Dowden, Hutchinson and Ross: Stroudsburg, Pa.

KAPLAN, S., KAPLAN, R. and WENDT, J. S. (1972) Rated preference and complexity for natural and urban visual material. *Perception and Psychophysics*, **12**, 334–56.

KATSIKITIS, M. and BREBNER, J. (1980) Individual differences in the effects of personal space invasion: A test of the Brebner–Cooper model of extraversion. *Personality and Individual Differences*, in press.

KEMSLEY, W. F. F. (1950) Weight and height of a population in 1943. *Ann. Eugenics*, **15**, 161.

KEMSLEY, W. F. F. (1957) *Women's Measurements and Sizes*. HMSO: London.

KING, B. G. (1948) Measurements of man for making machinery. *Am. J. Physical Anthropol.*, **6**, 341–52.

KING, B. G., MARROW, D. J. and VOLLMER, E. P. (1947) Cockpit studies—the boundaries of the maximum area for the operation of manual controls. *Naval Medical Institute Report No. 3*, Bethesda, Maryland, 15 July.

KLEITMAN, N. (1963) *Sleep and Wakefulness*. University of Chicago Press: Chicago.

KLEMMER, E. T. (1971) Keyboard entry. *Appl. Ergonomics*, **211**, 2–16.

KNOWLAND, R. (1976) Searching for the golden gift of peace and quiet. *Health and Social Services J.*, **86**, 1900–1.

KNOWLES, E. S. and BASSETT, R. I. (1976) Groups and crowds as social entities: Effects of activity, size and member similarity on nonmembers. *J. Personality and Social Psychol.*, **34**, 837–45.

KOFFKA, K. (1935) *Principles of Gestalt Psychology*. Harcourt: New York.

KOHFELD, D. L. and GOEDECKE, D. W. (1978) Intensity and predictability of background noise as determinants of simple reaction time. *Bull. Psychonomic Soc.*, **12**, 129–32.

KONEČNI, V. J. (1975) The mediation of aggressive behavior: Arousal level versus anger and cognitive labelling. *J. Personality and Social Psychol.*, **32**, 706–12.

KONEČNI, V. J., LIBUSER, L., MORTON, H. and EBBESEN, E. B. (1975) Effects of a violation of personal space on escape and helping responses. *J. Experimental and Social Psychol.*, **11**, 288–99.

KORTE, C. (1980) Helpfulness in the urban environment. In: *Advances in Environmental Psychology*. Eds. Baum, A., Singer, J. and Valins, S. Erlbaum: Norwood, N.J.

KORTE, C. and KERR, N. (1975) Responses to altruistic opportunities under urban and rural conditions. *J. Social Psychol.*, **95**, 183–4.

KRAU, E. (1977) Subjective dimension assignment through set to objective situations. In: *Personality at the Crossroads: Current Issues in Interactional Psychology.* Eds. Magnusson, D. and Endler, N. S. Erlbaum: Hillsdale, N.J.

KRAVKOV, S. V. (1936) The influence of sound upon the light and colour sensitivity of the eye. *Acta. Ophthal.*, **14**, 348.

KRAVKOV, S. V. (1939a) The influence of the loudness of the indirect sound stimulus on the colour sensitivity of the eye. *Acta. Ophthal.*, **17**, 324.

KRAVKOV, S. V. (1939b) The influence of loudness of accessory aural stimulus on colour sensitivity of the eye. *Vestn. Oftal.*, **15**, 100.

KRYTER, K. D. (1970) *The Effects of Noise on Man.* Academic Press: New York.

KRYZHANOVSKAYA, V. V. and NAVAKATIKAYAN, A. O. (1970) Age-related changes in the information processing capacities of the visual analysers in people working at intellectual tasks. *Gigena Truda i Professional'nye Zabolevaniza*, **7**, 28–32. (English summary.)

LANDSELL, H. (1954) The effect of form on the legibility of numbers. *Canadian J. Psychol.*, **8**, 77–9.

LANG, J., BURNETTE, C., MOLESKI, W. and VACHON, D. (Eds.) (1974) *Designing for Human Behavior: Architecture and the Behavioral Sciences.* Community Development Series, Vol. 6. Dowden, Hutchinson and Ross: Stroudsburg, Pa.

LANGE, K. O. and COERMANN, R. R. (1962) Visual acuity under vibration. *Human Factors*, **4**, 291–300.

LAUBACH, L. L., McCONVILLE, J. T., CHURCHILL, E. and WHITE, R. M. (1977) *Anthropometry of Women of the US Army.* Technical Report No. 1. Methodology and Survey Plan. Webb Associates Inc.: Yellow Springs, Ohio.

LAWSON, B. R. (1970) Open and closed ended problem solving in architectural design. In: *Proc. Architectural Psychol. Conf.* Kingston Polytechnic Institute: Kingston upon Thames, UK.

LE BON, G. (1968) *The Crowd.* Ballantine: New York. (Originally published in 1895.)

LEE, T. R. (1954) A study of urban neighbourhood. *Ph.D. Dissertation.* University of Cambridge, UK.

LEE, T. R. (1976) *Psychology and the Environment.* Methuen: London.

LEFF, H. S. and DEUTSCH, P. S. (1973) Construing the physical environment: differences between environmental professionals and lay people. In: *EDRA 1.* Ed. Preiser, W. F. E. Dowden, Hutchinson and Ross: Stroudsburg, Pa.

LEHMANN, G. (1962) *Pratische Arbeitphysiologie.* Thieme: Stuttgart.

LE MAY, M. and ARONOW, E. (1977) Some determinants of lingering behavior in a suburban shopping centre. *Perceptual and Motor Skills*, **45**, 1202.

LENNARD, S. H. and LENNARD, H. L. (1977) Architecture: Effect of territory, boundary, and orientation on family functioning. *Family Process*, **16**, 49–66.

LEOPOLD, L. (1972) Landscape aesthetics. In: *Human Identity in the Urban Environment.* Eds. Bell, G. and Tyrwhitt, J. Penguin Books Ltd: Harmondsworth, UK.

LEVY-LEBOYER, C., VEDRENNE, B. and VEYSSIERE, M. (1977) Differentiating sources of noise. *Psychol. Francaise*, **22**, 69–80.

LEWIN, K. and FREUND, A. (1930) Untersuchungen zur handlungsund affekt-psychologie, VII Psychische sattigung im menstruum und intermenstruum. *Psychologische Forschung*, **13**, 198–217.

LINDSAY, P. H. and NORMAN, D. A. (1972) *Human Information Processing.* Academic Press: New York.

LOCHER, J. L. (Ed.) (1974) *The World of M. C. Escher.* Abrams: New York.

LORD, B. and FINLAY, D. C. (1978) Effects of noise on access to recent memory. *Perceptual and Motor Skills,* **47**, 168–70.

LOWIN, A., HOTTES, J. H., SANDLER, B. E. and BORNSTEIN, M. (1971) The pace of life and sensitivity to time in urban and rural settings: a preliminary study. *J. Social Psychol.,* **83**, 247–53.

LÜSCHER, M. (1970) *The Lüscher Color Test.* Jonathan Cape: London.

LYTHGOE, R. J. (1932) The measurement of visual acuity. *MRC Special Report Series No. 173.* HMSO: London.

McCANCE, R. A., LUFF, M. C. and WIDDOWSON, E. E. (1937) Physical and emotional periodicity in women. *J. Hygiene,* **37**, 571–611.

McCARTHY, D. and SAEGART, S. (1978) Residential density, social overload, and social withdrawal. *Human Ecology,* **6**, 253–72.

McCORMICK, E. J. (1976) *Human Factors in Engineering and Design, 4th edn.* McGraw-Hill: New York.

MacDONALD, J. and McGURK, H. (1978) Visual influences on speech perception processes. *Perception and Psychophysics,* **24**, 253–7.

McFARLAND, R. A., DAMON, A., STOUDT, H. W., MOSELEY, A. L., DUNLAP, J. W. and HALL, W. A. (1954) *Human Body Size and Capabilities in the Design and Operation of Vehicular Equipment.* Harvard School of Public Health: Boston, Mass.

McKENNELL, A. (1971) *Second Survey of Aircraft Noise around London (Heathrow) Airport.* HMSO: London.

McLEAN, E. K. and TARNOPOLSKY, A. (1977) Noise discomfort and mental health. A review of the socio-medical implications of disturbance by noise. *Psychological Medicine,* **7**, 19–62.

MACHLE, W. (1945) The effect of gun blast on hearing. *Arch. Otolarnyg.,* **42**, 164–8.

MACKWORTH, N. H. (1950) Researches on the measurement of human performance. *MRC Special Report Series No. 268.* HMSO: London.

MARCOEN, A. and HOUBEN, M. L. (1975) Formal aspects of the behaviour of individually and collectively living elderly. *Ned. Tijdsch. voor Gerontol.,* **6**, 82–9.

MASLOW, A. H. and MINTZ, N. L. (1956) Effects of aesthetic surroundings 1. Initial short-term effects of three aesthetic conditions upon perceived 'energy' and 'well-being' in faces. *J. Psychol.,* **41**, 247–54.

MATTHEWS, K. E. and CANON, L. K. (1975) Environmental noise level as a determinant of helping behaviour. *J. Personality and Social Psychol.,* **32**, 571–7.

MAY, J. and WRIGHT, H. B. (1961) Heights and weights of businessmen. *Trans. Ass. Ind. Med. Off.,* **11**, 143.

MELTON, A. W. (1936) Distribution of attention in galleries in a museum of science and industry. *Museum News,* **14**, 5–8.

MELTON, A. W. (1972) Visitor behaviour in museums: Some early research in environmental design. *Human Factors,* **14**, 393–403.

MERTON, R. K. (1947) The social psychology of housing. In: *Current Trends in Social Psychology.* Ed. Dennis, W. University of Pittsburgh Press: Pittsburgh.

MILGRAM, S. (1970) The experience of living in cities. *Science,* **167**, 1461–8.

MILGRAM, S., BICKMAN, L. and BERKOWITZ, L. (1969) Note on the drawing power of crowds of different size. *J. Personality and Social Psychol.,* **13**, 79–82.

MILLER, G. A. (1956) The magical number seven plus or minus two: some limits on our capacity for processing information. *Psycholog. Rev.*, **63**, 81–97.

MILLER, T. L. (1978) Behavioral and spatial change in response to an altered behavioral setting. *Environmental Psychol. and Nonverbal Behavior*, **3**, 23–42.

MINISTRY OF MUNITIONS (Great Britain) (1917) *Health of Munitions Workers Committee. Industrial Efficiency and Fatigue.* (Cd. 8511). HMSO: London.

MINTZ, N. L. (1977) Studies extending Schachtel's developmental theories: Problematic aspects of aesthetic encounters. *Contemporary Psychoanalysis*, **13**, 261–86.

MITCHELL, R. E. (1971) Some social implications of high density housing. *Am. Sociology Rev.*, **36**, 18–29.

MONCRIEFF, R. W. (1970) *Odours.* William Heinemann Medical Books Ltd: London.

MOORE, G. T. (1979) Knowing about environmental knowing: the current state of theory and research on environmental cognition. *Environment and Behavior*, **11**, 1979.

MOOS, R. H. (1978) Social environments of university students living groups: Architectural and organizational correlates. *Environment and Behavior*, **10**, 109–26.

MORGAN, C. T., COOK, J. S., CHAPANIS, A. and LUND, M. W. (Eds.) (1963) *Human Engineering Guide to Equipment Design.* McGraw-Hill Inc.: New York.

MULLINS, P. and ROBB, J. H. (1977) Residents' assessment of a New Zealand public housing scheme. *Environment and Behavior*, **9**, 573–624.

MURRELL, K. F. H. (1971) *Ergonomics.* Chapman and Hall: London.

MYERS, D. H. and DAVIES, P. (1978) The seasonal incidence of mania and its relationship to climatic variables. *Psycholog. Medicine*, **8**, 433–40.

NATIONAL BUREAU OF STANDARDS (1977) *Power lawn mowers: Evaluation of anthropometric foot probes.* Human Factors Section, Consumer'Product Safety Commission Report No. NBSIR-77-1294, Washington, D.C.

NEWMAN, O. (1972) *Defensible Space.* Macmillan: New York.

O'BRIEN, R. and SHELTON, W. C. (1941) Women's measurements for garment and pattern construction. *US Dept Agric., Misc. Publication No. 454.* Prepared in co-operation with Textile and Clothing Division, Bureau of Home Economics.

ODBERT, H. S., KARWOSKI, T. S. and ECKERSON, A. B. (1942) Studies in synesthetic thinking: 1. Musical and verbal associations of color and mood. *J. Gen. Psychol.*, **26**, 153–73.

OGDEN, F. W. (1944) Ear plug protection against noise and concussion of gunfire. *USAF Av. Med. Tech. Report 1, Project 326.*

OLDFIELD, S. (1979) *The role of the pinna in auditory localization.* Invited Seminar given at the Department of Psychology, University of Adelaide, South Australia.

OOSTENDORP, A. and BERLYNE, D. E. (1978) Dimensions in the perception of architecture: III. Multidimensional preference scaling. *Scandinavian J. Psychol.*, **19**, 145–50.

ORLANSKY, J. (1948) The human factor in the design of stick and rudder controls for aircraft. *Report SPECDEVCEN-151-1-8.* US Naval Training Devices Center: Port Washington, New York.

OSHIMA, M., FUJIMOTO, T., OGURO, T., TOBIMATSU, N. and MORI, T. (1962) *Anthropometry of Japanese Pilot.* Japanese Air Self-Defense Force, Tokyo Aero-Medical Lab. Final Report, March 1961–March 1962.

OSMOND, H. (1957) Function as the basis of psychiatric ward design. *Mental Hospitals*, **8**, 23–9.

ÖSTBERG, O. (1976) *Designing CRT Workplaces. A Handbook.* (In Swedish.) Stätskontoret: Stockholm.

OTTENSMANN, J. R. (1978) Social behavior in urban space. *Urban Life*, **7**, 3–27.

OXFORD, H. W. (1969) Anthropometric data for educational chairs. *Ergonomics*, **12**, 140–61.

PARKES, D. and THRIFT, N. (1980) *Times, Spaces and Places: A Chronogeographic Perspective.* Wiley: New York.

PATTERSON, H. P. and CONNOR, W. K. (1973) Community responses to aircraft noise in large and small cities in the USA. In: *Proc. Internat. Congr. Noise as a Public Health Problem, Dubrovnik.* Washington Printing Office, Rept. No. 550/9-73-008.

PEDERSON, D. M., JOHNSON, M. and WEST, J. H. (1978) Effects of room hue on ratings of self, other, and environment. *Perceptual and Motor Skills*, **46**, 403–10.

PEPLER, R. D. (1958) Warmth and performance: An investigation in the tropics. *Ergonomics*, **2**, 63.

PERIN, C. (1974) The social order of environmental design. In: *Designing for Human Behavior.* Eds. Lang, J., Burnette, C., Moleski, W. and Vachon, D. Vol. 6, Community Development Series. Dowden, Hutchinson and Ross: Stroudsburg, Pa.

PETERS, G. A. and ADAMS, B. B. (1959) Three criteria for readable panel markings. *Product Eng.*, **30**, 55–7.

PETERSON, R. F., KNAPP, T. J., ROSEN, J. C. and PITTER, B. F. (1977) The effects of furniture arrangement on the behaviour of geriatric patients. *Behaviour Therapy*, **8**, 464–7.

PETROPOULOS, H. and BREBNER, J. (1980) Stereotypes for direction-of-movement of rotary controls associated with linear displays. In: *Proc. 17th Ann. Conf. Ergonomics Soc. Australia and New Zealand.* Eds. Croft, P. and Fisher, A. Printed at the University of N.S.W.: Sydney.

PIEHL, J. (1978) The golden section: The true ratio? *Perceptual and Motor Skills*, **46**, 831–4.

PLAGENHOEF, S. (1971) *Patterns of Human Motion—A Cinematographic Analysis.* Prentice-Hall, Inc.: Englewood Cliffs, N.J.

PONS, L. and BAUDET, M. (1978) Structure of response patterns to a repeated verbal stimulus and action of noise and odor on originality. *Psycholog. Reports*, **42**, 1323–31.

PORTER, T. and MIKELLIDES, B. (Eds.) (1976) *Colour for Architecture.* Studio Vista: London.

PRANDTL, A. (1927) Uber gleichsinnige Induktion und die Lichtverteilung in gitterartigen Mustern. *Zsch. fur Sinnesphysiologie*, **58**, 263–307.

PREISER, W. F. E. (1972) Application of unobtrusive observation techniques in building performance appraisal. In: *Performance Concept in Buildings.* Ed. Foster, B. E. Special Publication No. 361, Vol. 1, National Bureau of Standards: Washington, D.C.

PREISER, W. F. E. (1973) An analysis of unobtrusive observations of pedestrian movement and stationary behaviour in a shopping mall. In: *Architectural Psychology.* Ed. Kuller, R. Dowden, Hutchinson and Ross: Stroudsburg, Pa.

PREYER (1897) On certain optical phenomena. *Am. J. Psychol.*, **9**, 42–4.

PROSHANSKY, H. M. (1978) The city and self identity. *Environment and Behaviour*, **10**, 147–69.

PROVINS, K. A., STOCKBRIDGE, H. C. W., FORREST, D. W. and ANDERSON, D. M. (1957) The representation of aircraft by pictorial signs. *Occupational Psychol.*, **31**, 21–32.

RAHE, R. H. and CARTER, J. E. L. (1976) Middle-aged male competitive swimmers. Background and body structure characteristics. *J. Sports Medicine and Physical Fitness*, **16**, 309–18.

RAMAZZINI, B. (1713) *De morbis artificum diatriba*. (*Diseases of Workers*, Trans. Wright, W. C. Hafner Publishing Co.: New York, 1965.)

RAWLS, J. R., TREGO, R. E., McGAFFEY, C. N. and RAWLS, D. J. (1972) Personal space as a predictor of performance under close working conditions. *J. Social Psychol.*, **86**, 261–7.

REDGRAVE, J. A. (1971) Menstrual cycles. In: *Biological Rhythms and Human Performance*. Ed. Colquhoun, W. P. Academic Press: London.

RENT, G. S. and RENT, C. S. (1978) Low-income housing factors related to residential satisfaction. *Environment and Behaviour*, **10**, 459–88.

REYNOLDS, H. M. (1976) *A foundation for systems anthropometry. Phase 1*. Interim Scientific Report, June 30–November, 1976. Michigan University, Ann Arbor, Highway Safety Research Institute: Michigan.

RICHTER, C. P. (1965) *Biological Clocks in Medicine and Psychiatry*. Chas. C. Thomas: Springfield, Illinois.

ROBERTS, J. (1966) *Weight by height and age of adults. United States 1960–1962*. National Center for Health Statistics, Rockville, Maryland. Division of Health Examination Statistics, Bureau of the Census: Washington, D.C.

ROBINSON, E. S. (1928) The behaviour of the museum visitor. *Publication No. 5 Am. Assoc. Museums. New Series*. Washington, D.C.

ROBINSON, S. and WEIGMAN, B. (1974) Heat and humidity. In: *Environmental Physiology*. Ed. Slonin, N. B. C. V. Mosby Co.: St. Louis.

RODIN, J. (1976) Density, perceived choice and response to controllable and uncontrollable outcomes. *J. Experimental and Social Psychol.*, **12**, 564–78.

ROHE, W. and PATTERSON, A. H. (1974) The effects of varied levels of resources and density on behaviour in a day care center. In: *EDRA 5*. Ed. Carson, D. H. Dowden, Hutchinson and Ross: Stroudsburg, Pa.

RONCO, P. G. (1972) Human factors applied to hospital patient care. *Human Factors*, **14**, 461–70.

ROSE, R. M., JENKINS, C. D. and HURST, M. W. (1978) Health change in air traffic controllers: A prospective study. 1. Background and description: *Psychosomatic Medicine*, **40**, 142–65.

ROSENTHAL, A. M. (1964) *38 Witnesses*. McGraw-Hill: New York.

ROTTON, J., OLSZEWSKI, D., CHARLETON, M. and SOLER, E. (1978) Loud speech, conglomerate noise, and behavioural after-effects. *J. Appl. Psychol.*, **63**, 360–5.

RUMP, E. E. (1974) Cluster analysis of personal questionnaires compared with principal component analysis. *Brit. J. Social and Clinical Psychol.*, **13**, 283–92.

SADALLA, E. and BURROUGHS, J. (1978) Mobile homes in hyperspace: Recognition memory for architectural form. *Environmental Psychol. and Nonverbal Behavior*, **2**, 195–205.

SAEGART, S. (1976) Stress inducing and reducing qualities of environments. In: *Environmental Psychology. People and their Physical Settings.* Eds. Proshanksy, H. M., Ittelson, W. H. and Rivlin, L. G. Holt, Rinehart and Winston: New York.
SALAME, P. and WITTERSHEIM, G. (1978) Selective noise disturbance of the information input in short term memory. *Quarterly J. Experimental Psychol.*, **30**, 693–704.
SANDHAL, D. A. (1972) Conceptions of self as individual orientations to the spatial environment. In: *EDRA 3*, 1, 2.3.1–2.3.10. Ed. Mitchell, W. A. University of California Press: Los Angeles.
SANOFF, H. (1974) Measuring attributes of the visual environment. In: *Designing for Human Behavior.* Eds. Lang, J., Burnette, C., Moleski, W. and Vachon, D. Community Development Series, Vol. 6. Dowden, Hutchinson and Ross: Stroudsburg, Pa.
SCHACHAR, R. (1976) Cover picture. *Science*, **192**, No. 4237.
SCHELLEKENS, H. M. (1978) Appearance of streets and experience with them: Report on investigations in the field of environmental psychology. *Ned. Tijdschz voor de Psychol en haar Grensgebieden*, **33**, 403–21.
SCHMITZ, M. A. (1959) The effect of low frequency high amplitude vibration on human performance. *Progress Report No. 2a*, Office of Surgeon General, Dept of the Army.
SCHNEWLIN, H. (1959) Anatomical factors in work design. *Paper given at International Zurich Conference 'Fitting the job to the worker'.*
SCHURER, G. A. K. (1978) Chrono-geography: an interpretative review of related literature. *Urban and Regional Planning Working Paper, No. 6*, University of Adelaide: South Australia.
SCHWARZ, H. and WERBIK, H. (1971) Eine experimentelle Untersuchung uber den Einfluss due syntaktischen Information der Anordnung von Baukorpern entlang einer Strasse auf Stimmungen des Betrachters. *Zschr. f. exp. und angew. Psychol.*, **18**, 499–511.
SCHWARZ, W. (1959) The relation of functional periodicity to changes in the characteristics of emotional reactions and personality. *Dissertation Abstr.*, **19**, 3372.
SEEGER, B. R. and STERN, L. M. (Eds.) (1980) *Aids for Handicapped Children.* Published by the Crippled Children's Association of South Australia, Inc.
SFOGLIANO, C. (1964) Ciclo menstruale e rendimento lavorativo di giovani operaie addette alla produzione di transistors in uno stabilimento elettronico. *Rass. Med. Ind.*, **33**, 218–21.
SHABAN, J. and WELLING, G. (1972) Experiment on personal versus regulations responsibility. In: *Urban Stress: Experiments on Noise and Social Stressors*, 123. Eds. Glass, D. C. and Singer, J. E. Academic Press: New York.
SHERROD, D. R., ARMSTRONG, D., HEWITT, J., MADONIA, B., SPENO, S. and TERUYA, D. (1977) Environmental attention, affect, and altruism. *J. Appl. Social Psychol.*, **4**, 359–71.
SHERVEN, J. K. (1978) The therapy office as a projection of the therapist's personality. *Dissertation Abstr. Internat.*, **38**, 5759.
SHONYO, C. (1977a) *Anthropometry: Basic Studies and Applications, Vol. 1. 1964–1975.* (A Bibliography with Abstracts.) National Technical Information Service: Springfield, Virginia.
SHONYO, C. (1977b) *Anthropometry: Basic Studies and Applications, Vol. 2. 1976– August 1977.* (A Bibliography with Abstracts.) National Technical Information Service: Springfield, Virginia.
SHOOTER, A. M. N., SCHONFELD, A. E. D., KING, H. F. and WELFORD, A. T. (1972) Some field data on the training of older people. In: *Human Ageing.* Ed. Chown, S. Penguin Books Ltd: Harmondsworth, UK.

SIEGEL, P. V., GERATHWOHL, S. J. and MOHLER, S. R. (1969) Time-zone effects. *Science*, **164**, 1249–55.

SIMONS, A. K. and SCHMITZ, M. A. (1958) The effect of low-frequency, high amplitude whole-body vibration on human performance. *AD 157778 Research and Development Division*. Office of Surgeon General, Dept of the Army, April 1957–January 1958.

SINGLETON, W. T. (1966) Human factor problems of computer design and use. *AP Note 3*. Applied Psychology Centre, University of Aston in Birmingham, UK.

SLATTER, P. E. and WHITFIELD, T. W. (1977) Room function and appropriateness judgements of colour. *Perceptual and Motor Skills*, **45**, 1068–70.

SLESS, D. and CAIRNEY, P. (1978) Symbol design and testing methodology project: determination of need for a symbol. *Technical Paper No. 2, Centre for Applied Social and Survey Research*, The Flinders University of South Australia.

SLONIN, N. B. (Ed.) (1974) *Environmental Physiology*. C. V. Mosby Co.: St. Louis.

SMITH, S. L. and THOMAS, D. W. (1964) Color versus shape coding in information displays. *J. Appl. Psychol.*, **48**, 137–46.

SNYDER, R. G., SCHNEIDER, L. W., OWINGS, C. L., REYNOLDS, H. M. and GOLOMB, D. H. (1977) *Anthropometry of Infants, Children and Youths to Age 18 for Product Safety Design*. Michigan University, Ann Arbor, Highway Safety Research Institute Report UM-HSR1-77-17: Michigan.

SOAR, R. S. (1955) Height, width, proportion and stroke width in numeral visibility. *J. Appl. Psychol.*, **42**, 158.

SOMMER, R. (1959) Visitors to mental hospitals. *Mental Hygiene*, **43**, 8–15.

SOMMER, R. (1965) Further studies of small group ecology. *Sociometry*, **28**, 337–48.

SOMMER, R. (1969) *Personal Space*. Prentice-Hall: Englewood Cliffs N.J.

SOMMER, R. (1974a) Looking back at personal space. In: *Designing for Human Behavior: Architecture and the Behavioral Sciences*. Eds. Lang, J.. Burnette, C., Moleski, W. and Vachon, D. Community Development Series, Vol. 6, p. 207. Dowden, Hutchinson and Ross: Stroudsburg, Pa.

SOMMER, R. (1974b) *Tight Spaces*. Prentice-Hall: Englewood Cliffs N.J.

SRIVASTAVA, R. K. and PEEL, T. (1968) *Human Movement as a Function of Colour Stimulation*. Environmental Research Foundation: Topeka, Kansas.

STEELE, F. I. (1970) Problem solving in the spatial environment. In: *EDRA 1*. Ed. Preiser, W. F. E. Dowden, Hutchinson and Ross: Stroudsberg, Pa.

STEINITZ, C. (1968) Meaning and congruence of urban form and activity. *J. Am. Inst. Planners*, **34**, 233–48.

STEINZOR, B. (1950) The spatial factor in face to face discussion groups. *J. Assoc. Social Psychol.*, **45**, 552–5.

STEPHENS, S. D. G. (1970) *Studies on the Uncomfortable Loudness Level*. MRC Applied Psychology Research Unit, Cambridge Report 78,7/70.

STOKOLS, D., OHLIG, W. and RESNICK, S. (1978) Perception of residential crowding, classroom experiences and student health. *Human Ecology*, **6**, 233–52.

STOKOLS, D., RALL, M., PINNER, B. and SCHOPLER, J. (1973) Physical, social and personal determinants of the perception of crowding. *Environment and Behavior*, **5**, 87–115.

STOUDT, H., DAMON, A., McFARLAND, R. and ROBERTS, J. (1965) *Weight, Height, and Selected Body Dimensions of Adults*. National Center for Health Statistics, Rockville, Maryland. Division of Health Examination Statistics. Bureau of the Census: Washington, D.C.

STRINGER, P. (1974) Individual differences in repertory grid measures for a cross-section of the female population. In: *Psychology and the Built Environment*. Eds. Canter, D. and Lee, T. R. Architectural Press: London.

STRUGHOLD, H. (1952) Physiological day–night cycle in global flights. *J. Aviation Medicine*, **23**, 464–73.

SZAFRAN, J. (1948) *Problems of Ageing*. Nuffield Research Unit Reports 2 and 3. University of Cambridge: Cambridge.

SZOKOLAY, S. V. (1979) Ergonomics in architectural design. In: *Human factors and the quality of life: Proc. 16th Ann. Conf. Ergonomics Soc. Australia and New Zealand*. Ed. Devereaux, G. Printed at the University of Queensland: Brisbane.

TANNER, J. M. (1968) Earlier maturation in man. *Scientific American*, **18**, 21–7.

TARNOPOLSKY, A., BARKER, S. M., WIGGINS, R. D. and McLEAN, E. K. (1978) The effect of aircraft noise on the mental health of a community sample: A pilot study. *Psycholog. Medicine*, **8**, 219–33.

TAYLOR, R. B. and STOUGH, R. R. (1978) Territorial cognition: assessing Altman's typology. *J. Personality and Social Psychol.*, **36**, 418–23.

TAYLOR, W. (1972) The weavers of Dundee. *Trans. Soc. Occup. Med.*, **22**, 37–43.

TEMPLER, J. A. (1975) Stair shape and human movement. *Dissertation Abstr. Internat.*, **36**, 148.

THAYER, R. L. and ATWOOD, B. G. (1978) Plants, complexity, and pleasure in urban and suburban environments. *Environmental Psychol. and Nonverbal Behavior*, **3**, 67–76.

THOMAS, J. C., MALHOTRA, A. and CARROLL, J. M. (1977) An experimental investigation of the design process. *IBM Research Report No. RC 6702*, 32 pp.

THOMPSON, H. V. (1948) Watching marked rats taking plain and poisoned bait. *Bull. Animal Behavior*, **6**, 26–40.

THORSDEN, M. L., KROEMER, K. H. E. and LAUBACH, L. L. (1972) Human force exertions in aircraft control locations. *Aero. Medical Res. Lab. Technical Report*, 71–119.

TIFFIN, J. and WESTHAFER, F. L. (1940) The relation between reaction time and temporal location of the stimulus on the tremor cycle. *J. Experimental Psychol.*, **27**, 318–24.

TINKER, M. A. (1949) Trends in illumination standards. *Trans. Am. Acad. Ophthal. and Otolaryng*, **382**.

TOGNOLI, J. H., HAMAD, C. and CARPENTER, T. (1978) Staff attitudes toward adult male residents' behavior as a function of two settings for mentally retarded people. *Mental Retardation*, **16**, 142–6.

TRAVIS, L. E. (1929) The relation of voluntary movements to tremors. *J. Experimental Psychol.*, **12**, 515–24.

US MILITARY SPECIFICATION (1964) No. MIL-M-18012 B, July.

US MILITARY STANDARD AIR FORCE–NAVY DRAWING (1957) 10400—(width–height) based on Military Standard 33558, December 17.

VERDERBER, S. and MOORE, G. T. (1977) Building imagery: A comparative study of environmental cognition. *Man–Environment Systems*, **7**, 332–41.

VERHAEGEN, P., BERVOETS, R., DEBRABANDERE, G., MILLET, F., SANTERMANS, G., STYUCK, M., VANDERMOERE, D. and WILLENS, G. (1975) Direction of movement stereotypes in different cultural groups. In: *Ethnic Variables in Human Factors Engineering*. Ed. Chapanis, A. Johns Hopkins University Press: Baltimore.

VERNON, H. M. and BEDFORD, T. (1927) The relation of atmospheric conditions to the working capacity and the accident rate of coal miners. *IFRB Report No. 39*. HMSO: London.

VICKERS, D. (1980) *Decision Processes in Visual Perception*. Academic Press: London.

VINCE, M. A. (1948) Corrective movements in a pursuit task. *Quarterly J. Experimental Psychol.*, **1**, 85–103.

VITELES, M. S. (1932) *Industrial Psychology*. Norton: New York.

VON GIERKE, H. E. and CLARKE, N. P. (1971) Effects of vibration and buffeting on man. In: *Aerospace Medicine*. Ed. Randel, H. Williams and Wilkins: Baltimore.

WALKER, R. E., NICOLAY, R. C. and STEARNS, C. R. (1965) Comparative accuracy of recognizing American and international road signs. *J. Appl. Psychol.*, **49**, 322–5.

WALPAMUR CO. LTD (1959) *Colour in Buildings*. Thos. Forman and Sons Ltd: Nottingham, UK.

WALTER, F. (1971) *Sports Centres and Swimming Pools*. Thistle Foundation: Edinburgh.

WARD, L. M. and SUEDFELD, P. (1974) Human responses to highway noise. *Environmental Res.*, **6**, 306–26.

WARRICK, M. J. (1947) Direction of movement in the use of control knobs to position visual indicators. In: *Psychological Research on Equipment Design*. Ed. Fitts, P. M. USAAF Aviation Psychology Research Program, Department 19.

WEINSTEIN, N. D. (1978) Individual differences in reactions to noise: A longitudinal study in a college dormitory. *J. Appl. Psychol.*, **63**, 458–66.

WEISS, R. S. and BOUTOURLINE, S. (1962) *A Summary of Fairs, Pavilions, Exhibits, and their Audiences*. A circulated monograph.

WELLS, B. W. P. (1965) Subjective responses to the lighting installation in a modern office building and their design implications. *Building Science*, **1**, 57–67.

WESTON, H. C. (1949) *Sight, Light and Efficiency*. H. K. Lewis: London.

WESTON, H. C. (1961) Rationally recommended illumination levels. *Trans. Illum. Eng. Soc.*, **26**, 1.

WEXNER, L. B. (1954) The degree to which colors (hues) are associated with mood tones. *J. Appl. Psychol.*, **38**, 432–5.

WHITE, R. M. (1964) *Anthropometric Survey of the Royal Thai Armed Forces*. Army Natick Labs.: Mass.

WHITFIELD, T. W. and SLATTER, P. E. (1978) The evaluation of architectural interior colour as a function of style of furnishings: Categorization effects. *Scandinavian J. Psychol.*, **19**, 251–5.

WILLIS, F. N. (1966) Initial speaking distance as a function of the speakers relationship. *Psychonomic Science*, **5**, 221–2.

WILNER, D. L., WALKLEY, R. P., PINKERTON, T. C. and TAYBACK, M. (1962) *The Housing Environment and Family Life*. Johns Hopkins University Press: Baltimore.

WINKEL, G. H. and HAYWARD, D. G. (1971) *Some major causes of congestion in subway stations*. Center for Environment and Behavior, CUNY: New York.

WINKEL, G. H., MALEK, R. and THIEL, P. (1969) The role of personality differences in judgements of roadside quality. *Environment and Behavior*, **1**, 199–223.

WOHLWILL, J. F. (1968) Amount of stimulus exploration and preference as differential functions of stimulus complexity. *Perception and Psychophysics*, **4**, 307–12.

WOHLWILL, J. F. (1975) Children's responses to meaningful pictures varying in diversity: Exploration time vs. preference. *J. Experimental Child Psychol.*, **20**, 341–51.

WOHLWILL, J. F. (1976) Environmental aesthetics: the environment as a source of affect. In: *Human Behavior and the Environment, Vol. 1, Advances in theory and research*. Eds. Altman, I. and Wohlwill, J. F. Plenum Press: New York.

WOODSON, W. E. (1957) *Human Engineering Guide for Equipment Designers*. University of California Press: Berkeley, California.

YLLÖ, A. (1962) The bio-technology of card punching. *Ergonomics*, **5**, 75.

ZALOT, G. and ADAMS-WEBBER, J. (1977) Cognitive complexity in the perception of neighbours. *Social Behaviour and Personality*, **5**, 281–3.

ZEISEL, J. (1975) The design cycle. *Sociology and Architectural Design, Social Science Frontiers, No. 6*. Russell Sage Foundation: New York.

ZIMMER, J. W. and BRACHULIS-RAYMOND, J. (1978) Effects of distracting stimuli on complex information processing. *Perceptual and Motor Skills*, **46**, 791–4.

Author Index

Ertel, H., 162
Esser, A. H., 151
Eugen, T., 65
Evans, G. W., 57, 172
Eysenck, H. J., 176

Fairbanks, L. A., 133
Falk, S. A., 48
Faris, R. E. L., 143
Farrimond, T., 89
Fechner, G. T., 154
Festinger, L., 134
Field, H. H., 136
Fife, D., 54
Finkelman, J. M., 52
Finlay, D. C., 58
Fisher, J. D., 130, 140, 169
Fisher, M. B., 15
Floyd, W. F., 108
Foley, P. J., 79
Forrest, D. W., 81
Foveman, J. E. K., 53
Fowler, C. J., 57
Freedman, J. L., 135, 136
Freund, A., 22
Fried, M., 31
Fujimoto, T., 7
Fuller, P., 136

Gabriele, T., 137
Gallé, O. R., 143
Garfinkel, M., 127
Geen, R. G., 60
Geissler, L. R., 87
Gelfand, D. M., 138
Glanville, A. D., 15
Glass, A., 22
Glass, D. C., 52
Glencross, D. J., 95
Goedecke, D. W., 57
Goldman, D. E., 61
Goldman, R. F., 45, 46

Goldstein, K., 175
Golomb, D. H., 7
Gombrich, E., 166
Gotz, K., 175
Gotz, K. O., 175
Gove, W. R., 143
Grandjean, E., 16, 17, 42, 70, 71, 72
Greene, R., 22
Gregory, R. L., 3, 28
Gregory, W. L., 160
Grether, W. F., 63
Griffen, L., 137
Griffiths, I. D., 58
Guignard, J. C., 63
Guilford, J. P., 175
Gunn, W. J., 58

Haber, R. N., 81
Hakiel, S. R., 84
Halberg, F., 22, 23
Hall, E. T., 69
Hall, W. A., 9
Hamad, C., 143
Hansen, R., 7
Harris, C. S., 63
Harrison, J., 149
Hart, D. J., 113, 115
Hartman, D. P., 138
Hauty, G. T., 20
Hayward, D. G., 74
Hendy, K., 7
Herman, G., 57
Herren, K. A., 133
Hershberger, R. G., 151
Hertzberg, H. T. E., 7
Hewitt, J., 170
Hick, W. E., 119
High, T., 136
Hillier, B., 150
Hitt, W. D., 81
Holahan, C. U., 134, 135
Holm, A., 18
Honikman, B., 149

Subject Index

Access for disabled people, 119
  et seq.
  Australian Standard 1428-1977,
    125, 126
  braille maps, 120
  British Standard 5810:1979, 125,
    126
  lift dimensions, 125–6
  principles for, 121
Aesthetics, 154 *et seq.*, 161–3, 165
Alienation, 145
Alphanumeric symbols, 77 *et seq.*
Anthropometrics, 6 *et seq.*
  British company directors, 9
  chair and table height, 9–10
  decrease with ageing, 9
  dynamic, 12 *et seq.*
  height, 6–9
    estimation, 10
    height measures, 11
    normal distribution, 9, 10
    percentiles for selected, 9, 11
    popliteal height, 10
    racial and national differences,
      8
  movement
    arm, of, 15–16
    foot and leg, of, 16–17
    hand, of, 15
    head, of, 15
    sporting activities, 17
  reach
    maximum, 16
    seated, 16
  strength
    female parachuting fatalities, 13
    hand grip, 15
    leg, 17
    lifting, in, 16

Auditory communication, 85
  et seq.

Buildings
  complexity, 2
  mobility within, 69 *et seq.*
  remembrance, 152
Bystander apathy, 138, 141

Circadian rhythm, 17 *et seq.*
  interindividual variability, 18
  'jet-lag', 20
  performance, and, 18–19
  performance and time of day,
    19–20
  shift work, 20–1
  temperature, and, 19–20
Clutter overload, 171–2
Colour, 169, 174 *et seq.*
  thresholds, 4
Common-sense views, 2, 5
Complexity, 173, 174
Context effects, 127, 169–70
Control mechanisms, 89 *et seq.*
  control–display
    principles, 102–7
    relations, 100 *et seq.*
  foot-operated pushbuttons, 96
  forces for levers, 96–7
  handles, 90–1
  handwheels, 99–100
  keyboards, 93–5
  knobs, 91
  levers, 96–7
  locks, 92–3
  pedals, 97–9
  principles for, 90

211

Odour, 64 *et seq.*
Offices
  desk position, 132–3
  effects of furnishings, 127,
    169–70

Perceived control, 139
Perceptual illusions, 28, 157
Personal space, 72–4, 131, 139
Pro-social behaviour, 137–8
Psychological aspects of places,
  149, 151, 152, 160–1, 169

Rehousing, grief effect, 31

Seating, 107 *et seq.*
  principles for, 108 *et seq.*
Social interaction, 133 *et seq.*, 144,
  150
Sociofugal spaces, 129 *et seq.*, 146
Sociopetal spaces, 129 *et seq.*
Spatial arrangements, 129, 130
Staircases, 70 *et seq.*
Stimulus overload, 141
Stress, 142

Temperature, 42 *et seq.*
  effects on performance, 44–6
  regulatory mechanism, 43
  relative humidity, 43
Territory, 147, 151, 169

Ultradian cycles
  alpha rhythm, 23
  finger tremor, 23
  sleep and dreaming, 23
  time of day and food intake, 24
Urban dwellers, 141, 142

Vibration, 61 *et seq.*
Vision, 35 *et seq.*
  moving parts of the eye, 36–8
  retina and optic nerve, 38–9
  structure of the eye, 35–6
Visual display units, 113 *et seq.*
  ambient conditions, 114
  long-term memory, 117
  motor co-ordination, 118
  perceptual organisation, 116
  short-term memory problems, 117
  visual task, 115, 119

Walking speed, 72–4